Dustin Peone

Memory as Philosophy
The Theory and Practice of Philosophical Recollection

STUDIES IN HISTORICAL PHILOSOPHY

Editor: Alexander Gungov

Consulting Editor: Donald Phillip Verene

ISSN 2629-0316

1 *Dustin Peone*
 Memory as Philosophy
 The Theory and Practice of Philosophical Recollection
 ISBN 978-3-8382-1336-1

Dustin Peone

MEMORY AS PHILOSOPHY

The Theory and Practice of Philosophical Recollection

Bibliografische Information der Deutschen Nationalbibliothek
Die Deutsche Nationalbibliothek verzeichnet diese Publikation in der Deutschen Nationalbibliografie; detaillierte bibliografische Daten sind im Internet über http://dnb.d-nb.de abrufbar.

Bibliographic information published by the Deutsche Nationalbibliothek
Die Deutsche Nationalbibliothek lists this publication in the Deutsche Nationalbibliografie; detailed bibliographic data are available in the Internet at http://dnb.d-nb.de.

Cover Picture: "Reflecting Pool." Copyright © 2019 by Megan Lillie

ISBN-13: 978-3-8382-1336-1
© *ibidem*-Verlag, Stuttgart 2019
Alle Rechte vorbehalten

Das Werk einschließlich aller seiner Teile ist urheberrechtlich geschützt. Jede Verwertung außerhalb der engen Grenzen des Urheberrechtsgesetzes ist ohne Zustimmung des Verlages unzulässig und strafbar. Dies gilt insbesondere für Vervielfältigungen, Übersetzungen, Mikroverfilmungen und elektronische Speicherformen sowie die Einspeicherung und Verarbeitung in elektronischen Systemen.

All rights reserved. No part of this publication may be reproduced, stored in or introduced into a retrieval system, or transmitted, in any form, or by any means (electronical, mechanical, photocopying, recording or otherwise) without the prior written permission of the publisher. Any person who does any unauthorized act in relation to this publication may be liable to criminal prosecution and civil claims for damages.

Printed in the EU

For Erin Cozens Peone

Table of Contents

Abbreviations 9
Preface 11
Introduction: The Recovery of Memory 15

PART ONE: THEORY 27

Section One: The Idea of Memory 29
I: The Origins of Wisdom 31
II: What Memory as Philosophy is Not 39
III: Memory as Philosophy 53
IV: Forgetting 79
V: Memory in the Technological World 89

PART TWO: HISTORY 99

Section Two: The Memory Tradition 101
VI: The Speculative Line 103
VII: The Technical Line 119
VIII: Theatrum Mundi 133

Section Three: Memory in Modernity 147
IX: Montaigne's Monstrous Memory 149
X: Writing and Memory 175
XI: Memory versus Modernity 185
XII: Descartes and His Children 205
XIII: Hegel's Philosophy of *Erinnerung* 221
XIV: Hegel's Later Works 241

Postface 261
Bibliography 265
Index 277

Abbreviations

Unless otherwise noted, all citations of Greek and Latin authors refer to the Loeb Classical Library (Cambridge: Harvard University Press); Aristotle, *Complete Works*, ed. Jonathan Barnes, 2 vols. (Princeton, NJ: Princeton University Press, 1984); or Plato, *Complete Works*, ed. John M. Cooper (Indianapolis, IN: Hackett, 1997). I have also employed abbreviations for the works of Hegel and Montaigne:

HEGEL

EL = [*Encyclopedia Logic*] *Logic: Being Part One of the Encyclopaedia of the Philosophical Sciences*. Trans. William Wallace. New York: Oxford University Press, 1975. (References to the three *Encyclopaedia* volumes are to Hegel's paragraph numbers.)
FK = *Faith and Knowledge*. Trans. Walter Cerf and H.S. Harris. Albany: State University of New York Press, 1988.
LHP = *Lectures on the History of Philosophy 1825–6*. Trans. R.F. Brown and J.M. Stewart. 3 Vols. New York: Oxford University Press, 2009.
PH = *Philosophy of History*. Trans. J.M. Sibree. Mineola, NY: Dover, 2004.
PM = *Philosophy of Mind: Being Part Three of the Encyclopaedia of the Philosophical Sciences*. Trans. William Wallace and A.V. Miller. New York: Oxford University Press, 1971.
PN = *Philosophy of Nature: Being Part Two of the Encyclopaedia of the Philosophical Sciences*. Trans. A.V. Miller. New York: Oxford University Press, 1970.
PR = *Philosophy of Right*. Trans. T.M. Knox. New York: Oxford University Press, 1967. (References to *PR* are to Hegel's paragraph numbers, where applicable.)
PS = *Phenomenology of Spirit*. Trans. A.V. Miller. Oxford: Oxford University Press, 1976. (References to *PS* are to Miller's paragraph numbers.)
SL = *Science of Logic*. Trans. A.V. Miller. Atlantic Highlands, NJ: Prometheus Books, 1991.
W = *Werke*. Ed. Eva Moldenhauer and Karl Markus Michel. 20 Vols. Frankfurt am Main: Suhrkamp, 1969. (All citations of Hegel list the Eng-

lish page or paragraph number, followed by the volume and page or paragraph number in the Suhrkamp edition.)
Z = *Zusatz*. (This indicates that the reference is to the *Zusätze*, the later additions Hegel made to his texts.)

MONTAIGNE

CE = *The Complete Essays*. Trans. Donald M. Frame. Stanford, CA: Stanford University Press, 1958.
L = *Letters*. In *The Complete Works*. Trans. Donald M. Frame. New York: Modern Library, 2003, 1271–1336.
TJ = *Travel Journal*. In *The Complete Works*, 1047–1270.
V = *Les Essais*. Ed. Pierre Villey and V.-L. Saulnier. 3 vols. Paris: Quadridge/PUF, 1988. (All references to the *Essays* list the book and chapter, followed by the English page number and the French page number.)

Preface

The conception of the present work is the result of a long interest in memory on the part of its author. When I was a young man, I was for some years an amateur boxer. On one occasion, after sparring a few rounds in the afternoon, I realized that I could not remember anything that had happened that day prior to arriving at the gym. The entire morning had been effaced from my mind. Slowly, over the course of the next week, disconnected images would return to me of that lost span, but in a very hazy and dream-like form. I was unsure of their strict fidelity to actual events. I had attended classes that day, and presumably I had learned something or other, but this learning was annulled, which is to say that I had not learned anything. "All learning depends on memory," says Quintilian (*Inst. Orat.*, XI. ii.1.). The great terror of this event was the fact that the absence of memory stripped my own self of a period of its existence. The *cogito* found itself staring into a chasm. Education is memory and the key to selfhood. As Emerson says, "Memory is a primary and fundamental faculty, without which none other can work ... it is the thread on which the beads of man are strung, making the personal identity which is necessary to moral action."[1] The unrecalled past *has not happened* in any sort of substantial manner. This was the end of my career in pugilism.

I now know that this was an instance of retrograde amnesia, a phenomenon quite common amongst boxers and other athletes who suffer concussions, and not in itself a particularly profound or unique experience. The short-term memory is disrupted by the trauma of the brain and is unable to consolidate the recent past.[2] With time, the event lost its terror and became an article of curiosity. It inspired me to develop, for instance, a very rudimentary system of mnemonics for the sake of recollection. When I turned my mind toward philosophy some years later, my implicit assumption was that my old personal interest in memory—which I seldom considered anymore—was separated by a wide gulf from this new endeavor. Surely in an enlightened age, we no longer have any need to pay attention to such a primitive faculty. To even speak of "faculties"

---

1 Ralph Waldo Emerson, "Natural History of Intellect," in *The Complete Works of Ralph Waldo Emerson*, vol. XII (New York: Houghton Mifflin, 1921), 90.
2 Nobel Prize-winner Eric R. Kandel describes the experience well, from the external standpoint of a neuroscientist. See Kandel, *In Search of Memory* (New York: W.W. Norton & Co., 2006), 211–12.

in the classical sense is the worst kind of heterodoxy. I have found that this assumption was entirely false.

As a student of the history of philosophy, and a voracious reader of Hegel, it occurred to me that the historical advance of philosophy is largely powered by recollection. At any period in which philosophical thought becomes stagnant and bogged down, forgetfulness has set in. The naïve philosopher mistakes a few partial truths for the whole of wisdom, because the path traversed to reach that point, along with its initial aims and presuppositions, is forgotten. The transitions to new vistas always partially involve a return to the past, a recollection. The ingenious philosopher must discover where the wrong turn was taken, and pick up the thread from that point, in order to open new directions for speculation. Philosophy is always self-referential in this regard, inseparable from its own history. This is clear in periods like the Renaissance, but we need not look so far afield; one can find the same engine behind any truly original philosopher of the past century, from Bergson to MacIntyre.

My project became clear: to investigate the philosophical significance of memory. By the nature of the topic, the theoretical side of this investigation is not separable from the historical. We must begin with the Socratic question: "What is memory?" However, to show what memory really *is* in a philosophical sense is at the same time to show how it has been understood in the history of philosophy itself. If I am correct that there can be no "I," no world, nothing at all without memory, and that this was always understood by philosophers of the past, then how and why have we forgotten the importance of memory? How might this forgetfulness be overcome, and what is the future of memory—that is to say, in terms one might find in the meditations of T. S. Eliot, what is the future of the past? The two parts of this work, "Theory" and "History," are really inseparable, Yin and Yang of the inquiry.

There are many people whose assistance and encouragement I would like to acknowledge, far too many to name. The laurel wreath must be shared by my wife and children. Their love and support is the platform necessary for me to think at all.

Intellectually, I owe an enormous debt to Donald Phillip Verene, the man who first showed me the philosophical significance of *ingenium*. Professor Verene's work on philosophical memory and his excellent writings on Hegel have been a powerful influence on my own project, and his guidance has been indispensible. I must also thank Ann Hartle (who taught me how to read Montaigne), Susan Bredlau, Thomas Flynn, and Dilek Huseyinzadegan for reading versions of this book in manuscript form.

A version of the fourth chapter was presented at the Southeast Philosophy Congress in February, 2015. My thanks are due to the Clayton State University audience members who offered valuable feedback.

Regards are due to the artist, Megan Lillie, who allowed me to use her painting, "Reflecting Pool," for the cover of this book. Finally, particular thanks are due to my dear friend Zuzana Montagne for copyediting the entire project and offering her invaluable insights throughout. For those countless others willing to discuss various difficulties throughout the course of my writing, my gratitude is also due. Philosophy is and always has been fundamentally a dialogue; without such discussions, I could not produce anything of much value.

Introduction:
The Recovery of Memory

> O Muses, O high genius, aid me now!
> O memory that engraved the things I saw,
> Here shall your worth be manifest to all!
>
> Dante, *Inferno*, Canto II

The title of this work is a philosophical doctrine that I wish to propose and defend. It is not an original doctrine; it has its roots in the most ancient wisdom of the West, and it has persisted in various forms from deepest antiquity. In certain stages of its historical transformation it has been explicitly articulated, while in others it has only been implicit. At present, the doctrine of "memory as philosophy" has cycled into a phase of dormancy. Our modern world is one dominated by method (our inheritance from Francis Bacon and Descartes) and technique (our inheritance from the Industrial Revolution). Memory in its philosophical sense stands in an antagonistic relationship with method and technique. Philosophical memory is always the work of *ingenium*, which cannot ultimately be reduced to either of these modern inamoratas. Technique and method are consuming forces, which demand that all phenomena be taken up into themselves. There can, however, be no technique or method of *ingenium*.

What is this "philosophical sense" of memory? The title announces the central question of this work: How can we modern thinkers still hold a philosophical doctrine of memory? Answering this question is the topic of the first section. Prior to this question is a more immediate question: What is meant by this title, this theme? What *is* "memory as philosophy"?[1]

The key to this question concerns the conjunction, "as". One possible reading of the title might suppose that the "as" is convertible with the copula "is". "Memory *is* philosophy" would connote a very different

---

[1] I must acknowledge a debt to the Renaissance scholar Ernesto Grassi, the title of whose book, *Rhetoric as Philosophy*, serves as a model for the title of the present work. Grassi's claim, similar to my own, is not that *all* rhetoric is philosophy, but that there *is* a philosophical rhetoric, with its own long-standing tradition. See Grassi, *Rhetoric as Philosophy*, trans. John Michael Krois and Azizeh Azodi (Carbondale, IL: Southern Illinois University Press, 2001), 18.

claim than the one I advocate. In this rendering, the two terms would suggest a single identity: all memory is philosophy and all philosophy is memory. This is not the claim I wish to make. Memory is a much broader category than philosophy; it is as broad as all human experience. One may remember where one placed one's pen, one may remember the opening tune of Handel's *Messiah*, or one may remember the events of last Thursday evening. The historian may be able to recollect a long series of historical dates, and the auto mechanic to call to mind a great number of dimensions of different carburetors. One may remember, in psychologically interesting ways, a severe trauma. None of these instances are philosophical.

We can turn this identity equation around, and ask if all philosophy *is* memory. This comes closer to the claim I want to make, but it is still not entirely accurate. Philosophy is also a broader category than memory. Neither "memory" nor "philosophy" is a term that can entirely encapsulate the other. Memory is and always has been *for the most part* the central human faculty whereby philosophy progresses and transforms. However, there have always been great works of philosophy that seem to be anathematic to a doctrine of philosophical memory. Plotinus, for example, insists that the end of philosophy—the immediate apprehension of the "One"—is only possible through a transcendence of all modes of human thinking, memory included. Descartes, in his *Meditations on First Philosophy*, presents his ideal philosopher as an isolated thinker on a zetetic quest for pure knowledge and *a priori* principles. *A priori* knowledge must be independent of all human experience. In his private writings, Descartes unequivocally asserts that there is "no need at all for memory in any of the sciences."[2] Descartes is a philosopher of method, which, I have already said, is always opposed to philosophical memory. To claim that *all* philosophy is memory would involve either a perverse manipulation of the term "philosophy" to indicate some body of work that keeps Plotinus, Descartes, and other canonical figures on its outside, or else a thorough exegesis of these problematic figures that demonstrates that a philosophical memory in fact underlies their works.[3]

---

2   René Descartes, *Cogitationes privatae*, in *Œuvres* (Paris: Vrin, 1996), 10: 230 (my translation).
3   I, of course, believe the latter to be true. For both Plotinus and Descartes, while the eventual end of philosophy is immediately cognized and not memorial, the process for attaining it certainly entails memory. To complete even the simplest syllogism requires a rather complex process of recollection.

There is another way one could understand the claims "memory is philosophy" and "philosophy is memory". This is to read these as speculative sentences in the Hegelian sense, rather than as the A = A of Fichte or Schelling. For Hegel, the speculative sentence [spekulativer Satz] is a proposition in which subject and predicate are each broader than the other and can never fully encapsulate one another. The subject begins with a clear and objective meaning, but receives a new determination through its attachment to the predicate. The predicate, in turn, finds a new determination and meaning of its own through its connection back to the subject. This is a continuous relationship of reciprocity (PS, §61; W, III: 59). The speculative sentence expresses the inner form of the object.[4] The speculative sense of the claim "memory is philosophy" approximates what I wish to suggest. However, in ordinary language, the copula "is" is more suggestive of identity. For this reason, I have opted instead for the conjunction "as" in my title; its ordinary usage comes closer to expressing the theme of the present work.

Rather than a quantitative identity, "memory as philosophy" suggests that aspect of memory which is philosophical, and that aspect of philosophy which is memorial. This leads to the important question: What is the philosophical aspect of memory? What is meant here by the first word of the title, "memory"? I will suggest a preliminary definition of memory which will convey in broad terms the intent of this project, borrowed from Giambattista Vico. In the *Scienza nuova*, Vico says, "Memory thus has three different aspects: memory [*memoria*] when it remembers things, imagination [*fantasia*] when it alters or imitates them, and invention [*ingegno*] when it gives them a new turn or puts them into proper arrangement and relationship. For these reasons the theological poets called Memory the mother of the Muses."[5]

This tri-partition is not the ordinary way in which memory is understood. I will attempt to show, however, that it is a valid way of understanding what memory is, and that there is a tradition coeval with philosophy itself that views memory in this light. On this schema, *memoria* is memory in its broad sense, the simple psychological remembrance of things past. *Fantasia* taken by itself is not yet philosophy either; it is un-

---

4 Donald Phillip Verene writes, "Speculation captures in thought the inner life of the object. To speculate is to follow in language the inner movement of consciousness, to narrate the inner life of the object." *Speculative Philosophy* (Lanham, MD: Lexington Books, 2009), 3.
5 Giambattista Vico, *New Science*, trans. Thomas Goddard Bergin and Max Harold Fisch (Ithaca, NY: Cornell University Press, 1968), §819.

ruly and wild, just as much the province of the child or madman as the sage. Imagination and philosophy are closely related, but not strictly convertible. The third term, *ingegno* (*ingenium* in Latin) is what I take to be the properly philosophical aspect of memory. This is the act of giving a new turn to or finding a new, proper order for those things held fast within the simple *memoria*. *Ingegno* is therefore rooted in *memoria*. It depends no less upon *fantasia*, which is the potentiality for constructing new forms and the origin of human wisdom. *Ingegno* is the controlled imagination, which deliberately reworks the content of simple psychological memory for purposes of invention. Vico was the first to see this clearly, and it has since been demonstrated by the work on myth and so-called primitive cultures carried out in the twentieth century.[6] A doctrine of philosophical memory is ultimately a doctrine of *ingegno*, which is bound up with *memoria* and *fantasia*.

The only word in the title that remains unaccounted for is "philosophy," the most difficult by far to saddle with a fixed meaning. Philosophy is always a live process, always a transformation of its objects, but of what this process consists is itself always transformative. We cannot say in advance what philosophy is; we can only look back once the process is completed, and consider what it is that has just been done. Aristotle's *noēsis noēseōs*, thought thinking thought, is that ideal toward which most or all philosophers have striven. The ultimate object of philosophical thought is thought itself.

We can also investigate the meaning of "philosophy" by inquiring into the tradition of the word. Pythagoras is said to have been the first person to use this term to describe himself. Cicero tells us that Pythagoras, when questioned by Leon, king of Phlius, as to what this term meant, gave the following response:

> [Pythagoras] replied that the life of man seemed to him to resemble the festival which was celebrated with most magnificent games before a concourse collected from the whole of Greece; for at this festival some men whose bodies had been trained sought to win the glorious distinction of a crown, others were attracted by the prospect of making gain by buying or selling, whilst there was on the other hand a certain class, and that quite the best type of free-born men, who looked nei-

---

6 See Ernst Cassirer, *The Philosophy of Symbolic Forms, vol. 2: Mythical Thought*, trans. Ralph Manheim (New Haven, CT: Yale University Press, 1955): "None of [the basic forms of cultural life] started out with an independent existence and clearly defined outlines of its own; in its beginnings, rather, every one of them was shrouded and disguised in some form of myth" (xiv). See also Bruno Snell's *The Discovery of the Mind* and F. M. Cornford's *From Religion to Philosophy*. Both writers' central theses are that western philosophy has its origin in mythical thought.

ther for applause nor gain, but came for the sake of the spectacle and closely watched what was done and how it was done. So also we, as though we had come from some city to a kind of crowded festival, leaving in like fashion another life and nature of being, entered upon this life, and some were slaves of ambition, some of money; there were a special few who, counting all else as nothing, closely scanned the nature of things; these men gave themselves the name of lovers of wisdom (for that is the meaning of the word philosopher); and just as at the games the men of truest breeding looked on without any self-seeking, so in life the contemplation and discovery of nature far surpassed all other pursuits (*Tusc. Disp.*, V. iii.8–9).

Iamblichus gives a similar account, though without reference to Leon. He adds emphasis to the particular things loved by the lovers of wisdom. He writes, "Wisdom indeed, truly so called, is a certain science which is conversant with the first beautiful objects, and these divine, undecaying, and possessing an invariable sameness of subsistence; by the participation of which other things may be called beautiful. But philosophy is the appetition of a thing of this kind."[7]

Philosophy, as conceived by Pythagoras, is the disinterested love of the spectacle of the world. It is disinterested because it does not hope to gain anything from the spectacle. It is the drive of *eros* to contemplate the beautiful, and the beautiful is that which endures. This view of philosophy is first seriously challenged by Plato in the *Phaedo*. This dialogue takes place in Phlius, where Pythagoras gave Leon his definition. Phaedo is reporting on the last hours of Socrates' life to a group of Pythagoreans. In this context, Plato has Socrates say, "Those who practice philosophy in the right way are in training for dying [*hoi orthos philosophountes apothneskin neskein meletosi*]" (67e). Philosophy is here redefined as learning to die. Learning to die, of course, means learning to live rightly. The two moments of this conceptual framing give the impetus to the practice of philosophy for all future generations. Philosophy is the contemplation of the wondrous; the only debate is whether the greater wonder is in the world or within oneself, object or subject. Following this ancient tradition, philosophy will be understood throughout this work as contemplation of the wondrous. I leave it to the partisans of different conceptions of philosophy to determine what the doctrine of "memory as philosophy" has to offer their fields.

There are two guiding questions I wish to explore in this work. These are: (1) Is it possible at present to hold a philosophical doctrine of

---

7   Iamblichus, *Life of Pythagoras*, trans. Thomas Taylor (Rochester, VT: Inner Traditions, 1986), 29.

memory? Phrased differently, this question aims to consider whether it is possible to understand memory as the human faculty central to the work of philosophy. I believe that the answer is yes. The first section, "The Idea of Memory," is an attempt to demonstrate how we can and should think about "memory as philosophy." This section is the overtly theoretical portion of the work. It will suggest an approach to philosophy as a whole—not a new approach, but one that has been left behind for some time. In my presentation, I will seek to reattach philosophy in the age of technology to its origins in the sacred house of the Muses.

(2) Is there a tradition of viewing philosophy and memory in this way? The purpose of asking this question is to put this doctrine, unfamiliar to most, into a historical context, to show that it is not only possible to think in this way, but also that it has powered some of the most profound and effective philosophies the West has produced. The memory tradition exists in perambulations. Most obviously, memory is a central topic in the thinking of Plato and Aristotle. After this, however, it wanes and waxes. We find pronounced philosophical doctrines of memory in Cicero and St. Augustine, and then again throughout the Middle Ages and Renaissance. *Ars memoria*, the "art of memory" (thought to be Ciceronian) becomes a dominant pedagogical technique throughout Europe. The Hermetic tradition and Lullism intertwine with this "art of memory" when taken up by the Italian humanists. Memory and the occult become fused for a time, as we find in the work of colorful figures like Giulio Camillo and Giordano Bruno. The second section will explore some of the vicissitudes of the philosophical history of memory.

This discussion is not without precedent. There has been a good deal of excellent scholarly work in the past decades on *ars memoriae*. The present work is greatly indebted to Paolo Rossi's *Clavis Universalis* (1960), Frances Yates' *The Art of Memory* (1966), and Mary Carruthers' *The Book of Memory* (1990). Their careful and thorough research into the medieval memory arts leaves little to be desired. However, none of these authors is primarily concerned with the *philosophical* aspect of memory, and none follows the memory tradition beyond the Renaissance, though each suggests that one could do so. Part of my purpose is to give a philosophical history of memory. This history will not be exhaustive, but will rather focus on certain major figures in order to convey a sense of the movements of the tradition. Another part of my purpose is to consider the development of this tradition into modernity.

At the start of the modern period of philosophy, the memory tradition abruptly terminates. Modern science has no place in its operation and its great undertakings for the fragility of human recollection. When Descartes replaces memory with method, the faculty of reflection arises and steals the philosophical Caduceus. In part, this decline of the memory tradition had been prepared by its very ubiquity. In the hands of so many dilettantes, and making so many false promises to deliver divine power to its disciples, the art of memory had come, by the time of the Copernican Revolution, to look very much like a hollow pseudo-science. I will suggest, however, that the memory tradition does not simply die out, but continues on, becoming even more philosophically refined than at its height of popularity. To demonstrate two of the forms it takes in later thought, I have selected as my exemplars two thinkers not often put in dialogue with one another: Michel de Montaigne and G. W. F. Hegel. The third section of this work contains exegeses of their respective writings, in an attempt to show that the works of both men ultimately depend upon philosophical doctrines of memory. The purpose of this is twofold: both to show the functionality of philosophical memory in the age of science, and also to contribute something original to the scholarship on both philosophers. Very few commentators have fully grasped the role or contextual background of memory in either figure's thought.

I feel that I must justify my selection of these two men as exemplars. There are several reasons behind my choice to do so. Foremost, they represent (both chronologically and philosophically) the beginning and end of a linear period of modern philosophy. Montaigne, writing at the time of the final sickness of the classical memory tradition, is explicitly opposed to the "art of memory." His own, original doctrine of memory is much more philosophically productive than that of his time. Hegel, I propose, re-embraces this tradition at the end of the period called "modernity," though in his thinking it is thoroughly modified and transformed. What is the intellectual period that Montaigne and Hegel bookend? This period runs in a direct line from Descartes through Kant. It is the epoch of modern philosophy in which the faculty of *reflection* is elevated to the highest place, as we will see in the third chapter. Between my discussions of Montaigne and Hegel, I have included two chapters exploring those social and intellectual forces that contributed to the decay of the memory tradition (both without and within the arena of philosophy) in the age of modernity.

Montaigne's philosophy depends on memory. Descartes' method is in large part a response to Montaigne, and the Cartesian philosophy of reflection dominated the philosophical field through the time of Kant. Kant's *Critique of Pure Reason*, far from breaking with Descartes, in fact carries Cartesian dualism to its natural terminus, a point at which the two realms of being fail to touch at all. Hegel's philosophy is in large part a response to Kant, and his "absolute knowing" is ultimately a rejection of reflective thinking and a return to the primacy of memory. Approaching philosophical memory in this way will show us something about the history of modern philosophy that has not been adequately emphasized by commentators.

There are striking similarities between the two philosophers, but I do not intend to make a comparative study. Montaigne has a dialectical approach to thought that comes close to Hegel's. The essay as a form is naturally dialectical. Theodor Adorno is right in saying, "The essay takes Hegelian philosophy at its word ... the claim of the particular to truth is taken literally to the point where there is evidence of its untruth."[8] It is not yet Hegel's dialectic, though: the stark separation between the two concerns the question of system. For Hegel, valid philosophy is always a *Systematik*. Regarding Montaigne, Aldous Huxley is not speaking hyperbolically when he refers to the *Essays* as "one damned thing after another—but in a sequence that in some almost miraculous way develops a central theme and relates it to the rest of human experience."[9] Montaigne does not have a system. It is possible that Hegel is *not* in fact as systematic a thinker as he himself claims, but this is a question I will delay until the final two chapters.

Because of this affinity in methodological principle, reading the one project against the other is useful in understanding the similar role that memory plays in the thought of the two figures. There is also a certain affinity in the scope of both projects; both Montaigne's *Essays* and Hegel's systematic philosophy are undertakings that demonstrate enormous range of learning. They are the modern works of pansophism *par excellence*. The difference is that Montaigne is always skeptical of the human capacity to attain this universal wisdom, whereas Hegel, the philosopher of the Absolute, considers this to be the goal of all philosophy.

---

8   Theodor W. Adorno, "The Essay as Form," *New German Critique* 32 (Spring 1984): 166. Adorno is the only commentator I know of who has considered Montaigne and Hegel against one another. However, Adorno sees this relationship as one of irreconcilable opposition, which is not my position.
9   Aldous Huxley, *Collected Essays* (New York: Harper, 1955), vii.

It is highly unlikely that Hegel ever considered Montaigne a fellow traveler. He mentions Montaigne on two occasions, but there is no evidence that he ever read a word of the *Essays*. Both references appear in the *Lectures on the History of Philosophy*, and both seem to refer to the reputation of Montaigne rather than his actual writings. The first occurs in a section dealing with "Ciceronian popular philosophy." Montaigne's "popular writings" are mentioned along with those of his protégé, Pierre Charron. In reference to the work of Charron, and pertaining as well to the *Essays* of Montaigne, Hegel writes that "they belong to common sense" and not philosophy proper (*W*, XX: 17, my translation).[10] Charron, who bore the arms of Montaigne after the latter's death, was famous for writing in defense of Roman Catholicism against Protestantism. Donald Frame writes: "[Charron] rejects [Montaigne's] self-portrait, the play with ideas, the graceful irregularity, the serene acceptance of the human condition. Thus even in his most literal borrowings he changes Montaigne—perhaps without conscious intent—by making his ideas methodical, rigid, even dogmatic. Montaigne's distinction between religious belief and morality becomes a gulf in Charron."[11] The coupling of Montaigne with Charron certainly does not resound favorably to Montaigne, considering Hegel's commitment to the Lutheran faith. If it was through Charron that Hegel had a sense of Montaigne's work, this could only have been a one-sided sense.

For Hegel, the benefit of the Ciceronian form of philosophy is that it "deals with everything that takes place in the human soul and feelings. That is its merit, which is all the greater in view of the prevalent religious selflessness" (*LHP*, 59). However, this is also its shortcoming and the reason it fails to live up to true, systematic philosophy. In the second reference, Hegel lists Montaigne along with Charron and Machiavelli as "remarkable men" who "properly do not belong to philosophy but rather to general culture." They offer perceptive insights about human life, but "since they do not take the highest inquiry of philosophy as the topic of their investigation, and since they have not reasoned from thought as

---

10 This reference appears in neither of the two English-language translations of the *History of Philosophy* lectures: the nineteenth century version of E. S. Haldane and Frances H. Simson (from Michelet's second edition), nor the twentieth century translation of Robert F. Brown (from the 1825–26 lectures). I have translated directly from the Suhrkamp edition.
11 Donald M. Frame, *Montaigne's Essais: A Study* (Englewood Cliffs, NJ: Prentice-Hall, 1969), 98. A longer discussion of Charron's appropriation of Montaigne appears in Frame, *Montaigne: A Biography* (New York: Harcourt, Brace & World, 1965), 312–14.

such, they do not properly belong to the history of philosophy" (*LHP*, 74–5; *W*, XX: 48). Hegel seems to respect the man Montaigne and the practical utility of his ethical teachings, but he does not consider him anything more than a sort of philosophical dilettante. While a general *Bildung* would include Montaigne, he remains on the outside of Hegel's conception of philosophical *Bildung*.

The pairing of these two writers does not involve a claim of intellectual inheritance or transmission. For whatever similarities they evince, it is just as much their differences that make them an interesting tandem. This is the second major reason I wish to consider them together. The two objects central to philosophical investigation are the good and the true. It is Montaigne who teaches us how memory can reveal the good, and Hegel who teaches how it can reveal the true. Memory for Montaigne is ethical, and for Hegel it is metaphysical. By considering the two as a pair, we can understand the implicit role of memory in modern philosophy, and we can also understand something about the project of modernity writ large. This dialogue has never been attempted before. Adorno suggests that the essay is the natural opposite to any philosophy of the Absolute,[12] which in some ways is correct. However, it is worth noting in this context what Hegel says about polarity: the north pole *is* the south pole. The south is only south in reference to the north, but the north is itself south in reference to the south. Polar opposition is not a relationship that excludes its opposite, but one in which opposites meet (*EL*, §119).

I must respond to one potential criticism that I foresee. In the following work, as I have already said, I will attempt to show the centrality of memory to the history of philosophy, and in particular to the writing of Montaigne and Hegel. This is a heterodox reading of these thinkers, and I expect some version of the following objection: Is this not an imposition of your own interests? How can you claim that your interpretations of Hegel, Montaigne, and the history of philosophy are legitimate or "objective" and not perverse? These questions miss the fact that philosophy has yet to find an Archimedean point (though as an ideal, this is always worth seeking). Knowing a man's philosophy, we likewise know the

---

12 See Adorno, "The Essay as Form": "If the essay is accused of lacking a standpoint and of tending toward relativism because it recognizes no standpoint lying outside of itself, then the accusation implicitly contains the conception of truth as something 'ready-made,' a hierarchy of concepts, an image of truth that Hegel destroyed in his dislike of standpoints: in this the essay touches its polar opposite, the philosophy of absolute knowledge" (166).

man. Every commentator imposes his or her own interests upon the text at hand. This is the very manner in which philosophy progresses. The inner movement of philosophy is a dialectic between a body of received texts, with their claims to objective truth, and the subject's own history and *doxes*. The opposition between the two is what drives thought forward.

Great texts are the Pillars of Hercules. One may approach them from the west, and see them as the sign that one has—at last—come upon safe waters; from this point, we can stay close to the shores and come ever closer to the comforts of home. Or one may approach from the east, and look out upon the vast, open waters that lie beyond, unexplored. *All* commentaries, if not mere repetitions of the original, are shaded by the commentator's interests and background. The plurality of these interests is what proves great texts to be as limitless as the seas beyond the Pillars. Commentaries that add nothing foreign to the original and never get beyond orthodox standards neither instruct nor delight.

PART ONE: THEORY

Section One: The Idea of Memory

> Has it ever struck you, Connie, that life is all memory, except for the one present moment that goes by you so quick you hardly catch it going? It's really all memory, Connie, except for each passing moment.
>
> Tennessee Williams, *The Milk Train Doesn't Stop Here Anymore*

There can be no doubt that all our knowledge depends on memory. We have no knowledge antecedent to memory, and with memory all our knowledge begins. In the present section, I will explain in what manner I understand these claims, and I will offer a view of memory as the human faculty central to philosophy. There are five natural divisions of this section. The first, as decency demands of all written work, is an appeal to the wellsprings of the most ancient wisdom of the western world, the Muses and Isis. The second is a survey of what philosophical memory *is not*. Following this, the third will say what philosophical memory *is*. The fourth is a corollary: a philosophical doctrine of memory must be supplemented with a philosophical doctrine of forgetting. The fifth shows memory in its external relationships to the present world—that is, to those twin sisters, method and technology.

I: The Origins of Wisdom

The Muses

The earliest Greek wisdom that has come down to us is that of the theological poets.[1] The *Theogony* of Hesiod does not look like an authoritative text in the modern sense. There are no deductions and no arguments; Hesiod simply tells us how things are. But this was nonetheless a work of deep wisdom, as every Greek well knew. Hesiod is not a capricious "rhymester," to use an insult coined by Stephen Dedalus. He is a divine poet who simply tells us how things are, *rerum natura*. Mythical consciousness is perception itself as a way of thinking, and all myths are simple truths.[2] The great power of Hesiod's authority is evidenced by his ban from Kallipolis.[3]

Proper to the work of a poet, the *Theogony* begins with an appeal to the Muses, who are not first in time but first in knowing: "Muses of Helicon, let us begin our song with them" (*Theog.*, 1). The Muses are the sources of inspiration for the various human arts. More than this, they are the wellsprings of the wisdom of these arts, the source of Hesiod and Homer's simple truths. Homer's epics are equally contemporary to every age because of his pious deference to the Muse.[4] It is not human wisdom but the Muse's wisdom that tells us through Homer the universal history of man. The wise poet or artist must be sure to court the particular Muse set over his or her art. In some traditions, the Muses *are* the arts that they represent. To name the Muse is to name the art by metonymy.

---

1   Vico's three axioms of poetic wisdom are relevant here: "That all the histories of the gentile nations had fabulous beginnings, that among the Greeks (who have given us all we know of gentile antiquity) the first sages were the theological poets, and that the nature of everything born or made betrays the crudeness of its origin. ... Just as Manetho, the Egyptian high priest, translated all the fabulous history of Egypt into a sublime natural theology, so the Greek philosophers translated theirs into philosophy." *New Science*, §361.
2   See Ernst Cassirer's discussion of the *Ausdrucksfunktion* in the third volume of the *Philosophy of Symbolic Forms*, especially Part 1.2, "The Phenomenon of Expression as the Basic Factor in the Perceptive Consciousness."
3   See Plato, *Rep.*, II, III and X, especially 377d and 605a–c.
4   The *Iliad* and *Odyssey* open: μῆνιν ἄειδε θεὰ Πηληϊάδεω Ἀχιλῆος, and ἄνδρα μοι ἔννεπε, μοῦσα, πολύτροπον, ὅς μάλα πολλὰ, respectively. Each begins with an appeal to the Muse (reading θεὰ as μοῦσα). C.f. Bruno Snell, *The Discovery of the Mind in Greek Philosophy and Literature*, trans. T.G. Rosenmeyer (New York: Dover, 1982), 136–38.

The Muses are not first in time. Chaos is first in the genealogy of Hesiod, preceding all of the particularized gods and invisible powers. From whence do the Muses spring? Their father is Zeus, king of the later gods, whom they delight with their hymns. Their birthright through Zeus is their authority. Their mother, Hesiod tells us, is Mnemosyne—that is, memory personified (*Theog.*, 52–57). Mnemosyne is conceived, in the earliest poetic wisdom, as the mother, the fountainhead, of all of the human arts. Memory is the first principle of human invention, without which there is only brute existence. The epigraph from Dante at the start of the introduction to the present work shows that the Muses were still thought of as daughters of memory well beyond the Greco-Roman world.

The birthright of the Muses from their mother's side is the ability to sing of "what is and what will be and what has been" (*Theog.*, 38, translation mine). This line of Hesiod, which became a formulaic commonplace in antiquity, is crucial to understanding the foundation of a philosophical doctrine of memory. The Muses have complete knowledge of the *whole*, and we know that the true is the whole. The modality of this knowledge is necessity. What is, will be, and has been is the object sought by the *eros* of the philosopher; it is both the true and the good. It is also the proper object of memory. Memory in its philosophical sense is not limited to hindsight, but is rather concerned to envelop the whole, the complete speech. The philosopher must be Prometheus (foresight) as well as Epimetheus (hindsight)—Epimetheus by himself has no gifts for humanity.[5] Philosophical memory takes up the past, but not as dead matter. It sees in what it recollects the movement of necessity in things. In using the word "necessity" here, I mean to say that memory is able to root out the inner form and inner movement of its object. This necessary movement is that which obtains in the future just as much as the past. If we grasp the sources of all things past, we also know the sources of present and future things. We know things not just as they appear, but by their essence.

This is not a perverse reading of the meaning of the term "memory". Philologically, this evidence from Hesiod shows that from the earliest times, the wisdom of Mnemosyne was understood as projecting into all three dimensions of time. The western idea of memory derives from this *muthos*, or rather from the symbolic form of consciousness that expressed this *muthos* and knew it to be true. The human arts spring up from Mother Memory; the Muses, children of Memory that

---

5   See Plato, *Prot.*, 320d–322a.

guide and direct these arts, are able to guide humanity's institutions because of their memorial knowledge of past, present and future. A one-sided view of memory that limits its sphere to hindsight is a conception that has lost much from the rich ancient understanding of the faculty.

The Muses come to Hesiod and speak their wisdom directly to him. The Muses are *muthos* personified.[6] There is an etymological connection between the words, and a corresponding conceptual connection: the poetic wisdom of myth is the gift of the Muses. They say to Hesiod, "Field-dwelling shepherds, ignoble disgraces, mere bellies: we know how to say many false things similar to genuine ones, but we know, when we wish, how to proclaim true things" (*Theog.*, 26–28). Lewis Hyde interprets this passage as indicating that the Muses believe that the *human* capacity for lying is a result of the human's imperfect condition and submission to the appetites of the stomach.[7] Instead, it should be understood as the Muses announcing that they themselves can speak truth or falsehood, when they will. Only the intellect that already knows the whole can properly will to speak true or false. The Muses simultaneously hold all that was, is, and shall be in memory. Their decision to speak true or false to mankind is determined by man's status as an appetitive creature. They are prudent in their revelations. To Zeus, they always sing truly (*Theog.*, 36–38); mortal man must beware, but to man they *can* sing truly if they will. T. S. Eliot joins to this a second warning for those who would court the divine sisters: "Anyone who has ever been visited by the Muse is thenceforth haunted."[8]

There is another significant claim that Hesiod makes about the Muses, one which must not be taken to contradict their genealogy. He says that the *nature* of the Muses is "forgetfulness of evils and relief from anxieties" (*Theog.*, 55). How can the daughters of Mnemosyne have a nature of forgetfulness? This anticipates the philosophical doctrine of forgetting that I will articulate in the fourth chapter. These two items, "forgetfulness of evils" and "relief from anxieties," are not separate, juxtaposed things, but are one and the same. An indiscriminate memory that cannot forget is cut off from happiness. Happiness must embrace what is

---

6 See Lisa Atwood Wilkinson, *Socratic Charis: Philosophy without the Agon* (Lanham, MD: Lexington Books, 2013): "The Muses, then, are *muthos*. Much as Memory is inseparable from Mnemosyne, *muthos* is inseparable from the Muses" (58).
7 Lewis Hyde, *Trickster Makes this World* (New York: Farras, Straus & Giroux, 1998), 66–67.
8 T. S. Eliot, *The Use of Poetry and the Use of Criticism* (London: Faber and Faber, 1964), 69.

at hand, which is why it is so fleeting in this finite life. A capacity for forgetfulness is the condition (necessary, but not sufficient) for taking pleasure in life. Pleasure requires discrimination and judgment. There can be no freedom from cares or evils if these evils are at all times living, haunting images without relief.

The power to forget always depends upon the power to remember; again we find that the opposites touch one another. To say that the nature of the Muses is forgetfulness is at the same time to say that their nature is memory. It is to have a vital memory rather than one fixed in petrifaction. The Muses know all, but because they are divine they are able to forget when they will, just as they are able to speak falsely when they will. To deprive these goddesses of the art of forgetting would be to condemn them to unhappiness, and to give humankind an excellence lacking to divinity.

The veil of Isis

Much earlier than the Greek wisdom tradition, the dominant locus of Western mythical knowledge was Egypt. I wish to turn to a discussion of the goddess Isis, not in her original Egyptian context, but as transmitted to the Greek world. I am not here concerned with the popular story most associated with Isis: that of her role in the story of the death and resurrection of her brother and husband, Osiris.[9] This myth is interesting in its own right, but the importance of Isis in the present work concerns only her portrayal in the ancient European wisdom tradition.

This goddess is mentioned twice by Herodotus, who had visited Egypt in the fifth century BCE. At one point in his treatment of Egypt in the *Histories*, he mentions that cows are sacred to her and that her statues often portray her with a cow's horns (*Hist.*, II. 41). Later, he writes of a temple and festival at Busiris that honor the goddess. In this passage, he equates her to the goddess Demeter (*Hist.*, II. 60–61).[10] Demeter, whose counterpart in Roman mythology is Ceres, is the Greek goddess of the harvest and fertility, mother of Persephone.

Five centuries later, Plutarch, who had also visited Egypt at one point, composed *De Iside et Osiride*, a much more extensive treatment of Isis than that of Herodotus. Though cults of Isis had already sprung up in

---

9   For this story, and other prominent Isis myths, see R. E. Witt, *Isis in the Graeco-Roman World* (Ithaca, NY: Cornell University Press, 1971), 36–45.
10 Isis literally *is* Demeter, translated into the Egyptian milieu. See Bruno Snell, *Discovery of the Mind*, 24.

Greece by 330 BCE, this work, however inaccurate it may have been in its portrayal of Egyptian culture, was partially responsible for enflaming the ensuing European interest in these deities.[11] Plutarch writes: "Many writers have held [Isis] to be the daughter of Hermes, and many others the daughter of Prometheus, because of the belief that Prometheus is the discoverer of wisdom and forethought, and Hermes the inventor of grammar and music. For this reason they call the first of the Muses at Hermopolis Isis as well as Justice [*Dikaiosune*]: for she is wise[12], as I have said, and discloses the divine mysteries to those who truly and justly have the name of 'bearers of the sacred vessels' and 'wearers of the sacred robes'" (*Is. Os.*, 3, 352B).

Plutarch, with his Greek sensibilities, intuitively understood the kinship between the figure of Isis and the Muses. The link is made because of her great wisdom, which, as we will see, is of the same nature as that of the Muses: knowing what is and what will be and what has been. Hers is the wisdom of Mnemosyne, which recollects the inner movement of the whole. Not only is Isis wise, but she also discloses her wisdom to those who are deserving, in the manner of the Muses. She gives guidance in those matters human intelligence cannot penetrate. The figures suggested for the parentage of Isis are revealing: Prometheus is synonymous with foresight, the direction of memory that looks ahead in time. Hermes—that is, Hermes Trismegistus, the "thrice-great"—is a figure we will confront throughout this work because of his influence on the memory tradition of the Renaissance and the notion attributed to him of man as the cosmos in miniature.

In a later passage, Plutarch writes: "It is not right to believe that water or the sun or the earth or the sky is Osiris or Isis." He does not interpret these deities as anthropomorphic personifications of the natural elements, nor as limited to a single sphere of influence. This is a rejection of the identity that Herodotus found between Demeter (the harvest personified) and Isis. He continues, "If we revere and honor what is orderly and good and beneficial as the work of Isis and as the image and reflection and reason of Osiris, we shall not be wrong" (*Is. Os.*, 64, 376F–377A). Isis is the deity that brings into existence (a) order, in place of chaos, and (b) the "good and beneficial," that is, the human arts, whereby

---

11   See Frank Cole Babbitt's introduction to *Is. Os.*, 3. It is also noteworthy that Babbitt believes Plutarch's primary sources were priests and books present in Greece, rather than anything he may have learned while in Egypt (3–5).

12   Babbitt notes that σοφὴν οὖσαν appears in some manuscript editions as σοφίαν, which would change the translation to: "She is Wisdom itself."

humans are raised from the condition of savage being. It is Isis to whom one must pray for divine wisdom and inspiration. Again, we see her kinship to the Muses.

There is another deeply important passage in Plutarch. Just after he says that Egyptian philosophy is "veiled in myths and in words containing dim reflections and adumbrations of the truth," Plutarch relates a famous inscription found in the western Nile delta town of Saïs. He writes, "In Saïs the statue of Athena, whom they believe to be Isis, bore the inscription: 'I am all that has been, and is, and shall be, and my veil no mortal has yet uncovered'" (*Is. Os.*, 9, 354C, translation altered). Isis is identified by Plutarch with Athena, the Greek goddess of wisdom. The passage does not imply that the Egyptians have simply mistaken a temple of Athena for one of Isis; rather, Plutarch is claiming that the statue of Isis *is* Athena because in his view the two goddesses are, on a practical level, one and the same. Of what subjects does the wisdom of Isis partake? Isis *is* what has been, what is, and what shall be; her being is the inner form of the whole. Her wisdom is of herself. No mortal has lifted her veil because it is the privilege of the gods to hold in recollection the complete view of the inner necessity of the cosmos. Like the Muses, Isis can sing to mortals of her wisdom, but their limitations prevent them from fully understanding what they hear or receiving more than partial truths.

This notion of the veiled wisdom of Isis, like the "veil of Maya" of Oriental traditions, is the basis of an ancient mystery tradition of esoteric wisdom. Isis herself was often associated with magic, and the occult was thought to be the secret instrument for "lifting the veil" and attaining the complete memory of the gods.[13] This understanding of the role of the occult was taken up later by the Hermetic tradition.[14] The idea of wisdom as hidden behind a veil has come down to modernity as a cliché because of its ubiquity. We find the image in W.E.B. DuBois' veil between the races and John Rawls' "veil of ignorance," both of which owe something to the cultural diffusion of the idea of the veil of Isis. There were always those skeptical of this mystery tradition; Montaigne, for one, says: "The

---

13 See Geraldine Pinch, *Handbook of Egyptian Mythology* (Santa Barbara, CA: ABC-Clio, 2002), 151. Isis was called the "*Weret-Hekau*," that is, "the Great of Magic." The view of Isis as initiator into the mysteries was a view that preceded even Herodotus by some time (153).
14 See the two-volume *magnum opus* of H. P. Blavatsky, *Isis Unveiled*, on the efforts of esoteric science and theology to "lift the veil" of Isis. Umberto Eco uses "Isis Unveiled" as the title of a fictional series of esoteric and occult publications in *Foucault's Pendulum*.

Egyptians, with unwise freedom, forbade, under pain of hanging, that anyone should say that Serapis and Isis, their gods, had once been men; and no one was unaware that they had been. And their statues representing them with a finger to their lips signified, says Varro, that mysterious ordinance to their priests to hush up their mortal origin" (*CE*, II: 12, 384; *V*, 517). For Montaigne, the great secret that the statues of Isis conceal with finger to mouth is that there is no secret.

This passage in Plutarch was known and reflected upon by Hegel, which lends it much of its relevance in the current work. We will see in the fourth section that for Hegel—who was deeply interested in occult and magical traditions[15]—the veil "melts away before thought" (*PN*, §246, Z). Through philosophical thinking, we can acquire the memory of the gods. Unlike other Hegelian images, such as the "Owl of Minerva" in the *Philosophy of Right*, this image has inspired little or no significant commentary. I will suggest in the final two chapters that this image is the key to understanding the role of memory in Hegel's philosophy.

This discussion of the Muses and Isis provides the groundwork for the archaeological rediscovery of philosophical memory. In the most ancient wisdom traditions, wisdom and philosophy are transmitted through these parallel goddesses, whose gaze embraces the inner movement and providential order of past, present, and future. This complete view of the whole is memory in its original and richest sense; it is the secret and divine wisdom of Mnemosyne. Without a preliminary understanding of the Muses and Isis, and the origins of philosophy in theological poetry, one cannot rise to the concept of "memory as philosophy." The Muses' song and what lies behind the veil of Isis are the contents of the divine memory. They are also two ways of naming the obscure object of the philosopher's *eros, il dilettoso monte* away in the distance.

---

15 Glenn Alexander Magee has demonstrated Hegel's lifelong interests in magic, alchemy, etc., the influence of Hermetic thinkers on his work, and his correspondences with prominent occult figures of his time, in *Hegel and the Hermetic Tradition*.

II: What Memory as Philosophy is Not

Having given the philological foundation for the doctrine "memory as philosophy," I will now turn to say what a philosophical memory is not before saying what it is. The term "memory" has a great many applications and a great many aspects; its mantle has been taken up by every discipline. As I have said above, not every instance of memory is an instance of philosophy. In his *Naturalis historia*, Pliny the Elder claims, amongst other examples of men with prodigious faculties of recollection, that Cyrus I knew the names of all of the soldiers in his massive army, Lucius Scipio knew the names of the entire Roman populace, and the Greek Charmadas "recited the contents of volumes in libraries that anyone asked him to quote, just as if he were reading them" (*Nat. Hist.*, VII. xxiv.88–90).[1] Marsilio Ficino adds to this list Seneca, who "had taken two hundred verses recited by his disciples and repeated them in reverse order," Mithridates, who knew the languages of all twenty-two peoples he governed, and others.[2]

It is clear that these men, interesting as their feats of recollection may be, are not for all this philosophers. It is necessary, then, that limits be set so as to give definition to the idea of "memory as philosophy." These limits are discovered by considering what falls outside of the matter at issue. In the present section, I will discuss three competing views of memory that are prominent today, but that do not capture what is at stake with "memory as philosophy." Each of these views has a high social *value*, to be sure; my intention is not to undermine any of them or claim that the rediscovery of a philosophical doctrine of memory would cancel their importance in their own spheres. Memory is a house with many mansions. These three views are those of: (α) biology, (β) psychology, and (γ) Nietzsche.[3]

---

1   Pliny also mentions Simonides, the founder of the *memoria technica*, who will be discussed in the following chapter.
2   Marsilio Ficino, *Platonic Theology*, trans. Michael J.B. Allen (Cambridge, MA: I Tatti Renaissance Library, 2004), XIII. iii.9.
3   While these are the three most respected approaches to memory in the contemporary world, I must acknowledge a number of twentieth-century writers who have developed their own versions of "memory as philosophy." Henri Bergson, Ernst Cassirer, Stanley Cavell, R. G. Collingwood, Karl Jaspers, Paul Ricoeur, George Santayana, and Eric Voegelin immediately come to mind as thinkers with some doctrine of philosophical memory underlying some or all of their works. In the literary world, Augusto Roa Bastos, Jorge Luis Borges, James Joyce, and Marcel Proust have grasped the fun-

The biological view

The ultimate goal of science is always liberation from the yoke of the unpredictability of nature. If human beings can understand how nature works, understand the causes of things, then they can either control nature and turn it toward their own ends, or else replace nature altogether. The human will is set up over and against the purposiveness of natural laws, since each is the final limit of the other.

Neurobiology, which is a relatively embryonic field, has taken up the study of the brain as the place, the location, of thought. The goal of this science of the brain is to understand the functions of and interrelations between the physical structures of the brain, so as to understand the material processes that manifest themselves to us as thought. Despite its young age, this field has made remarkable progress in cerebral mapping, and it has yielded remarkable drugs for the treatment of cognitive disorders. In the near future, it promises even further advancements with regard to disorders of memory like Alzheimer's disease. I have no intention of claiming that mind and body are dissociable terms. It is clear that thought, and memory in particular, is bound to these structures of the anatomy that are slowly being uncovered, and that neurobiology is of great utility to humanity. The question is: what can neurobiology really say about "memory as philosophy"?

Eric Kandel received the 2000 Nobel Prize in Physiology or Medicine for his contributions to the field of memory. His work focuses on the physiology of memory storage in neurons, most of his research involving the large sea slug, *Aplysia*. Kandel is himself aware that research into memory is not the province of biology alone; in his textbook on memory, he (or his co-author) writes, "The analysis of how learning occurs and how memories are stored has been central to three intellectual disciplines: first philosophy, then psychology, and now biology. Until late in the nineteenth century, the study of memory was restricted largely to the domain of philosophy. However, during the twentieth century, the focus gradually moved to the more experimental studies, initially in psychology and more recently in biology. As we enter the next millennium, psychology and biology have begun to converge on common ground."[4] This is true as regards the study of the *mechanics* of memory, which is the

---

damental role of memory in human life. I will speak of many of these figures as this work unfolds.
4   Larry R. Squire and Eric. R. Kandel, *Memory: From Mind to Molecules* (Greenwood Village, CO: Roberts and Company, 2009), 2–3.

primary item of interest for biology and psychology. These two fields have come to work more and more closely in their research, while philosophers no longer dwell much upon the organic processes of memory, nor should they. This would be "philosophy *of* memory", which is distinct from "memory as philosophy". A philosophical doctrine of memory is not overly concerned with the structures of the brain. Aristotle's *noēsis noēseōs* is thought thinking thought, not thought thinking brains.

What are the leading questions of biological and psychological research into memory? "From the perspective of psychology these questions are: How does memory work? Are there different kinds of memory? If so, what is their logic? From the perspective of biology these questions are: Where in the brain do we learn? Where do we store what is learned as memory? Can memory storage be resolved at the level of individual nerve cells? If so, what is the nature of molecules that underlie the various processes of memory storage?"[5] The modern neurobiologist is concerned not with the metaphysics of memory, or its identification with the Muses and its role in human creativity and wisdom, but with how it operates on the material level of nerves and synapses. The neurobiological view of memory never bothers itself with the distinction in kind between Cyrus's mechanical memory of the names of his many soldiers and Homer's poetic memory of the *Iliad*.

In his part-history of biology, part-memoir, *In Search of Memory*, Kandel enumerates the five principles of the "new science" of neurobiology. The first of these is: "Mind and brain are inseparable. ... Mind is a set of operations carried out by the brain, much as walking is a set of operations carried out by the legs, except dramatically more complex." The second is, "Each mental function of the brain ... is carried out by specialized neural circuits in different regions of the brain."[6] Memory on this view is reduced to nothing more than a complex operation carried out by particular specialized neurons. The neurobiologist takes humans to be much closer to a *canard digérateur* than to the famous *Imago Dei*.

This view, along with its presuppositions, has yielded successful results with regard to the aims of biology. A neurobiology that began from the metaphysical assumption that mind is a divine thing, a microcosm, would never have discovered, for example, the role of cyclic adenosine monophosphate in short-term memory formation.[7] This knowledge

---

5   Ibid., 3.
6   Kandel, *In Search of Memory*, xii.
7   Ibid., 230ff.

is useful for treatments of pathologies or cognitive deviations from the norm, and such treatment is a human expression of mastery over nature. Hegel is correct when he says that a philosophy of nature must always agree with and take up the experimental discoveries of the empirical sciences (*PN*, §246). However, these presuppositions by themselves fall short of a philosophical anthropology and, while informing us how memory operates structurally, can never exhaust what memory is and can do.

We ought here to consider Heisenberg's uncertainty principle: "The knowledge of the position of a particle is complimentary to the knowledge of its velocity or momentum. If we know the one with high accuracy, we cannot know the other with high accuracy."[8] The *movement* of thought is its vitality, what makes it truly thought. To examine its location alone is to examine dead matter, a *caput mortuum*. We can never capture the full meaning and freedom of thought by simply mapping a physical network of cerebral places. When we pin down the butterfly to study it, we are no longer studying what makes it a butterfly: namely, its flight. Similarly, we can never attain a full understanding of a painting by Manet by studying only its brushstrokes and the chemical composition of the paint and canvas. Any reduction of human consciousness to infinitesimal physiological phenomena is a reduction that loses sight of the human. Memory *is* a complex of particular chemical saturations, but in its vitality it is also much more than this. As Donald Phillip Verene says, "Science is a kind of forgetting, a living in the present. It begins in a forgetting of the way and it will work itself out in an elaborate baroque line to the end of Spirit itself. Scientific *Wissenschaft* is the act of forgetting the self. Philosophical *Wissenschaft* is the act of recollecting it."[9] The self is the velocity that is lost when its location is pinned down by neurobiology.

This is a view of the human being that has always been shared by physiognomy and phrenology, though these practices were never able to rise to the level of true science. Physiognomists have existed at least as long as philosophers. Cicero relates a story about Socrates' encounter with a "physiognomist" [*physiognomon*] named Zopyrus: "Do we not read how Socrates was stigmatized by the 'physiognomist' Zopyrus, who professed to discover men's entire characters and natures from their body,

---

8 Werner Heisenberg, "The Copenhagen Interpretation of Quantum Theory," in *Physics and Philosophy: The Revolution of Modern Science* (New York: Harper Perennial, 2007), 23.
9 Donald Phillip Verene, *Hegel's Recollection: A Study of Images in the* Phenomenology of Spirit (Albany: State University of New York Press, 1985), 75.

eyes, face, and brow? He said that Socrates was stupid and thick-witted because he had not got hollows in the neck above the collarbone ... he also added that he was addicted to women" (*De Fato*, v.10).[10]

Montaigne was likewise familiar with the practice of physiognomy, which was popular enough in his time that the penultimate chapter of the *Essays* is titled "Of physiognomy." As a starting point, Montaigne writes, "There is nothing more likely than the conformity and relation of the body to the spirit" (*CE*, III: 12, 809; *V*, 1057), citing Cicero as evidence. However, this is followed almost immediately by a reversal. The "likeliness" of this claim does not hold of the two exemplars to whom Montaigne immediately appeals: Étienne de La Boétie (Montaigne's late boon companion, the subject of "Of friendship"), whose "ugliness ... clothed a very beautiful soul," and Socrates, whose physical ugliness is well known, but whose excellence of soul was natural and not, as Socrates himself claimed, "self-made" (ibid., 810; *V*, 1058). In a final turn, Montaigne relates two anecdotes about occasions on which he was personally delivered from danger because of "my face and the freedom and firmness of my speech, which made me undeserving of such a misadventure" (ibid., 814; *V*, 1062).[11] It is not the structure of Montaigne's skull but his bearing, the noble character presented by his *visage*, which delivers him. One's manner or behavior is its own mask, much more certain than one's physiognomy.

The formal "science" of physiognomy was founded by Johann Caspar Lavater in the second half of the eighteenth century. This discipline became the basis of the phrenology [*Phrenologie*] of Franz Joseph Gall, which attempted to account for human behavior through measurements of the features of the skull. These are the writers to whom Hegel is responding when he criticizes phrenology in the *Phenomenology of Spirit* (though Hegel uses the term *Schädellehre* rather than *Phrenologie*). The mistake of these pseudo-sciences is that they take the "outer shape" of organs to express the "inner individuality" of the organism (*PS*, §313; *W*, III: 236), and the skull to express the true being of a man, rather than his deeds (*PS*, §322; *W*, III: 242). Hegel writes, "The murderer is neither

---

10 This story is also related in *Tusc. Disp.*, IV. xxxvii.80.
11 This resonates with the speech of Alcibiades in Plato's *Symposium*. Alcibiades says that during the Athenians' retreat from Delium he saw Socrates "making his way exactly as he does around town," serenely, calmly observing everything. The enemy could clearly see "that this was a very brave man, who would put up a terrific fight if anyone approached him" (*Symp.*, 221a–b). Like Montaigne, the character of Socrates expressed itself in his countenance and carriage, his actual behavior, rather than his skeleton.

merely this abstraction of a murderer, nor does he have only one bump and one hollow" (*PS*, §335; *W*, III: 253). The murderer is such because of his act, not because of any physical structure. Phrenologists and physiognomists understand human behavior by referring it to a bone, but behavior and its meaning are not reducible to a physiological location in this way. In a passage striking for its violence, Hegel says that the proper retort to such a line of argument would "have to go the length of beating in the skull of anyone making such a judgment, in order to demonstrate in a manner just as palpable as his wisdom, that for a man, a bone is nothing *in itself*, much less *his* true reality" (*PS*, §339; *W*, III: 256–7). The inner workings of spirit cannot be explained away by any outer manifestation.[12]

Neurobiologists are not phrenologists, and they should not be answered by beatings to the skull. Though there is no correlation between the parietal bone and behavior, there *is* a correlation between neurons and behavior. However, the two practices share the assumptions that all human behavior is reducible to physical locations, and that all faculties of thought are nothing more than the by-products of local, material phenomena. The neurobiologist always ignores the observation of Berkeley: "When therefore you say, all ideas are occasioned by impressions in the brain, do you conceive this brain or no? If you do, then you talk of ideas imprinted in an idea, causing that same idea, which is absurd."[13] Memory on this view is always approached as a question for reflective thinking. Science forgets that memory is, as Henri Bergson says, "the intersection of mind and matter,"[14] not the reduction of the one to the other. Science always forgets the self while studying the organism.

The psychological view

There are several different psychological standpoints in regard to memory. (i) One branch of research, that which Kandel mentions as moving ever closer to biology, is interested in the diagnosis and treat-

---

12   Verene sees B. F. Skinner and the behaviorist movement as the psychological heirs to this anthropology. See his discussion in *Hegel's Recollection*, 83–86.
13   George Berkeley, *Three Dialogues Between Hylas and Philonous* (New York: Bobbs-Merrill, 1954), 53.
14   See Henri Bergson, *Matter and Memory*, trans. N.M. Paul and W.S. Palmer (New York: Zone Books, 1988): "Memory—we shall try to prove in the course of this work—is just the intersection of mind and matter. ... No one, at any rate, will deny that, among all the facts capable of throwing light on the psychophysiological relation, those which concern memory, whether in the normal or in the pathological sense, hold a privileged position" (13).

ment of pathologies of memory. This branch of psychology is subject to the same analysis as neurobiology insofar as it ultimately views and treats these pathologies as the result of biochemical processes located in the brain or nervous system. Thought is valued primarily as an index of internal processes.

(ii) A second branch of psychology, more properly called "popular psychology," is a body of literature targeted at a mass audience. This branch abounds with advice for strengthening memory in its most general sense, the everyday memory of facts and trivialities. This field is always profitable, and usually does have some basis in hard empirical research. Its primary utility is its suggestion to the student of principles for more efficient learning. One can always find small books by small psychologists, suggesting some mnemonic techniques which are usually quite unoriginal. One such book, of a much higher quality than most others, is I. M. L. Hunter's *Memory: Facts and Fallacies*. Hunter's definition of memory is the commonsense view. He writes, "Memory refers to this pervasive and many-sided characteristic of biographical change. It refers to the effects which a person's past can exert on his present activities. It refers to the relationships that exist between what a person is doing and experiencing, here and now, and what he did and experienced at some point in his past. It refers to the ways in which past experiences are utilized in present activity."[15]

In Hunter's view, memory is simply the influence of the past on the present. This is the sense in which memory is most commonly taken, the type of memory the pedagogue strives to inculcate in the student. We might refer to this as retentive memory. Hunter gives a wealth of statistical data from learning trials, most of which correlate the quantity of material retained with the time between study and recitation. He suggests a few learning techniques to maximize the retention of material. These consist of organizing the task at hand, practicing and internalizing learning strategies, and repeating the same material several times.[16] Though this work is over fifty years old and the research practices of psychologists have become increasingly scientific, the general conclusions are the

---

15 I. M. L. Hunter, *Memory: Facts and Fallacies* (Baltimore: Penguin, 1966), 15.
16 See ibid., Chapter VII: "Improving Memory." Hunter is notably skeptical of the mnemonic systems of *ars memoriae*, to be discussed in the following chapter. He writes, "The writer's guess would be that few people would find it worthwhile to master a repertoire of mnemonic systems for the sole purpose of the contributions they would make to his everyday learning requirements. ... It is probably true to say that most people could get their best practical results by directly considering the requirements of those memory tasks which most trouble them in their daily life" (301–2).

same in all such popular books. These works are in line with the movement of modernity and the spirit of the technological world. Rather than take memory in its vital philosophical sense, they reduce the scope of memory to the techniques of learning. The sense of memory associated with the Muses is lost.

(iii) The third branch of psychology that must be mentioned fully appreciates memory and makes it the central element of its theorizing: psychoanalysis. In 1901, Freud wrote, "No psychological theory has yet succeeded in giving a connected account of the fundamental phenomenon of remembering and forgetting; in fact, the complete analysis of what can actually be observed has so far scarcely been begun."[17] At this time, psychology proper was a new scientific field. Sir Francis Galton, the British polymath, had conducted some "psychometric" memory experiments with himself as subject in the 1880s, concluding, "The subject must have a continued living interest in order to retain an abiding place in the memory. The mind must refer to it frequently, but whether it does so consciously or unconsciously is not perhaps a matter of much importance."[18] Galton found that some old memories that at first seemed utterly buried could be resuscitated and brought to clarity through a focus of attention, which became a general presupposition of psychoanalysis.[19]

Another predecessor of Freud who wrote on memory from a psychological standpoint was William James. In the sixteenth chapter of his *Principles of Psychology* (1890), James analyzes the phenomenon of memory extensively, along with its causes and the interrelationship in daily life between recollection and forgetting. He understands memory in its psychological sense as "the knowledge of a former state of mind after it has already dropped from consciousness; or rather *it is the knowledge of an event, or fact, of which meantime we have not been thinking, with the additional consciousness that we have thought or experienced it before.*"[20] Freud did not consider either James or Galton to have presented a

---

17 Sigmund Freud, *The Psychopathology of Everyday Life*, trans. James Strachey (New York: W.W. Norton & Co., 1960), 176.
18 Francis Galton, *Inquiries into Human Faculty and Its Development* (London: The Eugenics Society, 1951), 138. Plato's Timaeus gives a similar account of laboring to recover and illuminate buried memories; see *Tim.*, 26a–c.
19 Ibid.: "Every one of the fleeting, half-conscious thoughts that were the subject of my experiments, admitted of being vivified by keen attention ... but I strongly suspect that ideas which have long since ceased to fleet through the brain, owing to the absence of current associations to call them up, disappear wholly" (139). Freudian psychoanalysis understands itself as a method of uncovering these "disappeared" ideas.
20 William James, *The Principles of Psychology* (New York: Dover, 1950), 1: 648.

thorough psychology of memory, insofar as neither had grasped the phenomenon of the subconscious, or fully worked out the relationship of memory to the development of individual character and its pathologies—that is, neither offered a doctrine of repression.

How does psychoanalysis understand memory? Pathologies are believed to arise from disorders of memory. Freud writes, "The theory of repression is the corner-stone on which the whole structure of psychoanalysis rests. It is the most essential part of it; and yet it is nothing but a theoretical formulation of a phenomenon which may be observed as often as one pleases."[21] Repression is the menace of memory; it is the phenomenon of consciousness turning back on itself, the super-ego burying one's unproductive instincts toward the pleasurable within the unconscious. These instincts are not annihilated, but retain a "cathexis of energy" that influences conscious life from the hidden depths. These energies are immortal; so long as they are unconscious, they do not deteriorate in time. They erupt in the form of myriad psychological pathologies.[22] It is the work of psychoanalysis to disarm these repressed impulses: catharsis cancels cathexis. Freud writes: "[Repressed memories] can only be recognized as belonging to the past, can only lose their importance and be deprived of their cathexis of energy, when they have been made conscious by the work of analysis, and it is on this that the therapeutic effect of analytic treatment rests to no small extent."[23] Psychoanalysis works by making explicit the structures that the patient retains implicitly in his or her memory. Once explicit, and recognized as existing in time, they lose their manipulative eternality.[24]

William Faulkner understood the general principle of psychoanalysis: "The past is never dead. It's not even past."[25] Repressed memory preserves without sublating. It retains its power in ways that are not consciously recognized, and becomes the unacknowledged framework of the present. The past is always contemporary in the patient's unconscious.

---

21 Sigmund Freud, *On the History of the Psycho-Analytic Movement*, trans. Joan Riviere, revised James Strachey (New York: W.W. Norton & Co., 1990), 15.
22 Amongst his numerous writings on repression, see the relevant sections in Freud's *History of the Psycho-Analytic Movement*; *New Introductory Lectures on Psychoanalysis*; and *An Outline of Psycho-Analysis*.
23 Sigmund Freud, *New Introductory Lectures on Psychoanalysis*, trans. James Strachey (New York: W.W. Norton & Co., 1966), 66.
24 Freud's theory of repression owes much to Arthur Schopenhauer's theory of madness. For Schopenhauer, all pathologies arise from disturbances of memory. Repression is "the Lethe of unbearable sufferings." See Schopenhauer, *The World as Will and Representation*, trans. E.F.J. Payne (New York: Dover, 1966), 2: 399–402.
25 William Faulkner, *Requiem for a Nun* (New York: Vintage, 1975), 80.

Psychoanalysis entails a direct confrontation with memory, necessary for liberating oneself from its hold. The patient remembers in order to vitiate his or her own memories—in order to forget.

Freudian psychoanalysis has a certain kinship with "memory as philosophy" insofar as it highlights the productive potency and cathectic energies of memory, and illuminates the co-temporality of past, present and future in memory. In these respects, Freud comes close to the philosophical doctrine of memory. Ultimately though, psychoanalysis views memory as a *problem* rather than as a solution. It is the "corner-stone" of the work of psychoanalysis to bring the patient to a state of catharsis, which is to annihilate the potency of memory. This is to sacrifice the past for the sake of the present. It is to live in the world of immediacy, to be what one *is*, at the expense of what one *has been*. Essence is lost so that being may be found.

This is not to say that psychoanalysis has no utility. It has fallen out of favor in recent times because of its highly speculative character, but for many neuroses, psychoanalytic treatment may be of great benefit to the patient, especially when coupled with the insights and pharmaceutical innovations of neurobiology. The deeply distressed patient or trauma victim is not misguided to pursue a cathartic annihilation of the past. The cathectic energies of memory can be overwhelming. Nonetheless, while admitting its practical efficacy, we must stress that the view of memory that psychoanalysis holds is not that of "philosophy as memory."

Nietzsche

Kandel is correct in observing that in the twentieth century, the study of memory has shifted from philosophy to psychology and biology. However, by "study" we must understand experimental research into the functions and bio-chemical bases of memory. It would be false to say that the philosophy of the late nineteenth and twentieth centuries has not concerned itself at all with memory. Many philosophers have remained deeply interested in the phenomenon, and have tried to understand the role of memory in the development and vitality of both the human individual and society in general. This is true both of thinkers who have remained primarily on the theoretical side of philosophy, and in certain fields of applied philosophy and applied ethics. Consider that the headings of topical sections in a recent publication, *Theories of Memory*, include: "Collective Memory," "Jewish Memory Discourse," "Trauma,"

"Gender," "Race/Nation," and "Diaspora."[26] These views are too numerous to treat independently, and none by itself can offer more than a partial speech about memory. Likewise, I cannot treat at length the recent grammatological, phenomenological, or hermeneutical treatments of memory offered by Ricoeur, Derrida, Deleuze, Edward Casey, and others.[27] However, I must address the major theoretical figure who stands most overtly opposed to a philosophical doctrine of memory: Friedrich Nietzsche.

Nietzsche is the intellectual impetus for many of the philosophical movements of the twentieth century. He is the first philosopher to express a genuine suspiciousness about memory, and to view it as an altogether deleterious faculty. This position is announced as early as 1874, in his essay, "On the Uses and Disadvantages of History for Life". Nietzsche writes, "It is possible to live almost without memory, and to live happily moreover, as the animal demonstrates; but it is altogether impossible to *live* at all without forgetting. Or, to express my theme even more simply: *there is a degree of sleeplessness, of rumination, of the historical sense, which is harmful and ultimately fatal to the living thing, whether this living thing be a man or a people or a culture.*"[28] The arguments of this essay, ostensibly about history, apply equally to memory, as Ricoeur has pointed out.[29] Nietzsche's is a doctrine of forgetting, both on an individual and cultural level, which views memory as harmful. It is a doctrine of forgetting without a doctrine of memory, which is a philosophy that idolizes barbarism.

Nietzsche's most complete and systematic critique of memory appears in his *Zur Genealogie der Moral* (1887). Here, forgetting—in fact, "active" forgetting—is advocated as the natural, healthy condition of spirit, its pre-reflective nature. He writes, "A little stillness, a little *tabula*

---

26 Michael Rossington and Anne Whitehead, eds., *Theories of Memory: A Reader* (Baltimore: Johns Hopkins University Press, 2007). The notions of memory held by all such applied fields fall short of "memory as philosophy" for the simple reason that—as applied—they are exclusive to a certain group or certain time.

27 See Paul Ricoeur's *Temps et Récit* and *La mémoire, l'histoire, l'oubli*, Jacques Derrida's *De la grammatologie* and *Différance* essays, Gilles Deleuze's *Différence et Répétition*, and Edward S. Casey's *Remembering: A Phenomenological Study*.

28 Friedrich Nietzsche, "On the Uses and Disadvantages of History for Life," in *Untimely Meditations*, trans. R.J. Hollingdale (Cambridge: Cambridge University Press, 1992), 62.

29 Paul Ricoeur, *Memory, History, Forgetting*, trans. Kathleen Blamey and David Pellauer (Chicago: University of Chicago Press, 2006): "To be sure, the polemic raised here concerns history above all, more precisely the philosophy of history and its place in culture. But the tone is set for a similar treatment of memory, in particular, collective memory" (68–69).

rasa of consciousness so that there is again space for new things ... that is the use of this active forgetfulness, a doorkeeper as it were, an upholder of psychic order, of rest, of etiquette: from which one can immediately anticipate the degree to which there could be no happiness, no cheerfulness, no hope, no pride, no *present* without forgetfulness."[30] Forgetting is not a passive event, but "a strong force, a form of strong health."[31] Memory represents a degradation of this ecstatic state of forgetfulness. It arises in the human condition as the result of pain and weakness. The "I will not" is the wellspring of memory; the violence of punishment is the source of the "I will not." Citing the oldest psychology on earth, Nietzsche writes, "Only what does not cease to give pain remains in one's memory."[32] Pain breeds retention, and retention is the precondition for discontent and, finally, *ressentiment*.

In what way does memory change the human condition for the worse? When Nietzsche's likely story begins, the human being, in its state of airy forgetfulness, is a raw quantum of power, a cathexis (to borrow Freud's term) of creative-destructive energies that exists only in the immediate present. Man is unbound because his potentialities are open to the limitless. The introduction of memory is the origin of a consciousness of past, and likewise the origin of a consciousness of future. The implication of a history extending backward is that it can likewise extend forward. A future means the possibility of control, of preparation and prediction with regard to futurity. But, Nietzsche writes, "In order to have this kind of command over the future in advance, man must first have learned to separate the necessary from the accidental occurrence, to think causally ... in general to be able to reckon, to calculate,—for this, man must first of all have become *calculable, regular, necessary*, in his own image of himself as well, in order to be able to vouch for himself *as future*."[33]

Nietzsche is suspicious of this transformation, this new genesis of man as a fixed and calculable creature. In his view, this is something unnatural and contrived. There is a positive practical yield, of course: society, the possibility of living and working in concord, the feeling and assurance of safety and well-being, the entire superstructure of the world of human civilization. What is lost is the savage and unbounded existence

---

30 Friedrich Nietzsche, *On the Genealogy of Morality*, trans. Maudemarie Clark and Alan J. Swenson (Indianapolis: Hackett, 1998), II.i.35.
31 Ibid.
32 Ibid., II.iii.37–39.
33 Ibid., II.i.36.

of man as a magnitude of creative-destructive energies. The calculable creature is no longer free to express these energies as it will. Lost along with this is man's brute happiness, the gay whimsicality that can only come from an absence of all troubles and memories. The ideal of happiness for Nietzsche recalls the Muses' nature: "forgetfulness of evils and relief from anxieties." The great tension in Nietzsche's work is always between these two tendencies: memory and forgetting, civilization and barbarism.

This insight is a partial truth, but it is not the whole of the matter. The idea of "memory as philosophy" affirms that both a philosophical doctrine of memory and a doctrine of forgetting are necessary, but that these two can and must co-exist, as they do in the nature of the Muses. What Nietzsche misses is the nature of determinate forgetting, which always forgets some particular content. Complete indetermination is identical to nothingness. Determinate forgetting, like determinate remembering, is a form of becoming. As a becoming, the content of either pole is a transition from its opposite; the two poles always exist in tandem. The gay forgetfulness is a constant annihilation of the contents of memory. But this presupposes a memory from which that content is annihilated. A becoming forgetfulness begins in memory. It is not metaphysically coherent to claim that the human condition begins with forgetfulness as its first principle and that memory is a later perversion.

Moreover, the capacity to have a world at all is a wonder performed by memory. Nothing in the cosmos could have any steady character or any meaning without the power of recollection. Each moment would present an entirely novel panoply of colors and sounds, the blooming, buzzing confusion of William James. To thrive in the world (not yet to speak of words like culture or society) requires a higher level of memory than this, one that is able to retain feelings of suffering. For a people to survive, they must be able to recognize basic natural signs, like the shrinking supply of food that alerts them it is time to move on and the meteorological or zoological warnings to seek shelter. This recognition is a recollection of the pains of hunger, the suffering brought on by the elements, and the agony of the tiger's claws. The success of the gay heroes of the *Genealogy*, those cruel and noble beasts of prey, depends on avoiding extinction. This is impossible without the cultivation of a memory for suffering.

Memory must be a presupposition of any philosophy at all. Nietzsche is himself willing to admit this, but he remains suspicious of both memory *and* philosophy. This suspicion cannot, however, be answered. No amount of evidence can ever overcome what is only suspect.[34] While certainty is able to answer doubt, suspicion is answered only by more suspicion. It may be true that the beginning of philosophy is the beginning of the decline of civilization; Vico also held a version of this view.[35] However, finding ourselves within the social world, the world of philosophy and memory, we must make the best of it, and pervasive suspicion is not the way to do so. Philosophy always begins with the given phenomena and received knowledge of its time; it can do no better. "Memory as philosophy" does not share Nietzsche's nostalgia for the barbarism of his "blonde beasts of prey," and rather than viewing memory as a symptom of decline, sees it, along with Vico, as the instrument by which decline is repulsed.

---

34 Ricoeur writes, "Three masters, seemingly mutually exclusive, dominate the school of suspicion: Marx, Nietzsche, and Freud. ... 'Truth as lying' would be the negative heading under which one might place these three exercises of suspicion." Ricoeur, "Interpretation as Exercise of Suspicion," in *Freud and Philosophy*, trans. Denis Savage (New Haven, CT: Yale University Press, 1977), 32. For Ricoeur's justification of this claim, see 32–36. We should also recall the old proverb that a hundred suspicions do not make a proof.

35 See Vico, *New Science*, §1106. Unlike Nietzsche, Vico's position ultimately takes memory to be the great bulwark against the progress of barbarism. Memory is the one thing able to preserve "the institutions and laws that bind [men] within society" (§811).

III: Memory as Philosophy

Bergson and the problem of reflection

We must consider the perennial philosophical *problem* that memory is meant to address. Henri Bergson describes this problem at the beginning of his 1912 *Introduction à la Métaphysique*. He writes, "A comparison of the definitions of metaphysics and the various concepts of the absolute leads to the discovery that philosophers, in spite of their apparent divergencies, agree in distinguishing two profoundly different ways of knowing a thing. The first implies that we move round the object; the second, *that we enter into it* [*entre en elle*]. The first depends on the point of view at which we are placed and on the symbols by which we express ourselves." This external view depends on a collection of attributes, built up through observation. Bergson continues, "The second neither depends on a point of view nor relies on any symbol. The first kind of knowledge may be said to stop at the *relative*; the second, in those cases where it is possible, to attain the *absolute* [*l'absolu*]."[1]

The object of thought exists in the flux of temporal reality; its attributes are always accidental and transitional. This is why, examined from without, the object grants only a relative knowledge about its nature. The internal view of the object captures its inner stability and permanent character, and it knows the thing, all at once, as an absolute. For Bergson, the internal view is proper to metaphysics. What he does not make clear in the *Introduction* is *how* one is to get inside the object, how one is to make one's start on this metaphysical path. He writes, "An absolute could only be given in an *intuition*, whilst everything else falls within the province of *analysis*. By intuition is meant the kind of *intellectual sympathy* by which one places oneself within an object in order to coincide with what is unique in it and consequently inexpressible. Analysis, on the contrary, is the operation which reduces the object to elements already known, that is, to elements common both to it and other objects."[2] This solution inaugurates a new question: what are we to understand by "intuition"? "Intellectual sympathy" is a vague answer, but we must avoid thinking that Bergson has in mind the sort of mysticism one finds in the thought of Heidegger.

---

1 Henri Bergson, *An Introduction to Metaphysics*, trans. T.E. Hulme (Indianapolis: Hackett, 1999), 21 (emphasis mine).
2 Ibid., 23–24.

What Bergson has raised here is the very problem that a philosophical doctrine of memory is meant to confront. He is correct in naming these two approaches to metaphysics. We recognize in the external, analytic approach the philosophical method of Bergson's immediate interlocutor, Kant, as inherited from Descartes and Locke. Bergson has in mind any philosophy in which the human faculty of *reflection* is central. Reflection is always relative. It can never get beyond the flux of appearance and the aggregation of various standpoints. The Heraclitean view of the flux of the cosmos is correct insofar as visible being is concerned, which is the level upon which reflection seizes. Reflection is a term borrowed from optics, a term that is always related to visibility. The mirror image that we apprehend always appears to us as an external image. It is at a distance, and must be surveyed from without. A metaphysic of reflection assumes the visibility of the object, at the same time assuming that this object is external to the seeing eye. The analyst saunters around the object, taking it in from as many vantage points as possible, constructing an idea of the thing from this collection of angles and vectors. The process of reflection is a cognitive land survey.[3]

Descartes' method is not merely to doubt. Doubt must be coupled with reflection, the engine by which thought attains positive knowledge. In his *Discours de la méthode*, Descartes writes: "Reflecting [*faisant réflexion*] upon the fact that I was doubting and that consequently my being was not wholly perfect ... I decided to inquire into the source of my ability to think of something more perfect than I was; and I recognized very clearly than this had to come from some nature that was in fact more perfect."[4] Doubt cannot, under its own power, pull itself from the quagmire it creates. It is only when Descartes projects his doubt outward and considers it reflectively, as an external thing, that he is able to subject it to analytic critique. He later writes, "I have noticed certain laws which God has so established in nature, and of which he has implanted such notions in our minds, that after adequate reflection [*réflexion*] we cannot doubt

---

3   The pervasive authority of the form of optical thinking in the modern period is paralleled in the rise of historical thinking. At the same time as Descartes articulates his philosophy of reflection, we notice an optical trend in the labeling of historical periods. The "dark ages" are contrasted to the "Enlightenment," *Aufklärung*, with its doctrine of illuminism. Historical progress is understood as a matter of bringing the dark into the light.
4   René Descartes, *Discourse on the Method of Rightly Conducting One's Reason and Seeking the Truth in the Sciences*, in *The Philosophical Writings of Descartes*, trans. John Cottingham, Robert Stoothoff and Dugald Murdoch (New York: Cambridge University Press, 1985), disc. 4 (1: 127–28).

that they are exactly observed in everything which exists and occurs in the world."[5] Only by holding nature at a distance and gathering a plurality of points of view are we able to apprehend these divine laws.

Following Descartes, John Locke was the first English writer to use the word "reflection" in a philosophical sense. In his *Essay Concerning Human Understanding*, after dismissing the doctrine of innate ideas, Locke argues that there are two sources of ideas, namely sensation and reflection. He writes, "I call this reflection, the ideas it affords being such only as the mind gets by reflecting on its own operations within itself. By reflection then ... I would be understood to mean, that notice which the mind takes of its own operations, and the manner of them, by reason whereof there come to be ideas of these operations in the understanding."[6] Reflection is the source of ideas concerning those immaterial mental processes, such as knowing or willing, the originals of which cannot be acquired through sensation. These internal processes are held at a distance, as though reflected in a mirror, in order to be assessed. In the second edition of the *Essay*, Locke emphasizes that one's memory can have no contents "before impression from sensation or reflection."[7]

It is Kant, however, at whom Bergson's critique is primarily aimed. Kant's critical philosophy is the perfection of the metaphysics of reflection. The moment he establishes that the *noumenon*, the thing-in-itself, is inaccessible to human apprehension, all that remains knowable is the phenomenal world, the world of vision, vectors, and perspectives.[8] If we can never approach the *noumenon*, then we are condemned to being permanently outside of the real object. The phenomenal object is always an external thing for us to analyze under a lens. This is the point at which reflection becomes paramount. Kant writes: "*Reflection (reflexio)* does not concern itself with objects themselves with a view to deriving concepts from them directly, but is that state of mind in which we first set ourselves to discover the subjective conditions under which [alone] we are

---

5   Descartes, Ibid., disc. 5 (1: 132).
6   John Locke, *An Essay Concerning Human Understanding* (New York: Dover, 1959), 1: 124.
7   Ibid., 1: 111.
8   Kant defines the *noumenon* in the following way: "If I postulate things which are mere objects of understanding, and which, nevertheless, can be given as such to an intuition, *although not one that is sensible* ... such things would be entitled *noumena*." Immanuel Kant, *Critique of Pure Reason*, trans. Norman Kemp Smith (New York: St. Martin's Press, 1965), A 249 (emphasis mine). Kant asserts that the *noumenon* can never be known: "This something, thus conceived, is only the transcendental object; and by that is meant something = X, of which we know, and with the present constitution of our understanding can know, nothing whatsoever" (ibid., A 250).

able to arrive at concepts. It is the consciousness of the relation of given representations to our different sources of knowledge; and only by way of such consciousness can the relation of the sources of knowledge to one another be rightly determined."[9] Reflection means turning away from the thing, toward the conditions of conceptualization, which is at the heart of the Kantian critical philosophy. Beginning with this idea of reflection, philosophy must ultimately become fully analytic and shade into empirical science. Entering into the thing-in-itself must be given up. Kant has inherited this position directly from Descartes.[10]

Bergson writes, "Having once overlooked the ties that bind science and metaphysics to intellectual intuition, Kant has no difficulty in showing us that our science is wholly relative, and our metaphysics entirely artificial."[11] Kant's demonstration here is only a conditional proof. Bergson continues, "Doctrines which have a certain basis in intellectual intuition escape the Kantian criticism exactly in so far as they are intuitive; and these doctrines are the whole of metaphysics, provided we ignore the metaphysics which is fixed and dead in *theses*, and consider only that which is living in *philosophers*."[12] This is to say that any philosophy that gives up the idea of intuition and allows Kant his *noumena* is a philosophy that the Kantian critique can dominate.

What is the problem with the sovereignty of reflection? All knowledge becomes arbitrary: everything is relative to the standpoint one takes.[13] Because reflection depends on one's vantage point and abandons the task of coming to know the thing-in-itself, there can be no appeal to any higher, ultimate truth. Whatever one sees from one's position *is* the

---

9   Ibid., A 260, B 316. Kant's German term for reflection is *Überlegung*. The parenthetical reference to the Latin *reflexio* appears in the original text: "Die Überlegung (reflexio) hat es nicht mit den Gegenstäden selbst zu tun ..." This underscores the connection Kant wishes to make with earlier philosophies of reflection.
10 My critique of the historical role of reflection in Descartes and its inheritance in Kant owes something to the analysis of Alfred North Whitehead in Chapter VI of *Process and Reality*. It also agrees with Richard Rorty's critique of "man's glassy essence" and the "mirror of nature" in *Philosophy and the Mirror of Nature*, even though Rorty avoids the term "reflection" and tends to write in the context and vernacular of the analytic tradition.
11 Bergson, *Introduction to Metaphysics*, 57.
12 Ibid., 60.
13 My thanks to Donald Phillip Verene for suggesting this problem. This section owes much to his *Philosophy and the Return to Self-Knowledge*. Its first chapter, "Barbarism of Reflection," illuminates the nature of philosophies of reflection. Verene gives a critique of reflection at 57ff that demonstrates its arbitrariness as a foundation for ethics. His solution to the insidiousness of reflection is a return to philosophical memory.

truth of the matter. As John Findlay says, "This new [Kantian] pose of reason cannot take us far. As we look on a matter from one angle or another, practically any rule for action can be rendered self-consistent, or can be made to seem self-contradictory."[14]

Today, philosophers forget that *ars critica*, which makes deductions from first truths (*topoi*, places) depends upon *ars topica*, which is the art of discovering these *topoi*. However, *ars topica* is vanquished when reflection is undertaken. There are only relative positions, never fixed *topoi* from which to begin. This can be highly dangerous: any stance one wishes to take seems clear and valid from some angle of reflection or other. Reflection depends on the source of illumination one chooses. One can always reflect the appearance of society in such a way that fascism, for instance, appears reasonable. One can turn out the lights altogether, and then pronounce anything one likes. Hegel has this in mind when he laughs at the vacuous cognition that embraces "the night in which ... all cows are black" (*PS*, §16; *W*, III: 22).[15] Giordano Bruno makes the same point when he writes, "If you add enough ink to your lamps, Ethiopians look like anybody else."[16] Finally, James Joyce proclaims, "The rose is white in the darik! ... So all rogues lean to rhyme."[17]

Bergson is not alone in questioning the efficacy of the great philosophy of reflection. Vico, with the Cartesian philosophy in mind, discusses the "barbarism of reflection" in his *Scienza nuova*. This is contrasted against the simple barbarism of primitive peoples, against which one had only to defend oneself bodily. The barbarian of reflection, "with a base savagery, under soft words and embraces, plots against the life and fortune of friends and intimates."[18] Reflection, when used improperly, is "the mother of falsehood."[19] Ill-used reflection creates the night in which all cows are black. The bad can be made good, and the good can be made

---

14 John N. Findlay, *Hegel: A Re-Examination* (New York: Collier, 1962), 112.
15 C.f. *PN*, (§270, *Z*): "At night all cows are black. The quantum is to vanish; but if with its vanishing, the qualitative element, too, is effaced, then we can prove anything we like." Regarding the nature of night, Hegel says, "Night contains the self-dissolving ferment and destructive conflict of every power, it is the absolute possibility of everything, Chaos" (*PN*, §320, *Z*). It is possible to prove anything by exercising reflection in the darkness of night.
16 Giordano Bruno, *De umbris idearum*, trans. Scott Gosnell (Huginn, Muninn & Co, 2013), 13. Hegel deeply respected Bruno's work. His "night in which all cows are black" may be an adaptation of this line.
17 James Joyce, *Finnegans Wake* (New York: Penguin, 1986), 96.
18 Vico, *New Science*, §1106.
19 Ibid., §817. In the same paragraph, Vico says that barbarism proper, the "barbarism of sense", "for lack of reflection does not know how to feign."

bad. The barbarian of reflection, with his fountain pen, is more dangerous than the barbarian of force with his axe because we no longer know how to defend ourselves.

Hegel was equally critical of philosophies of reflection. One of his earliest published works, *Faith and Knowledge*, was subtitled: *or the Reflective Philosophy [Reflexionsphilosophie] of Subjectivity in the Totality of Its Forms as Kantian, Jacobian, and Fichtean Philosophy*.[20] Jacobi and Fichte self-identified with the term Reflexionsphilosophie. It is not a great stretch for Hegel to include Kant in his discussion. In the introduction to this work, he writes that these philosophies of reflection "all amount to nothing but the absolute restriction of reason to the form of finitude ... they make limitedness into an eternal law both in itself and for philosophy. So these philosophies have to be recognized as nothing but the culture of reflection raised to a system. This is a culture of ordinary human intellect" (FK, 64; W, II: 298).[21]

The preface of the *Phenomenology of Spirit* focuses on the weaknesses of reflection and the need for speculative philosophy as an alternative. This entails a new form of reflection, one that turns back on itself. Hegel writes, "Only this self-*restoring* sameness, or this reflection in otherness within itself—not an *original* or *immediate* unity as such—is the True" (*PS*, §18; *W*, III: 23). Speculation takes up this new form of reflection: "Reason is, therefore, misunderstood when reflection is excluded from the True, and is not grasped as a positive moment of the Absolute. It is reflection that makes the True a result, but it is equally reflection that overcomes the antithesis between the process of its becoming and the result" (*PS*, §21; *W*, III: 25). Reflexionsphilosophie holds the object in abeyance. The higher form of reflection, which reflects this very process, is necessary for the sublation of this differentiation. John H. Smith calls this transformed notion of reflection a "self-contained process of philosophical self-representation."[22]

---

20 *Glauben und Wissen oder Reflexionsphilosophie der Subjektivität in der Vollständigkeit ihrer Formen als Kantische, Jacobische und Fichtesche Philosophie*. This essay was published in the second volume of the *Critical Journal of Philosophy*, edited by Hegel and Schelling, in 1802. For a more substantial analysis of Hegel's critique of the philosophy of reflection in this essay, see my forthcoming article, "Ethical Negativity: Hegel on the True Infinite," in *The Meaning and Power of Negativity*, ed. Ingolf U. Dalferth and Marlene A. Block (Tübingen: Mohr Siebeck).
21 See John H. Smith, *The Spirit and Its Letter: Traces of Rhetoric in Hegel's Philosophy of Bildung* (Ithaca, NY: Cornell University Press, 1988), 164–73, for a discussion of Hegel's treatment of *Reflexion* in this early essay.
22 Smith, *Spirit and Its Letter*, 171.

In the *Encyclopedia*, without any knowledge of Vico's similar coinage, Hegel uses the phrase "barbarisms of the worst form of reflection" [*Barberei ... der schlechtesten Reflexions-Form*] in reference to Isaac Newton (*PN*, §320, Z, my translation). Reason is barbarous because it thinks of live bodies as dead matter and cannot see beyond external relationships (*PN*, §324, Z). Elsewhere, Hegel writes, "It is the customary mistake of reflection to take the essence to be merely the interior. If it be so taken, even this way of looking at it is purely external, and that sort of essence is the empty external abstraction" (*EL*, §140). Reflection that does not turn back on itself takes the external for the whole. It rests at a level of fixed opposition, in which the many and the one, or the "I" and the body, are irreconcilable (*PM*, §389, Z). Because of this, it is inadequate for absolute knowing. The faculty of the absolute is *Erinnerung*, recollection.

Because Montaigne wrote his *Essays* prior to Descartes' introduction of *réflexion* as a philosophical term, he was not acquainted with philosophies of reflection *per se*. However, the *Essays* are a measure of Montaigne against things, never a reflection on things held up for measurement. Montaigne writes, "I speak my mind freely on all things, even on those which perhaps exceed my capacity and which I by no means hold to be within my jurisdiction. And so the opinion I give of them is to declare the measure of my sight, not the measure of things" (*CE*, II: 10, 298; *V*, 410). This is reflection turned back upon itself. It has been argued convincingly that the analytic method of Descartes is in large part a critical response to Montaigne.[23] Kant is the inheritor of Descartes' method. Hegel's system is in large part a critical response to Kant. We are now in a position to give a name to this particular philosophical period that Montaigne and Hegel bookend: it is the period of reflective philosophy.

Reflection is the problem with which Bergson is centrally concerned in the *Introduction*, though he speaks in terms of the "external view" of philosophers. A metaphysical approach that encounters the object strictly from without is limited. What is needed is a philosophy that can get inside the object and apprehend its very essence rather than its

---

23 For example, the opening line of the *Discours*, "Good sense is the best distributed thing in the world ..." (111), is a direct response to Montaigne's "Of presumption": "The only thing that makes me think something of myself is the thing in which no man ever thought himself deficient: ... for who ever thought he lacked sense?" (*CE*, II: 17, 498; *V*, 656). Donald Frame writes that Descartes viewed Montaigne "as the man he had to reckon with and whose skepticism he had to refute." Frame, *Montaigne*, 314.

accidents. However, Bergson's "intuition" is not the solution I offer. Rather, it seems to me that Bergson offers a more concrete answer to this problem twenty years before writing the *Introduction*. *Matière et mémoire* is the seminal text that reinvigorated the idea of memory for twentieth-century philosophy. In this volume, the central problem is resolving spirit with matter, while affirming the reality of both. Bergson approaches this through a discussion of memory, which is "just the intersection of mind and matter. ... Among all the facts capable of throwing light on the psychophysiological relation, those which concern memory, whether in the normal or in the pathological sense, hold a privileged position."[24]

Memory is the arena in which objective fact is transformed into a subjective possession. For Bergson, memory is always "psychical," as opposed to cerebral. The brain is the necessary physical mechanism whereby pure memories are converted into particular images. However, pure memories are not localized in the material of the brain. They can never be destroyed in a corporeal sense, though the brain's mechanism of recollection may be inhibited.[25] Pure memory is entirely psychical or spiritual. Being-in-itself is transformed into being-for-itself. Though this earlier text may appear to be a work of psychology rather than metaphysics,[26] the faculty of memory continues to holds a privileged position in regard to Bergson's later problem, that of metaphysics, though he does not explicitly make this connection himself.

Memory is Vico's answer to the barbarians of reflection. It is Hegel's answer in a different era. In the twentieth century, Karl Jaspers states the same view: "In the process of reconstitution the mental substance can only be preserved by a sort of historical remembrance which must be something more than a mere knowledge of the past and must take the form of a contemporary vital force. In default of this, man would slip back into barbarism."[27] In the present age, memory can be our answer once again. A developed memory is always necessary to hold off the tides of barbarism.

---

24 Bergson, *Matter and Memory*, 13.
25 Along with the general argument of Chapter 3 of *Matter and Memory*, see Bergson's elucidation of this view in his essay "Memory of the Present and False Recognition," in *Mind-Energy*, trans. H. Wildon Carr (New York: Henry Holt and Company, 1920), 156–57.
26 Bergson himself stresses the interdependence of psychology and metaphysics at ibid., 15.
27 Karl Jaspers, *Man in the Modern Age*, trans. Eden Paul and Cedar Paul (Garden City, NY: Doubleday Anchor Books, 1957), 130.

Recollection and essence

How can we have an internal approach to the object through the faculty of memory? Bergson is correct that memory is a nexus between mind and matter. The object as such stands opposite us in its brute immediacy, on the level of raw being. Of course, as soon as we become aware of it, it is already mediated by our thought. By simply casting our gaze upon it, we can never get beyond its phenomenal appearance, which is always a view contingent upon ourselves, the situation, and the superstructure of circumstance. External change is accidental; it can never lead us to the discovery of necessity. By keeping the object in consciousness as a present sensual actuality, we can never internalize the object or grasp its *inner* movement. Mind cannot penetrate matter through the senses.

When we hold the object in our *memory*, however, matter becomes mind, or, as Hegel says, substance becomes subject. This is what Hegel has in mind when he makes the following claim in the preface to the *Phenomenology*: "That the true is actual only as system, or that substance is essentially subject, is expressed in the representation of the absolute as *spirit*—the most sublime concept [*Begriff*]" (*PS*, §25; *W*, III: 28). We do not attain absolute knowing until the Hegelian circle closes in the final pages of the work, at which point we learn that the absolute is recollection [*Erinnerung, Er-Innerung*].[28] Subject takes up and internalizes substance through an act of recollection. The *Phenomenology* is the process of this transformation.[29]

Memory transforms matter into a spiritual form. As a content of active memory, the object ceases to be an *actuality*. It loses its character as an immediate being over and against the subject. It becomes a spiritual object, an object *for* thought, *for* the thinking subject. The external thing ceases to be external; it is now one's own, internal to consciousness. Taken up in this way, the object's foreignness and otherness are cancelled. Donald Phillip Verene writes, "The vacuous actuality that characterizes the nature of the object of reflection is not overcome by giving the object an 'inside.' It is overcome by *making the object itself part of the inside*, the actuality of the knowing self. Critical reflection is overcome through the recollective, memorial nature of the speculative act that produces the

---

28 I have included a translation of the final paragraph of the *Phenomenology* in the thirteenth chapter.
29 Hegel's view on this matter does not change as his system develops. In the *Encyclopedia*, he writes that memory [*Gedächtnis*] is "the reduction of this outwardness to inwardness" (*PM*, §460). *Gedächtnis*, though, is not equivalent with *Erinnerung*.

inward being of the real."[30] Memory answers Bergson's dilemma by a simple inversion. The problem of getting inside of the object, which he answers by an appeal to intuition, becomes a matter of getting the object inside of oneself.

How is this approach different from any view that emphasizes the imaginary character of the perceptual object—that is, any view of perception, like Kant's, that claims that the phenomenal appearance of the object is already an internal apprehension, dependant of the categories of cognition? If the percept is nothing more than a mental image, then in a sense we do have the object already within the subject. Memory, however, avoids the problem of temporality and change in a way that reflection cannot. The object is always in motion. The analytic approach of Descartes or Kant, as an external view of an object, concerns itself only with what it *is*, but the object changes with time. The change that is apprehended is accidental, the change of Heraclitus' river. It is one thing after the next, movement without order. This change in time goes on infinitely. Because no necessity can possibly be found governing this movement, this change is as vacuous as the actuality of raw being. Absent is the inner necessity comprehended by the Muses. At most, reflection collects an aggregate of moments and tries to piece them together to create a whole.

Memory, on the other hand, cancels time. In recollection, all moments are coeval and all are equally immortal. Memory is not bound to temporal (or spatial) limits. It lifts the object from its particularity in space and time, so that its history can be viewed at once, start to finish. When I call to mind a dear friend, the entire past opens like a flower, not as a series of images, one after the next. Though he is a vital, changing, inconsistent creature, yet I understand the fellow; he is not to me a new mystery at each moment. Why? Hegel writes, "In placing the content of feeling in the inwardness of intelligence"—that is, in recollecting the object—"and thereby making it a mental representation, I lift it out of the *particularity* of space and time to which, in its immediacy, it is tied and on which I, too, am dependent in feeling and intuition" (*PM*, §452, Z). Holding the various historical moments in a single atemporal view, memory is able to discover or invent an inner movement of the object that reveals its essence. This inner movement becomes a historical narrative. We can see this inner movement all at once because memory is al-

---

30 Verene, *Hegel's Recollection*, 113 (emphasis mine). "Vacuous actuality" is a term borrowed from Alfred North Whitehead, which I will use several times myself. See Whitehead, *Process and Reality* (New York: Macmillan, 1929): "The term 'vacuous actuality' here means the notion of a *res vera* devoid of subjective immediacy" (34).

ways the annulment of time. The historical narrative that memory creates is playful.[31] *Ingenium* is always a playful power, and the children of the Muses always have something of the child at play in their work. Reflection can only invest its object with an inner history if it presupposes and falls back upon memory.

"Essence" is a word that philosophers avoid in the present century. Overuse and over-application have reduced "essence" (much like "substance") to an ambiguous term without analytical precision. However, Hegel offers a doctrine of essence with great conceptual clarity. In the *Science of Logic*, the truth of being is essence [*Wesen*]. By "being" Hegel means immediate, vacuous being, that impenetrable something that simply stands before us. Knowing [*Wissen*] seeks to "penetrate" being "on the supposition that at the back of this being there is something else, something other than being itself, that this background constitutes the truth of being" (*SL*, 389; *W*, VI: 13). This approach can only succeed when it entails a recollective act. Hegel writes, "Not until knowing *inwardizes, recollects* [*erinnert*] itself out of immediate being, does it through this mediation find essence. The German language has preserved essence in the past participle [*gewesen*] of the verb *to be*; for essence is past—but timelessly past—being [*zeitlos vergangene Sein*]" (ibid.). *Wesen* is *gewesen*. Shortly after this, Hegel continues, "The reflection that immediately forces itself on one is that this *pure being*, the *negation* of everything finite, presupposes an *internalization*, a *recollection* [*Erinnerung*] and movement which has purified immediate, determinate being [*Dasein*] to pure being" (ibid.; *W*, VI: 13-4).

For Hegel, being is what *is*, and essence is what *was*. Being is accidental immediacy. Essence is what one seeks when one attempts to penetrate immediate being and discover what lies behind it. In this non-reflective inquiry, we require a history of the object, which is an appeal to recollection. We must know what the thing has always been, not what it happens to be at this moment in time. Recollecting is always internalizing (*Er-Innerung*) and transforming substance into subject by way of the memory. Not until we recollect the object can we get behind it to its essence, to what it has always been. This is the sense in which essence is the truth of being. What *was* gives verity and significance to what *is*, and

---

31 An example of such a playful, atemporal historical narrative can be found in the Creation stories of Genesis 1 and 2, which fail to agree on the specific order of Creation. The reason is simple: the divine recollection is not bound to temporality; all moments are coeval. The inner form and reason of Creation is not exhausted in any particular history.

what *was* is found in recollection. This is what Bergson means when he writes, "Memory ... [constitutes] the subjective side of the knowledge of things."[32] The objective side by itself is vacuous. Meaning in the world is a spiritual creation, and yet we can have no world without meaning. Spirit creates the world, and creates it by the discovery of essences. The sublime act of world-creation, of which we all partake, is an act of recollection.

But how are we to know what *was*? When we approach the object, it does not sing to us its own past, present and future. This is the moment at which memory must be more than mere *memoria*, and must become ingenious. Angelica Nuzzo has argued that this recollection of essence is an act of thought, which precedes memory. A past is artificially imposed upon the internalized being. She writes, "*Erinnerung* is not reproduction of a meaning or sense that has been; it is rather the first time creation and production of a meaning that is—a meaning that is projected back onto the beginning as origin precisely by this act of production. Thus, the pure being of the original word is nothing else but pure thinking, which is absolutely self-referential thinking ... listening only to itself."[33]

If by this Nuzzo has in mind a fantastic recollection that is completely unmoored, which has its basis only in capricious fancy rather than in any actual experience, then this would be a far more arbitrary manner of philosophizing than the method of reflection.[34] "Memory as philosophy" is never an appeal to fancy. Proust is correct to insist that recollection is not necessarily the remembrance of things as they were, but this is only to say that a philosophical recollection grasps the way things always are and must be. Memory makes essence by referring being to past being, to past experience. Recollection fills in what is missing to give the object its history. Like Homer and Hesiod, it tells a likely story. This story is an ingenious fabrication, but it is not fanciful. The essence of the thing is what it has always been, is now, and will always be; it is the musical thread of its internal transformation. As Jaspers says, "A sincere historicity is a readiness to discover the sources which feed all life and therefore the life of the present as well."[35]

---

32 Bergson, *Matter and Memory*, 34.
33 Angelica Nuzzo, "Dialectical Memory, Thinking, and Recollecting: Logic and Psychology in Hegel," in *Mémoire et souvenir: Six études sur Platon, Aristote, Hegel et Husserl*, ed. Aldo Brancacci and Gianni Gigliotti (Napoli: Bibliopolis, 2006), 111.
34 This may be what Nuzzo is suggesting. She writes, "This is essence: it is the recollection of something that has never taken place and has never been there but that, precisely by being recollected, is posited for the first time as something that has taken place and has been there—*gewesen*" (ibid., 108).
35 Karl Jaspers, *Man in the Modern Age*, 133.

The Idea of Memory 65

Vico's *ingegno*

The playful construction of this inner order cannot, however, be attained by method. The likely narrative is probable, not certain. Probability is the hobgoblin of the post-Cartesian mind. As probable, the idea of essence is always subject to possible revision. It never yields absolute certainty. However, the idol of certainty is a relatively new idea in the world, which was not defended as the golden standard of knowledge until the seventeenth century. We forget that even in the hardest sciences, there are still many basic assumptions that are probabilistic, and these increase as we delve deeper into the macro and micro levels of science. Quantum mechanics and astrophysics alike contain much that is probabilistic, but nonetheless functionally true. To accept the idea of "certainty" as the *sine qua non* of knowledge is to lose sight of the most profound question ever posed, that of Pilate. "What is truth? said jesting Pilate; and would not stay for an answer."[36]

The fabrication of the inner order of things is instead the work of the *ingenium* that Vico says is the crown of memory. Ingenium [*ingegno*] is the aspect of *memoria* that is properly philosophical. Nonetheless, it is not a method, because it cannot have rules or guidelines. *Ingenium* is an art, the art whereby one views the matter at hand in a new order or gives it a new twist. In order for this fabrication to take place, *ingenium* requires a view of the whole and its parts, a view of the history of the object as though upon a stage. *Ingenium* requires a theater of memory. Because it is not method, a doctrine of philosophical memory cannot say precisely what is entailed in the ingenious act. In the third section, we will see this inventive memory at work in Montaigne's *Essays*, and in the fourth section we will see it in Hegel's system, but it is not the same in these two cases, nor is any instance of *ingenium* ever like any other. To borrow an image from Schopenhauer, the ingenious mind is shooting at targets it alone sees. One simply sees, or one does not see. One has the good eye, the *buon occhio*, or one does not. Philosophy is not for everyone, nor is it democratic. The Muses can sing true if they will, but they can also sing false.

Though there is no technique of *ingenium*, we may say something more regarding Vico's claim about memory, first quoted above in the Introduction. This claim is made in a section of the *Scienza nuova* in which

---

36 Francis Bacon, "Of Truth," in *Essays and New Atlantis* (New York: Walter J. Black, 1942), 3.

Vico is arguing that poetic wisdom is embedded with historical significations, and that these histories are preserved in the shared memories of a people. In this context, Vico writes: "Memory is the same as imagination, which for that reason is called *memoria* in Latin. (In Terence, for example, we find *memorabile* in the sense of imaginable, and commonly we find *comminisci* for feigning, which is proper to the imagination, and thence *commentum* for a fiction.) Imagination is likewise taken for ingenuity or invention [*ingegno*]. (In the returned barbarian times an ingenious man was called imaginative, *fantastic*; so, for example, Cola di Rienzo is described by his contemporary biographer.)" Vico's evidence for these connections is philological. James Joyce, for one, thought that the identity of imagination and memory was the most profound claim of the *Scienza nuova*.[37]

As quoted above, Vico continues, "Memory thus has three different aspects: memory [*memoria*] when it remembers things, imagination [*fantasia*] when it alters or imitates them, and invention [*ingegno*] when it gives them a new turn or puts them into proper arrangement or relationship. For these reasons the theological poets called Memory the mother of the Muses."[38] Because these three words are (supposedly) interchangeable in the Italian language, there exists a natural conceptual affinity. Vico had already expressed this idea twenty years before the second edition of the *Scienza nuova*. In his 1710 work, *De antiquissima Italorum sapienta*, Vico writes: "The Latins called the faculty that stores sense perceptions 'memory' [*memoria*]; when it recalls perceptions they called it 'reminiscence' [*reminiscentia*].[39] But memory also signified the faculty that fashions images (which the Greeks call *phantasy* and the Italians call *immaginativa*). For in ordinary Italian, *immaginare* is equivalent to the *memorare* of the Latins."[40] This convertibility is the justification that Vico gives for the Greek notion that the Muses, "forms of imagination, were the daughters of Memory."[41]

---

37 Richard Ellmann writes that Joyce, who was deeply influenced by Vico, believed that the most important line in the *Scienza nuova* was "Memory is the same as imagination," and told friends that "imagination is memory." See Ellmann, *James Joyce* (New York: Oxford University Press, 1982), 661.
38 Vico, *New Science*, §819. This is a longer excerpt of a passage partially quoted in the Introduction.
39 This is a division first posited philosophically by Aristotle in his work *De memoria et reminiscentia*.
40 Vico, *Most Ancient Wisdom*, 95–96.
41 Ibid., 96.

This discussion is followed by an account of *ingenium* (Vico is here writing in Latin rather than Italian). "*Ingenium* is the faculty that connects disparate and diverse things. ... An acute wit penetrates more quickly and unites diverse things. ... Furthermore, *ingenium* (mother wit) and *natura* (nature) were one and the same to the Latins. ... Is it because, just as nature generates physical things, so human wit gives birth to mechanics and, as God is nature's artificer, so man is the god of artifacts?"[42] Vico, long before Bergson, already has a sense of "penetration," an understanding of the need for philosophy to get inside of or behind its objects. Also, we see that *ingenium* is not conceived by Vico as an arbitrary or ungrounded process. Rather, it is synonymous with nature; it discovers the necessary order of things, *rerum natura*. The discovery of this order turns men into gods, into artificers. This connects to Vico's famous claim that the true is convertible with the made.[43]

When called to account by the anonymous critic of the *Giornale de' letterati d'Italia* for merging these three terms into one, Vico appeals to the authority of Terence, the Roman comic playwright. He writes, "There is a fine case of [*ingenium* converting with *memoria*] in the *Andria* [of Terence], where Davus, eager to arrange a great trick with Mysis, tells her, 'Mysis, now I need your memory and cunning ready for this business.'" Regarding the imagination, he continues, "What we call 'imagination' and 'to imagine' is called by the Latins 'to remember' and 'memory' ... as in that other passage of the *Andria* which is worthy of note, where Corinus complains of Pamphilius's maliciousness and treachery: 'Is it believable or within all memory that anyone should be so completely mad that he takes pleasure in disasters, evils, and gets his own advantages from the misfortunes of others?'"[44] It is fitting that Vico turns to a comic writer rather than a deeply serious tragedian like Seneca.[45] Method is deeply serious and tolerates no mockery. Memory cannot be serious, since it has no rules. Where it is most successful, it is most

---

42   Ibid., 96–97.
43   See ibid.: "For the Latins, *verum* and *factum* are interchangeable" (45).
44   Ibid., 161. Vico's exposition of the same topic in the *Scienza nuova* also relies on Terence's *Andria* as its primary philological justification.
45   Vico had the option of turning to Seneca for his justification. Seneca writes, "We must digest [the food which nourishes our mind]; otherwise it will only come into our acquired memory-store [*memoria*] and not pass on to become a part of our own abilities [*ingegno*]." This passage, from Seneca's *Epistulae morales*, is quoted and translated in Mary Carruthers, *The Book of Memory* (New York: Cambridge University Press, 1992), 192.

playful; its courtship of the Muses is whimsical. Ultimately, comedy is the genre of memory.

How are we to understand Vico's three terms? *Memoria* is the psychological memory of Proust's narrator, as depicted in the overture of *La recherche du temps perdu*. Upon tasting the crumbs of a *petite madeleine*, the images of the past come flooding back: grandmother, Combray, Swann's park, and eventually the whole of the *Recherche du temps perdu*.[46] Simple *memoria* is also the object of Francis Galton's self-experimentation. This *memoria* is necessary for holding together the reference points of experience. *Fantasia* is the artistic imagination. The images of *memoria* are repeated or altered, manipulated into new forms or preserved through pious mimesis. A highly developed capacity for *fantasia* gives us Ovid's *Metamorphoses* and Raffaello's frescos. It requires an openness toward what is possible. *Ingenium* is the completion of the first two terms, the philosophical act *par excellence*. Vico tells us, "*Ingenium* is the discovery of new things, and the ... power of imagining is the mother of poetic inventions."[47] This definition preserves the Latin sense of *inventio*, which is best translated as "discovery."

The ingenious twist depends upon the power to hold the whole of experience in one view. One's gaze must fall all at once, like that of the Muses, upon the three temporal dimensions of past, present, and future.[48] It must be open to the possible, willing to transform these memorial images. From this platform, the discovery of their necessary arrangement is the lightning flash of genius. Ernst Cassirer writes that the Renaissance idea of "genius" was the discovery of necessity in nature, a sense to which "memory as philosophy" remains faithful.[49] *Ingenium* is something distinct from memory and imagination, but this distinction does not

---

46 The narrator of the *Recherche* expresses *memoria* in its simple form. On the other hand, the memorial work of Proust himself—that is, the creation of the entire *Recherche*—is an act of deep *ingenium*.
47 Vico, *Most Ancient Wisdom*, 162.
48 Vico enjoins the reader of the *Scienza nuova* to direct his thought at discovering the ideal eternal history, "so far as he himself makes it for himself by that proof 'it had, has, and will have to be' [*dovette, deve, dovrà*]." *New Science*, §349. C.f. Verene, *Philosophy and Self-Knowledge*: "In largest terms, *ingenium* lets us make the connections needed to recollect an order among things past, present, and to come. The Muses offer us the power of memory as *narration*" (211).
49 Ernst Cassirer, *The Individual and the Cosmos in Renaissance Philosophy*, trans. Mario Domandi (Mineola, NY: Dover, 2000): "The power of mind, the power of artistic and of scientific genius does not reside in unfettered arbitrariness but in the ability to teach us to see and to know the 'object' in its truth, in its highest determination. Be it as artist or as thinker, the genius finds the necessity in nature" (164).

entail a separation. The relationship of the three terms is difference in identity.

Philosophy has been intertwined with *ingenium*, or philosophical invention, since its earliest days. In Plato, this connection is obvious, but the doctrine of "memory as philosophy" predates Plato by centuries. All of the pre-Socratic sages simply tell us what the world is like. They are ingenious seers. In lieu of a mechanistic analysis, which is not possible, I will give an illustration of this ingenious recollection.

Rousseau's *Discours sur l'origine et les fondements de l'inégalité* is a perfect example. The promise of this discourse is: "To mark, in the progress of things, the moment when, right taking the place of violence, nature was subjected to law. To explain the sequence of wonders by which the strong could resolve to serve the weak."[50] An inventive rethinking of the inner movement of political history is required for this explanation. The basis of this invention is a survey of the phenomenon of the political, the moments of which are taken from Rousseau's own experience and extensive research. In holding these moments together and contemplating their connections and possible re-connections, Rousseau is able to discover the necessary inner movement of all political life. He lights upon the necessary "progress of things" and the hidden order of the "sequence of wonders." The new order given in Rousseau's political narrative—its new twist—emphasizes the inherent goodness of the natural man (*contra* Hobbes) and the deleterious effects of *amour propre*. *Ingegno* fills in the missing threads of the story, not as a "real" history, but as an ideal history, the history which *has always been and will always be*.

This history is not found in experience, but experience leads to its discovery. Rousseau's story applies to the political as such, not to any one contingent event in the history of a particular polity. This is the internal view, as opposed to the external. This narrative is a likely story. All ingenious narratives are likely stories, lacking the "clear and distinct" predicates of Cartesian knowledge. The likely story is the oldest trope of philosophy. It is the gift that the Muses sing from memory, the song of what was, is, and shall be. As with mythical consciousness, this ingenious apprehension of the inner movement of the object is simply true, even if there are many particular instances in which it is not factually

---

50 Jean-Jacques Rousseau, *Discourse on the Origin and Foundations of Inequality Among Men*, in *The Basic Political Writings*, trans. Donald A. Cress (Indianapolis: Hackett, 1987), 38.

true. We must, however, beware the false songs of the Muses. The history of philosophy and the humanities in general is a battlefield between conflicting likely stories. We find, though, that certain stories outlast others, and we can continue to tell them to ourselves under different circumstances. Locke's story outlasts Filmer's; Hegel's outlasts Jacobi's; Twain's outlasts Cooper's. The true songs of the Muses are those we can sing to ourselves over and over again without growing stale.

Only the outside of the object can ever be clear and distinct. The outside, though, shows itself only in its contingency and relativity, never in its necessity. Anyone can be taught the Cartesian method, insofar as this is just a matter of refusing whatever is not clear and distinct and reflecting upon what is. Likewise, anyone can be taught to be an adequate astronomer or chemist. One cannot, however, be taught to think with ingenuity. One cannot through training become a Rousseau any more than one can through training become a Kepler or a Lavoisier.

Cicero and the ethics of prudence

In *De inventione*, Cicero gives a description of *prudentia*, one of his four cardinal virtues (along with justice, fortitude and temperance). He writes, "Prudence [*prudentia*] is the knowledge of what is good, what is bad, and what is neither good nor bad. Its parts are memory [*memoria*], intelligence [*intelligentia*], and foresight [*providentia*, i.e. providence]. Memory is the faculty by which the mind recalls what has happened. Intelligence is the faculty by which it ascertains what is. Foresight is the faculty by which it is seen that something is going to occur before it occurs" (*De Inv.*, II. liii.160, translation altered). This description of the three parts of *prudentia* was pictorially represented in Titian's painting, *The Allegory of Prudence*, in which *memoria*, *intelligentia* and *providentia* are represented by the heads of a wolf, a lion, and a dog, respectively.

Prudentia is understood by Cicero to embrace what has been, what is, and what shall be. *Prudentia* is therefore the Latin name for the wisdom of the Muses. It is the art of discovering the providential order of things.[51] This Ciceronian understanding of *prudentia*, which contains all three temporal directions of apprehension under one act, is the ethical el-

---

51 Donald Phillip Verene develops this point. See "Two Sources of Philosophical Memory: Vico versus Hegel," in *Philosophical Imagination and Cultural Memory: Appropriating Historical Traditions*, ed. Patricia Cook (Durham, NC: Duke University Press, 1991), 40.

ement of the philosophical idea of memory that I am defending.[52] There are three historical sources for moral systems. Religions have based their systems on revelation and authority. Many modern philosophers, such as Kant and Mill, have attempted to discover the first principles of a universal moral philosophy through pure reason alone. Dependent on the limits of human reason, such systems are always liable to be refuted by human reason. The third source is memory, which is the motor behind what the Romans called *prudentia* and the Greeks called *phronesis*.

A moral philosophy based on *prudentia* or *phronesis* discovers the good by remembering what has been beneficial to man in the past. Further, it is open to adaptation in reference to future human experience in a way that the rigorously closed systems of revelation and pure reason are not. A moral system based on *prudentia* is tied much closer to human life in the world, with its shifting needs and circumstances, than one based on supposed absolutes. For Kant, the notion of duty is the cornerstone of ethical action.[53] The ethics of duty is problematic because all possible concrete ethical situations have many sides. There never arises concrete situation in which one's decision does not entail some opportunity cost. Careful analysis can uncover categorical duties that both compel and prohibit every action. Reflective thinking, which always fixes its oppositions in place, cannot adequately resolve these contradictions. The choice of action in a given situation therefore always falls back upon subjective choice, which is arbitrary and not motivated by duty. Hegel observes that the primary yield of absolute ethics is a good conscience for bad men (who can thereby justify their self-serving actions) and a bad conscience for good men (who are always aware of the duties they must violate in order to fulfill other duties) (*FK*, 184–85; *W*, II: 426–27). A true Kantian, for Hegel, is never able to decide on an action in good faith, for the fulfillment of every duty is a violation of other duties.

---

52 It is often argued that Cicero is simply a jurist, not really a philosopher. His notion of *prudentia* is viewed as an apology for the Roman legal code rather than as a real moral doctrine. What makes Ciceronian *prudentia* philosophical is its penetration into the providential, inner order of things and its connection to *ingenium*.

53 In articulating the project of the *Grundlegung zur Metaphysik der Sitten*, Kant writes, "In order, then, to unravel the concept of a will to be highly esteemed in itself ... this concept that always comes first in estimating the entire worth of our actions and constitutes the condition of everything else: we shall inspect the concept of duty, which contains that of a good will." Kant, *Groundwork of the Metaphysics of Morals*, trans. Mary Gregor and Jens Timmerman (New York: Cambridge University Press, 2012), 12.

Prudentia also has marked advantages for life over any morality based on revelation or authority. An ethical code of action handed down for all time by an infallible master cannot adapt itself to changing circumstances. The working out of such a code, even by human agency, would be of the utmost value were we only assured that the present conditions would last forever. However, all temporal conditions must grow and change, decline and fall. For human action to remain effectual through time, humans must be able to adapt to the world of flux. The right action, at one time and in one place, is not the right action in a very different climate and epoch. Living well is not a monolithic art; it requires understanding and coming to terms with the world as it is given, and as it is changing. Worldly wisdom is the knack for knowing what rules to apply to the concrete situation at hand. This is art of prudence, which is memory joined to intellect.

Concordantly, the moral standpoint of a doctrine of memory must always be that of *prudentia* or *phronesis*. The Muses teach this practical wisdom to those who know how to listen. Purely rational principles always present major problems when the attempt is made to put them into effect in concrete situations. *Prudentia* begins with the concrete, ascends to probable universals, and returns to the concrete in novel situations. It follows what C. S. Peirce called abductive logic, the logic of probability. If it turns out that the best received wisdom regarding past situations is ineffective under current conditions, then the prudent actor will revisit his or her assumptions, and search for other precedents. *Prudentia* is thoroughly tied to the past and to tradition, but not in bondage to the past. Tradition is a platform for action, not an ultimatum. In modern times, the ethics of prudence has been best developed by Montaigne, and it will be more thoroughly elucidated in the third section.

Self-knowledge

Hermes Trismegistus, Thrice-Great Hermes, teaches that "unlike any other living thing on earth, mankind is twofold—in the body mortal but immortal in the essential man."[54] Elsewhere, in a passage dear to Pico della Mirandola, he teaches: "Thus, O Asclepius, Man is a great miracle, a being to be adored and honoured. He passes into the nature of God as though he were God. ... Of all living beings it is in humans alone that

---

54 [Hermes Trismegistus], *Corpus Hermeticum*, in *Hermetica*, trans. Brian P. Copenhaver (New York: Cambridge University Press, 1992), 1: 15.

consciousness provides the intelligence of divine reason; consciousness both raises and sustains this intelligence."[55]

The Hermetic corpus was thought for over a thousand years to have been the most ancient wisdom of Egypt, received from the god Hermes, thrice-great "because he was the greatest philosopher and the greatest priest and the greatest king."[56] We now know that these texts were actually composed several centuries after the fall of the Roman Republic. Nonetheless, the Hermetic tradition has always been attractive to humanist philosophy. This philosophy elevates the human being to the position of divinity and accords humans access to the divine consciousness. If this divine consciousness is possible, then the whole of nature, the whole of the *cosmos*, can be known. The Hermetic anthropology views the individual human as a microcosm (a micro-cosmos) and, as such, we need only look within to fully comprehend what is without.[57]

On what faculty does this inward looking rely? It is always an act of memory. The Hermetic sage says, "Man knows himself and knows the cosmos, so that he remembers what is fitting for his role and recognizes what is useful for him and what he should serve."[58] Through recollecting what he himself is, the individual is able to recollect simultaneously the necessary thread of the cosmos. "With the four elements of mind, consciousness, memory and foresight he may know all things divine and contemplate them."[59] This schema bears a resemblance to the elements of Cicero's *prudentia*, namely memory, intelligence and foresight. All of these elements are properly memory, in the sense Vico gives the term. Finally, Hermes teaches, "Man's consciousness depends on the tenacity of his memory, that is, the memory of all that he has experienced. But the

---

55 [Hermes Trismegistus], *Asclepius*, trans. Clement Salaman (London: Gerald Duckworth & Co.), 58–59. I prefer the Salaman translation to that of Copenhaver because it emphasizes the use of "cosmos" in the Hermetic text.
56 This is the explanation of Marsilio Ficino, who first translated most of the *Corpus Hermetica* into Latin. It is quoted by Brian Copenhaver in his translator's introduction to *Hermetica*, xlviii.
57 Good summaries of the main points of Hermeticism can be found in Glenn Alexander Magee, *Hegel and the Hermetic Tradition* (Ithaca, NY: Cornell University Press, 2001), 13, and in the first three chapters of Frances A. Yates, *Giordano Bruno and the Hermetic Tradition* (Chicago: University of Chicago Press, 1964). Yates writes that Hermes sees "within himself, in his own *Nous* or *mens*, the light and an innumerable number of Powers, a limitless world and the fire enveloped in an all powerful force" (23). In *Individual and Cosmos*, Cassirer says of the Hermetic tradition: "Man ... viewed in his essence, [includes] within himself all things. In man as a microcosm all lines of the macrocosm run together" (40).
58 [Hermes Trismegistus], *Asclepius*, 63.
59 Ibid., 64–65.

divine consciousness in its descent reaches as far as the human being. ... Now the intelligence of human consciousness, be it of whatever kind of capacity, consists totally in the memory of past events, and through the tenacity of this memory it has become the ruler of the Earth. But the intelligence of Nature can be attained through the capacity of cosmic consciousness from everything which is subject to the senses in the cosmos."[60]

This final passage suggests that there are two lines of memory, one that apprehends the strictly human things and one turned toward the cosmic and divine. Through the recollection of those contingent and fluctuating external earthly things, the subject is equipped to predict and control his or her environment. This is the aim of science. On a higher level, however, by looking internally and recollecting oneself, the human being is able to partake of the divine. The recollection of one's own inner movement is at once the recollection of the inner movement of the cosmos. This is the original sense of the term "microcosm." In this cosmology, which is also an anthropology, self-knowledge is identical to the knowledge of the whole.[61]

"Memory as philosophy" does *not* depend on a Hermetic view of man as microcosm. The two are compatible, but my own thesis is not reliant upon so mystical a view of the universe. I do not claim that the secrets of the universe are there to be unraveled by an inward turn; this would undermine the role of experience. No anchorite ever discovered more than the limits of his or her own piety. "Memory as philosophy" claims that the elements of the cosmos can be comprehended through *ingenium*, but that the ingenious twist depends upon moments of experience, which it manipulates into new connections and new orders. It depends upon the memory of actual lived experience, *Erlebnis*. Nonetheless, the Hermetic view lays stress upon an important element of the philosophical idea of memory, namely the centrality of self-knowledge.

Self-knowledge has been the object of philosophical thought since the time of Socrates. The inscription in the temple of the Oracle of Apollo at Delphi enjoins the pursuit of self-knowledge to all who enter: *gnōthi*

---

60 Ibid., 88–89.
61 Magee has given a compelling argument that the Hermetic tradition had a profound influence on Hegel. He writes that the two central aims of his *Hegel and the Hermetic Tradition* are (a) to demonstrate this influence and (b) "to situate Hegel's thought *within* the Hermetic tradition; to show that Hegel self-consciously appropriated and aligned himself with Hermeticism; to show that Hegel's thought can best be understood as Hermetic" (17). I agree with Magee's overall claims, even though I am not convinced by every article of evidence he invokes.

seauton, know thyself. When Chaerephon asked the oracle whether any man was wiser than Socrates, the answer was negative (*Apol.*, 21a). The sense that Socrates makes of this claim is well known: "I am wiser than this man; it is likely that neither of us knows anything worthwhile, but he thinks he knows something when he does not, whereas when I do not know, neither do I think I know; so I am likely to be wiser than he to this small extent, that I do not think I know what I do not know" (*Apol.*, 21d).

This is the cry by which philosophy's turn toward self-knowledge is announced. Every philosopher who considers Socrates a kinsman must take up this concern for self-knowledge and must ruthlessly pursue the examined life.[62] As Shaftesbury says, "'Tis the hardest thing in the world to be a good thinker without being a strong self-examiner."[63]

Montaigne announces a novel subject for his *Essays* in his brief introductory note "To the Reader," placed before at the start of the first series of essays. He writes, "I want to be seen here in my simple, natural, ordinary fashion, without straining or artifice; for it is *myself* that I portray" (*CE*, 2; *V*, 3, emphasis mine). Montaigne is himself the object of curiosity, which his *Essays* one and all investigate. He is himself the thing under scrutiny, at turns miraculous and monstrous, the thing subjected to tests, measurements, and essays. This may be read as Montaigne's answer to the skepticism of which he is so often accused.[64] In the "Apology for Raymond Sebond," at the very point when he is most vociferously arguing that humans can have no knowledge, he turns about and allows that one *can* have knowledge of oneself. All controversies regarding external things are open to a thousand irreconcilable points of view and always admit of antinomies that can never be settled. However, the inward gaze can still be a starting point for wisdom, which begins with the Ecclesiastical recognition that all is vanity. "From the

---

62 See Ann Hartle, *Self-Knowledge in the Age of Theory* (Lanham, MD: Rowman & Littlefield, 1997). Hartle articulates the aim of her book as a defense of "the claim that philosophy is the search for self-knowledge and that the search for self-knowledge must ultimately be or become philosophical" (xiii).

63 Anthony Ashley Cooper, third Earl of Shaftesbury, *Characteristics of Men, Manners, Opinions, Times* (New York: Bobbs-Merrill, 1964), 112

64 This reputation is based primarily on Montaigne's "Apology for Raymond Sebond," the longest of his *Essais*. Emerson's essay, "Montaigne; or, the Skeptic," reinforced this reputation. Emerson reads "our Saint Michel de Montaigne" as asserting "that there is no line, but random and chaos, a calamity of nothing, a prosperity and no account of it, a hero born from a fool, a fool from a hero." Ralph Waldo Emerson, "Montaigne; or, the Skeptic," in *Representative Men* (New York: Marsilio, 1995), 115–17. The prominent role taken by the faculty of judgment in the later *Essais* shows, however, that Montaigne ultimately rejected this skeptical position.

knowledge of this mobility [*volubilité*] of mine I have accidentally engendered in myself a certain constancy of opinions" (*CE*, II: 12, 428; *V*, 569).⁶⁵ Taking up oneself as one's guiding question is the Socratic turn to self-knowledge.

The attainment of self-knowledge always requires an act of recollection. It is one's essence that is in question, what one *has* been, and by extension what one will be. Self-knowledge is not an external grasp of the facts and moments of one's own history. By combining an agglomeration of dates and addresses, one does not arrive at the *philosophical*, Socratic ideal of self-knowledge. One arrives only at a legal affidavit, which is never adequate to encapsulate the self. Self-knowledge is the grasp of the inner movement of the self and its necessity. It is attained only by recollecting the whole of this movement, including all of its misadventures and errors, in one complete view. This is the ideal of the stage of *das absolutes Wissen* with which Hegel's *Phenomenology* ends, as we shall see in the thirteenth chapter. It is also the ideal of Montaigne's *Essays*. The many perspectives of the individual essays are an attempt to capture the movement of the self.⁶⁶ Montaigne's rhetorical philosophy and Hegel's systematic philosophy share the same fundamental goal: the recollection of the inner form and movement of the self, self-knowledge. Insofar as philosophy is always concerned with self-knowledge, philosophy must always take a sympathetic orientation toward memory.

How is the inward gaze a starting point for wisdom? Montaigne tells us that "man" is the subject of the study he is making (*CE*, II: 17, 481; *V*, 634). This reference to "man" writ large would seem to give the lie to his claim that he himself is always the subject of his essays. However, Montaigne's self-study is at its core the study of the human condition because each human individual ultimately represents all of humanity. Montaigne writes, "I offer a humble and inglorious life; that does not matter. You can tie up all moral philosophy with a common and private life just as well as with a life of richer stuff. Each man bears the entire form the human condition [*l'humaine condition*]" (*CE*, III: 2, 611; *V*,

---

65 Donald Frame writes, "What is left for us as creatures of flux incapable of true knowledge? To learn the lesson of flux, to become 'wise at our own expense' [*CE*, II: 12, 423; *V*, 563] by knowing ourselves." Frame, *Montaigne's Essais*, 31.
66 See Jean Starobinski, *Montaigne in Motion*, trans. Arthur Goldhammer (Chicago: University of Chicago Press, 1985), 214–43. Starobinski examines the role of movement in Montaigne's *Essais*, as it pertains to the work of self-knowledge. He writes, "'Being consists in movement and action' [*CE*, 2: 8, 279] ... it is to human actions and movements that [this statement] pertains" (217).

805, translation altered).⁶⁷ On the Hermetic view, the individual human is literally a micro-cosmos. On Montaigne's view, the individual is a type of microcosm, but in relation to the whole of humanity rather than to the universe. Any and every individual bears in himself or herself the entirety of *l'humaine condition*.

Erich Auerbach captures the issue of Montaigne's claim. He writes, "Any random human destiny, *une vie populaire et privée*, is all he needs for his purpose. ... And then follows the famous sentence upon the *humaine condition* which is realized in any and every human being. With this sentence he has evidently answered the question of the significance and use of his undertaking. If every man affords material and occasion enough for the development of the complete moral philosophy, then a precise and sincere self-analysis of any random individual is directly justified."⁶⁸ Because Montaigne the individual is a "representative specimen"⁶⁹ of the human race, his self-knowledge is human knowledge.

L'humaine condition is not "human nature." Human nature implies that there is a set of distinguishing characteristics shared by all individuals, inborn in the species. Hegel writes, "For philosophy, however, this knowledge of human nature is devoid of interest. ... This knowledge of human nature can even be harmful for philosophy" (*PM*, §377, Z). The human *condition* implies only that all individuals exist in relation to the same socio-physical structures, that all individuals share some collection of external pressures and limits that weigh upon them, such as death, pain, the other. The objective world is common to all, and all of these factors are conditions that the self must confront in its growth and formation. We do not need to understand every single member of the human species to understand the human condition; as this condition is universal, we need only understand any particular individual. This requires a starkly honest pursuit of self-knowledge, a Socratic self-examination. It requires the utmost endurance and fortitude. Joseph Conrad is correct when he writes, "No man ever understands quite his own artful dodges to escape from the grim shadow of self-knowledge."⁷⁰ Montaigne is the first man of modernity because he is the first to stand naked before the world. He-

---

67 "Je propose une vie basse et sans luster: c'est tout un; on attaché aussi bien toute la philosophie morale à une vie populaire et privée, que à une vie de plus riche estoffe: chaque home porte la forme entire de l'humaine condition."
68 Erich Auerbach, "L'humaine condition," in *Mimesis: The Representation of Reality in Western Literature*, trans. Willard R. Trask (Princeton, NJ: Princeton University Press, 1953), 297.
69 Frame, *Montaigne's Essais*, 35.
70 Joseph Conrad, *Lord Jim* (New York: Barnes & Noble, 2004), 71.

gel stands naked in the *Phenomenology*. Nudity is the precondition for self-knowledge, and self-knowledge is the knowledge of the human condition. Because the human being is a microcosm of humanity, the complete recollection of oneself is also philosophical wisdom.[71]

Conclusion

To sum up this section, which contains the entire theory of "memory as philosophy": Memory transforms substance into subject. Only through the act of *ingenium* are we able to penetrate the object standing before us. In internalizing and making the object our own, we first discover its essence. Through this act of *ingenium*, we arrive at the most general principles of the matter at hand. It is therefore akin to the classical *ars topica*, rather than *ars critica* on which reflection depends.[72] *Prudentia* is the moral form that "memory as philosophy" must take. The likely story or myth is its narrative form, the Muses are its inspiration, and comedy is its genre. Self-knowledge is its ultimate aim.

This may seem like bad science, but the insights of *ingenium* are the basis of all science. These elements of the doctrine of philosophical memory, dubious to modern ears, have always been and will always be the central elements of the love of wisdom. He who has ears to hear, let him hear. This approach is what we must remember if we are to get beyond the external view of reflection. As Socrates showed, every *aporia* is answered by recalling the point at which we first began to wander astray. Philosophy has forgotten itself, but the inner movement of philosophy is nothing other than a recurrent self-forgetting and self-recollecting.

---

71 C.f. Verene, "Two Sources": "The product of memory is self-knowledge, which memory offers in two senses. It provides us with the autobiography of humanity and the autobiography of the individual to the extent that the individual is a microcosm of the life of humanity. Such autobiography, once understood, provides us with a practical wisdom because memory shows that all which has been in the past is in the present and will be in the future" (41).

72 Mary Carruthers writes, "One does not simply parrot forth some previously recorded *dictum* word for word by rote, but builds a 'topic' or '(common-)place' out of one's memorial inventory." Carruthers, *Book of Memory*, 34. *Ingegno* is the key to the discovery of these *topoi*, on which all deduction depends. Aristotle writes, "a demonstrative proposition is the assumption of one of two contradictory statements (the demonstrator does not ask for his premise, but lays it down)" (*Pr. An.*, 24a21–24).

IV: Forgetting

Philosophy depends upon memory. No less, however, does it depend upon forgetting. William James rightly suggested in his *Principles of Psychology* that forgetting is as useful to everyday life as recollecting.[1] The two powers must coexist in a dialectical relationship. A complete memory of all things past lacks any standard by which to judge these things. A memory unsullied by forgetfulness is a library of books without titles, in which one cannot be sure what one should read and what one should pass by. There are two aspects from which we may view this need. From a practical standpoint, a memory without the capacity for forgetting yields a state of consciousness in which pain can never dissipate; it retains at all times the full force of immediacy. From a cognitive standpoint, the subject whose memory is not intermixed with forgetfulness is never very good at *thinking*. Since the nature of even the Muses is "forgetfulness of evils and relief from anxieties," our philosophical doctrine of memory requires as its correlate a philosophical doctrine of forgetting.

Forgetting and *ataraxia*

The Athenian politician Themistocles was gifted with great wisdom and genius; Plato referred to him in the *Meno* as a "good and wise man" (93e). Cicero writes, "It is said that a certain learned and highly accomplished person went to [Themistocles] and offered to impart to him the science of mnemonics ... and that when Themistocles asked what precise result that science was capable of achieving, the professor asserted that it would enable him to remember everything; and Themistocles replied that he would be doing him a greater kindness if he taught him to forget what he wanted than if he taught him to remember" (*De Or.*, II. lxxiv.299).

Why did Themistocles prefer the science of forgetting to that of remembering? Presumably, it is because forgetting is the balm of all pains, the solace of all failures. The Greek school of philosophy most centrally concerned with pleasure and pain is that of Epicurus. In the philosophy of Epicurus, memory holds a privileged position: "Remembering previous goods is the most important factor contributing to a pleasant

---

1   James, *Principles of Psychology*, 679–80.

life."[2] Pleasure is always accessible to the individual through the recollection of those pleasant experiences of the past. The absence of immediate pleasure is not an obstacle to happiness. The supplement suggested by this doctrine is that, mercifully, pain is always subject to annihilation through the act of forgetting. The writings of Epicurus that specifically address forgetting have been lost, but Cicero affirms that this was a part of Epicurus' teaching. He writes, "If you 'recall' me to goods like this, Epicurus, I obey, I follow, I take you as my guide, I 'forget' evils too, as you bid, and the more readily because I think they are not so much as to be reckoned as evils" (*Tusc. Disp.*, III. xvii.37).[3] Epicurus bids us to forget the evils we have suffered, as a necessary condition for attaining pleasure free of pains. Epicurean pleasure depends on a perspicacious selectivity of memory. There is no doubt that Epicurus learned this lesson from the song of the Muses.

Because of their differences on ethical matters, Cicero is never more than a luke-warm supporter of Epicurus. For this reason, he does not ultimately align with Themistocles either, saying through the mouth of Antonius, "I am not myself as clever as Themistocles was, so as to prefer the science of forgetting to that of remembering" (*De Or.*, II. lxxxvi.351). As we shall see in the following section, Cicero is one of the classical advocates of the technical art of memory. Nonetheless, Themistocles is still presented as a man of great genius in the text. Cicero recognizes the importance of an art of forgetting, though he is more interested in pursuing its opposite. Because memory is one of the three parts of *prudentia*, its great value for Cicero is ethical. Forgetting, though, has its role in personal happiness: "Then again, emotions of the soul, anxieties and distresses are alleviated by forgetfulness when the thoughts of the soul are diverted to pleasure" (*Tusc. Disp.*, V. xxxviii.110). Cicero sees that Epicurus has hit on something, however misguided the twist he gives to it. In this passage, we see what is at issue in a doctrine of forgetting: *ataraxia*—that is, tranquility—requires the capacity to forget not the factual events of the past, but one's own emotions and opinions concerning them. So long as the preserved image persists in its attachment to the an-

---

2   Epicurus, *The Epicurus Reader: Selected Writings and Testimonia*, trans. and ed. Brad Inwood and L.P. Gerson (Indianapolis: Hackett, 1994), Text 137 (from Plutarch, *A Pleasant Life*, 1099d).

3   C.f. *Tusc. Disp.*, III. xvi.35: "Under the smart of circumstances which we regard as evil, concealment or forgetfulness is not within our control. ... And do you, Epicurus, bid me to 'forget,' though to forget is contrary to nature, while you wrest from my grasp the aid which nature has supplied for the relief of long-standing pain?"

ger or terror with which it was originally conjoined, there is always something disturbing one's tranquility, some eternal cathexis of energy, as Freud would say, lurking in the unconscious. Emotion is always contingent. The need to forget the emotional element of the past for the sake of *ataraxia* is the one point on which Cicero and Epicurus agree.

Montaigne, neither an Epicurean nor a Ciceronian but always eclectic in his sources, inherits this doctrine of forgetting. In the "Apology for Raymond Sebond," amidst quotations from both Cicero and the Epicurean philosopher Lucretius, Montaigne argues that human knowledge is inadequate against the ills of the world. His evidence is that under their pressure even philosophy enjoins us to turn to ignorance. He writes, "When not even a philosopher, but simply a sound man, feels in reality the burning thirst of a high fever, what kind of coin to pay him in is the memory of the sweetness of Greek wine? This would be rather to make his bargain worse, 'For to recall the joy doubles the pain'" (*CE*, II: 12, 365; *V*, 494, the quotation being an adaptation of Dante). Even the recollection of joy is a hollow ruse. The suffering individual does not achieve *ataraxia* through whimsical reminiscence; rather, consciousness of the distance from the past increases the anguish of the present. In Montaigne's version of "memory as philosophy" all emotive elements must be selectively forgotten.[4] *Ataraxia* comes from learning to die, and terror is disarmed by disimpassioned familiarity (see *CE*, I: 20).

There is, however, an immediate reversal: "Of the same sort is that other advice that philosophy gives, to keep in our memory only past happiness, and to efface from it the troubles we have suffered; as if the science of forgetting [*science de l'oubly*] were in our power. ... For memory sets before me not what I choose, but what it pleases. Indeed there is nothing that imprints a thing so vividly on our memory as the desire to forget it: a good way to give our mind something to guard, and to impress it on her, is to solicit her to lose it" (*CE*, II: 12, 365; *V*, 494). To enjoin forgetfulness is a confession on the part of philosophy, an admission of its own impotence. Stripping the memory altogether of its contents is the "road to ignorance," which (following Seneca) "is a poor remedy for ills" (ibid., 365; *V*, 495).

The question does not concern the value of forgetfulness. Montaigne does not doubt that some amount of forgetting is necessary for *at-*

---

4   Along similar lines, George Santayana says that all "healthy" memory excludes the emotional reversion to the past, and must "forget in remembering." See Santayana, *Scepticism and Animal Faith* (New York: Dover, 1955), 152–57.

araxia. What is at issue is whether selective forgetting is in the power of the subject. If it is not, then the philosophers must be recommending a wholesale forgetfulness, which is ignorance. I will suggest in the third section that the *Essays* as a whole are in part Montaigne's answer to what he sees as a bankrupt art of memory and an equally bankrupt science of forgetting. The radical nature of this critique can only be properly understood if we recognize that in Montaigne's time, *ars memoriae* were at the peak of their authority and ubiquity. His criticism of the "science of forgetting" is in fact a call for a new, more useful science of forgetting. What he desires is a science of forgetting that promotes *ataraxia* but does not lead to complete ignorance. As Sarah Bakewell says, "[Forgetfulness] freed [Montaigne] to think wisely rather than glibly; [it] allowed him to avoid the fanatical notions and foolish deceptions that ensnared other people; and [it] let him follow his own thoughts wherever they led."[5]

Jorge Luis Borges writes, "As the years pass, every man is forced to bear the growing burden of his memory."[6] Recent studies by neurobiologists have described a certain type of cognitive abnormality that has been termed "Highly Superior Autobiographical Memory" (HSAM), or hyperthymesia. Subjects with hyperthymesia "are able to recall events from their personal past, including the days and dates on which they occurred, with very high accuracy."[7] The subject can recollect nearly every moment of his or her personal history, and there seem to be no quantitative limits to this autobiographical memory. What influence does this condition have on behavior? These subjects tend toward obsessive compulsion, reporting "that they hoard items, need organization in their physical environment, and/or are germ-avoidant. ... They expressed aversions to touching public doorknobs, restaurant utensils, items that are near or have touched the ground, and/or a need to wash their hands excessively. ... HSAM participants express significantly more obsessional tendencies than controls."[8] This is the ever-growing burden of memory: one cannot escape the constant awareness of the potential dangers and disorders of life that beset one on all sides.

---

5   Sarah Bakewell, *How to Live, or A Life of Montaigne in One Question and Twenty Attempts at an Answer* (New York: Other Press, 2010), 73.
6   Jorge Luis Borges, "Shakespeare's Memory," in *Collected Fictions*, trans. Andrew Hurley (New York: Penguin, 1998), 514.
7   Aurora LePort, et al, "Behavioral and Neuroanatomical Investigation of Highly Superior Autobiographical Memory (HSAM)," *Neurobiology of Learning and Memory* 98 (2012), 78.
8   Ibid., 84.

In his *Art of Worldly Wisdom* (1647), Baltasar Gracián advises, "Folly consists not in committing folly, but in not hiding it when committed. ... One should conceal [one's failings] from oneself if one can. But here one can help with that other great rule of life: learn to forget." In a later maxim, Gracián writes, "Be able to forget. ... Memory is not only unruly, leaving us in the lurch when most needed, but stupid as well, putting its nose into places where it is not wanted. ... Very often the only remedy for the trouble is to forget it, and all we forget is the remedy. Nevertheless one should cultivate good habits of memory, for it is capable of making existence a paradise or an inferno."[9] It is worldly wisdom (*prudencia*) to learn to forget what can only cause us prolonged suffering. Gracián's unusual and astute mind well understood the capacity of memory to infect our entire world with pain or pleasure.

Life *is* dangerous and disordered, without question. This truth is part and parcel of the human condition, but it does not exhaust the human condition. The individual must strive to transcend the merely factical reality of danger and pursue spiritual well-being. *Ataraxia*, tranquility, requires a musical "forgetfulness of evils and relief from anxieties." The great philosophers of forgetting—we must recall Nietzsche as well as Epicurus, Montaigne, and Gracián—all tie their doctrines to well-being and happiness. One must be able selectively to annihilate the past if one is to flourish in the present and build toward the future. The recollection of past suffering is always present suffering. The entirety of the past presses down upon us; learning to live requires that we forget this enormity.

Forgetting and thinking

The profound imagination of Borges produced the story of Ireneo Funes, a young nineteenth century Uruguayan who is left crippled when bucked from a horse. The strange side effect of this accident is that Funes is able to remember everything he has ever experienced, to its smallest detail: "Now his perception and his memory were perfect."[10] Funes' memory is tied to perception; the visual is linked to muscular and thermal sensations, so that the entirety of every moment can be reconstructed in a perfectly mimetic image. Funes undertakes several memorial projects of an

---

9 Baltasar Gracián, *The Art of Worldly Wisdom*, trans. Joseph Jacobs (Boston: Shambhala, 2006), maxims 126 and 262, respectively.
10 Borges, "Funes, His Memory," in *Collected Fictions*, 135. This story, "Funes el memorioso" in Spanish, is often translated by the more provocative and literal title, "Funes the Memorious."

enormous scope: the construction of an infinite vocabulary for all natural series of numbers and an exhaustive mental catalogue of every image contained in his memory. His accomplishments in learning are miraculous. Nonetheless, Borges' narrator is correct in his assessment: "He had effortlessly learned English, French, Portuguese, Latin. I suspect, nevertheless, that he was not very good at thinking. To think is to ignore (or forget) differences, to generalize, to abstract. In the teeming world of Ireneo Funes there was nothing but particulars—and they were virtually *immediate* particulars."[11]

Funes' *memoria* (to recall the Vichian distinction of aspects of memory) is perfect. However, he is unable to deal with the world of general ideas and universals. His mind isolates each thing as a unique particular. Every apple falls from the tree for its own particular reasons. This is a poor way of thinking. The move from particulars to universals is the most important practical yield of philosophical consciousness. Funes is a fictional character, but we can easily find evidence that Borges' insights about the gap between memory and thinking are correct. Funes predicts the Russian mnemonist S. V. Shereshevskii, whose powerful and limitless memory was described at length twenty-four years after the publication of "Funes" by the neuropsychologist Alexandr Luria, in *The Mind of a Mnemonist*.

Shereshevskii, called S. throughout the book, was a professional mnemonist, who gave public performances demonstrating his extraordinary powers of memory. Audience members would recite long strings of words or numbers or nonsense syllables, which he would then repeat back, either forward or backward. He could phonetically memorize poetry in languages he did not know. In all of the tests S. was subjected to by Luria, he never demonstrated any limitations either to the quantity of material his memory could retain, or the duration for which it would be retained. Decades removed from first hearing a series of words, S. could repeat their sequence perfectly. Nothing was ever lost from his memory, nothing ever forgotten. However, this perfect retention was, as Borges predicted, deeply problematic. Luria writes, "Many of us are anxious to find ways to improve our memories; none of us have to deal with the problem of how to forget. In S.'s case, however, precisely the reverse was true. The big question for him, and the most troublesome, was how he

---

11 Ibid., 137.

could *learn to forget*."¹² S. finally found that he could block off his memories through an act of will: "Aha! ... If I don't want the chart to show up it won't."¹³ This act of will was not able, however, to utterly efface the particular memory-image. At best, it allowed S. some relief from the constant barrage of memory-images, some respite from the *petites madeleines* of his mind.

This depiction of S. accords with Borges' characterization of Funes. Like Funes, despite his miraculous powers of memory, S. was not very good at thinking. His memory, lacking a dialectical relationship to forgetfulness, prevented his thought from grasping anything with more than a turbid depth. Luria records a few illuminating insights: "As he put it: 'Other people *think* as they read, but I *see* it all.' As soon as he began a phrase, images would appear; as he read further, still more images were evoked, and so on."¹⁴ S.'s mind was unable to follow the thread of a story as a whole, unable to keep from associating each word, each single element, with an image. This is an empirical proof of Vico's claim that *memoria* is *fantasia*. Rather than abstracting the meaning from a story, S. was left with a series of meaningless images representing only the semantic structure of the narrative. The individual words obfuscated the meaning of the whole. "Given such a tendency, cognitive functions can hardly proceed normally. The very thought which occasions an image is soon replaced by another ... a point is thus reached at which images begin to guide one's thinking, rather than thought itself being the dominant element."¹⁵

S. could only think figuratively. He was unable to generalize or abstract. Luria writes, "The conventional use of language is such that abstraction and generalization are most basic. ... [S.'s problem with poetry] clearly indicates that figurative thinking is not always helpful in understanding language."¹⁶ Metaphor, which Ernesto Grassi calls "the root of knowledge,"¹⁷ was altogether beyond S.'s power of understanding. The very perfection of S.'s memory prevented his cognition from understanding abstract ideas. If each thing is a unique particular, a difference with-

---

12   Alexandr R. Luria, *The Mind of a Mnemonist*, trans. Jerome S. Bruner (Cambridge: Harvard University Press, 1987), 67. The sub-heading for this section of the book is "The Art of Forgetting."
13   Ibid., 71.
14   Ibid., 112.
15   Ibid., 116.
16   Ibid., 117, 120.
17   See Ernesto Grassi, *The Primordial Metaphor*, trans. Laura Pietropaolo and Manuela Scarci (Binghamton, NY: Medieval & Renaissance Texts & Studies, 1994), 10–14.

out identity, we can never ascend to the universal, which is an identity of difference. I. M. L. Hunter observes, "The more efficient and logical the thinking, at least of a logical nature, the less it is accompanied for most people by imaging. It would appear images are too concrete and specific to be of great service in reaching solutions by higher-level thinking."[18] The capacity for forgetting is necessary to make this leap. One must be able to forget specific differences and remember only qualitative identities in order to think in terms of universals or generalizations. Likewise, one must forget identity and remember only difference to think in terms of particulars.

In the *Encyclopedia*'s treatment of psychology, Hegel analyzes memory [*Gedächtnis*] in its general Aristotelian sense, rather than in its philosophical sense. *Gedächtnis* is mechanical, psychological memory, in the sense of Vico's simple *memoria*. Hegel writes that *Gedächtnis* is "a passage into the function of *thought* [*das Denken*], which no longer has a *meaning*, i.e. its objectivity is no longer severed from the subjective, and its inwardness does not need to go outside for its existence" (*PM*, §464). What is the relationship in which the two terms stand? "Memory *qua* memory is itself the merely *external* mode, a merely *existential* aspect of thought, and thus needs a complementary element. The passage from it to thought is to our view or implicitly the identity of reason with this existential mode: an identity from which it follows that reason only exists in a subject, and as the function of the subject. Thus active reason is *thinking*" (ibid.). Memory is the external mode, and thinking is the internal. The external and internal depend on one another: memory and thinking exist in a reciprocal unity. We see from the examples of Funes and Shereshevskii that memory is not yet thinking, and that memory and imagination can lead thought itself if there is no control. The control needed to bridge the distance between memory and thinking is forgetting.

Forgetting is just as necessary for thinking well as it is for the attainment of *ataraxia*. Happiness depends on the capacity for forgetting the emotive element of experience. Thinking depends on the capacity for forgetting identity and difference by turns. The mythical form of thinking never rises to universals or generalities; it takes each thing to be a unique particular. Even the identity of the same thing is not fixed through time, as we learn from primitive cultures: when the shaman puts on the mask and becomes the god, he literally *becomes* the god during the ritual. There is a peculiar logic at play, but one that is akin to the logic of

---

18 Hunter, *Memory*, 193.

dreams, or the logic of sense.[19] Our logical thinking—that is, all thinking that depends on the Aristotelian notion of class logic—requires the capacity to move back and forth between universal, particular, and individual; between genus, species, and singular member. Memory without a relationship to forgetting leaves one at the level of mythical consciousness. Difference *always* obtains between any two things; immediate, vacuous actuality is always unique. This difference must be effaced. The immediate character of the object must be forgotten in order to ascend to universals.[20]

The form in which the capacity for forgetting becomes philosophical is *ingenium*, just as *ingenium* is the philosophical form of memory. There is nothing philosophical about common absent-mindedness. The leap from the particular to the universal (and the reverse leap, back to the particular) is always an ingenious act of thinking. There is no method or technique by which it can be learned. One simply *sees* identity.[21] Through *ingenium* we discover similarity in difference. The great difficulty of making this leap is evidenced by those primitive cultures around the world that persist in mythical thinking. The profound philosophical act requires that one hold a collection of individual things in one's mind and give them a new twist, recognizing an order, an identity amongst the set that one did not see before. This is an act of memory, but also an act of forgetfulness. To find the common thread of inner movement, one must annul the apparent differences. To return to the particulars, one must annul this identity. These moments of annulment or cancellation are ingenious lapses of memory. The dialectic between memory and forgetting is the basis of all logical or "rational" thinking. In this sense, Hegel is right when he writes that *Gedächtnis* is the external mode of thinking. The complete act of thinking is the truth of the tension between memory and forgetting.

---

19 See Cassirer, *Philosophy of Symbolic Forms*, 3: 58–91.
20 Schopenhauer writes, "[The concept] is able to take up into itself all the results of perception, in order to give them back again unchanged and undiminished even after the longest period of time; only in this way does *experience* arise. But the concept does not preserve what is perceived or what is felt; rather it preserves what is essential thereof in an entirely altered form, yet as an adequate representative of these results. Thus, flowers cannot be preserved, but their ethereal oil, their essence ... can." *The World as Will and Representation*, 2: 63–64.
21 Aristotle writes, "The greatest thing by far is to be a master of metaphor. It is the one thing that cannot be learnt from others; and it is also a sign of genius, since a good metaphor implies an intuitive perception of the similarity in dissimilars" (*Poet.*, 1459a5–8). William James, following Alexander Bain, similarly writes, "Superior intellect ... seems to consist in nothing so much as in a large development of the faculty of association by similarity." *The Varieties of Religious Experience* (New York: Signet Classic, 2003), 22n7.

V: Memory in the Technological World

It still remains to consider memory in its relation to the present world. This is a natural conclusion to our discussion: having said what "memory as philosophy" is not and what it is, it must finally be situated within its context. "*Yo soy yo y mi circunstancia,*"[1] the famous maxim of José Ortega y Gasset, must be applied to the idea of memory. It is not enough to say what a philosophical memory is as a solitary concept; it must also be related to its relevant circumstances. The abstract discussion of memory must be made concrete by bringing it into the present. We will then have a platform from which to investigate the history of memory in the following section.

Frances Yates, the pioneer of scholarly interest in the classical memorial arts, grasped the problem of modernity, which is the problem of technology. She writes, "The progressive deterioration of memory brought about by the march of technical invention—from printing to television—makes it almost impossible for us to imagine what a memory built up by the classical mnemonic can have been like."[2] Technology cancels memory because *efficiency*, the measure of technology, demands the sacrifice of the old. In the technological world, to say that something is outdated is to say that it is fully dead, without hope of resurrection. The present is not informed by the past because the past was less efficient.

The philosophical sense of memory is not a science that can be taught. It is not a method, and therefore cannot be quantified, predicted, or mastered. The ingenious art of seeing is not susceptible to control. The search for a philosophical method is the search for *clear and distinct ideas*, as we learn from Descartes (and, in different terms, from Kant and Francis Bacon). The value of clear and distinct ideas is their promise to facilitate the scientific control of their objects. "Memory as philosophy" can never convince those who simply do not see the internal form of things—it can never produce the sort of dumb certainty desired by technology. Memory uncovers the probable, never the certain. Reflection,

---

1   José Ortega y Gasset, *Meditaciones del Quijote: Ideas sobre la novella* (Madrid: Espasa-Calpe, 1963): 30.
2   Frances A. Yates, "The Ciceronian Art of Memory," in *Medioevo e Rinascimento: studi in onore di Bruno Nardi* (Firenze: Sansoni, 1955), 883. A version of this claim is repeated in the opening sentences of the preface to *The Art of Memory*: "In the ages before printing a trained memory was vitally important" (xi). This is to say that the rise of technology signals the end of the classical memory.

which never gets behind the exterior of vacuous actuality, *is* method. Technology is the application of technique, *technē*. Technology and method go hand in hand; the efficiency of method is perfected by the final technique.

The relationship between memory and method is more complex than one of simple opposition. It is the relationship of Cronus to Zeus. Yates writes, "If Memory was the Mother of the Muses, she was also to be the Mother of Method. Ramism, Lullism, the art of memory—all those confused constructions compounded of all the memory methods which crowd the later sixteenth and early seventeenth centuries—are symptoms of a search for a method. Seen in the context of this growing search or urge, it is not so much the madness of [Giordano] Bruno's systems as their uncompromising determination to find a method which seems significant."[3] Yates correctly observes that the memory arts of the late Middle Ages and Renaissance are attempts at discovering a method for producing clear and distinct ideas, certainty, and control over nature. These attempts finally bear fruit in the Baconian and Cartesian methods of the seventeenth century.

How are we to understand this claim? The history of the memory tradition follows two lines: what Paolo Rossi calls "the 'speculative' line and the 'technical' line."[4] The "mnemotechnic," which originates with Simonides, is already a technique, which attempts to dominate the speculative, philosophical line of memory. As we will see in the seventh chapter, mnemotechnic is the mother of method, and it is this technique that Montaigne ultimately rejects in his own memorial philosophy. The "speculative" line—that is, "memory as philosophy"—cannot be reduced to or replaced by technique, though it can utilize the mnemotechnic as a tool. *Ingenium* is mother wit, the gift of the Muses.

Memory is more than *ingenium*; we have seen that this aspect of memory depends on *memoria*, the psychological remembrance of things past, for its material. This is what technology *can* replace, and this substitution removes the foundation from a truly philosophical memory. Yates mentions the printing press and television. When one has access to books, one does not have a pressing need to hold a great many things in one's memory. Reference can always be made to an artificial paper memory. The book, however, is properly a supplement to memory, not a replacement.

---

3   Yates, *Art of Memory*, 306.
4   Paolo Rossi, *Logic and the Art of Memory: The Quest for a Universal Language*, trans. Stephen Clucas (New York: Continuum, 2006), 12.

Mary Carruthers writes, "In none of the evidence I have discovered is the act of writing itself regarded as a supplanter of memory, not even in Plato's *Phaedrus*. Rather books are themselves memorial cues and aids, and memory is most like a book, a written page or wax tablet upon which something is written."[5] In a similar spirit, Marshall McLuhan, the philosopher of media, writes, "Print provided a vast new memory for past writings that made a personal memory inadequate."[6] The printed word answers that inadequacy, but does not challenge the sovereignty of memory. It is a very recent phenomenon that books are written for the sake of conveying information or for being consulted and referenced. Printed books were originally intended to be read, not consulted.

There is more to be said concerning printing, which I shall bracket until the eleventh chapter. It is not actually the technique of printing, but the rise of the computer that has accelerated this assault on memory exponentially. Computers are unlimited data banks, and in the age of the computer there is no need to retain anything whatsoever in one's memory. Access to *information* is available everywhere, at every time. We can now wear our computers on our wrists or (as an excellent, unintentional metaphor for the modern human condition writ large) over our eyes, so that we are never separated from the technological storehouse of information. Information replaces real knowledge, real wisdom.

To be well-informed is not to be wise. Information is ubiquitous and has no natural end; it is only a means for the particular moment. We give the proper information on an application, or we acquire the information needed to diagnose an automotive problem. Technology itself is, as Jacques Ellul has said, "nothing more than *means* and the *ensemble of means*."[7] Knowledge, which is internalized information, has an influence on thinking, but information itself is always external to thinking, always localized to a particular situation. However, information is susceptible to control in a way that knowledge and thinking are not. It is potentially infinite, and it is now the best distributed thing in the world, supplanting *le*

---

5   Carruthers, *Book of Memory*, 16. The reference is to Plato's claim that writing is a deterrent to memory rather than an aid (*Phaedrus*, 274d–275b). Carruthers does not explain why her claim does not contradict Plato's.
6   Marshall McLuhan, *Understanding Media: The Extensions of Man* (New York: McGraw-Hill, 1964), 158.
7   Jacques Ellul, *The Technological Society*, trans. John Wilkinson (New York: Vintage, 1964), 19. Ellul continues: "Our civilization is first and foremost a civilization of means; in the reality of modern life, the means, it would seem, are more important than the ends." The present section of this work is deeply indebted to Ellul's analysis of technique.

bon sens. The "Cloud", with its promise of unlimited information storage, is the latest idol of technology. Its ephemeral name is appropriate. Nonetheless, once we apprehend the vastly superior efficiency of the Cloud, it would surely be foolish to concern ourselves with the fragile *memoria* of human individuals.

Without *memoria*, there can be no *ingenium*. The latter requires a rich field of memorial content. Putting a new twist on things, or finding their proper order and inner form, presupposes that these things are the inventory of one's memory, in such a way that they can be surveyed in one glance. The matter at issue must be internalized for this to occur. Information is never internalized because it never serves anything more than the end of the particular moment. It is always external; technology substitutes the external for the internal because the external memory is more efficient. It is subject to neither deterioration nor ambiguity. Reflection is the faculty of the technological world. However, when the content of memory is external, it can never be reorganized and thus can never elicit the ingenious flash of creative vision. The Internet gives us one thing after another, not the complete speech. The computer can only ever repeat what is programmed into it. It can never create, in the sense in which human art creates, or discover, in the sense of the Latin *inventio*. Mnemotechnics have sought and discovered that *telos*, the discovery of which has annulled mnemotechnics. The parent, as we see, is castrated by its offspring.

The problem of the modern world is this: once we have technique, we can only go forward. This is an inviolable existential principle. Technology pulls efficiency ahead, and the refusal to maximize efficiency is irrational. Technique carries us along, and there is no turning back. Ellul writes, "Technique engenders itself. When a new technical form appears, it makes possible and conditions a number of others."[8] Ellul calls this process the self-augmentation of technology. Its two laws are these: "(1) In a given civilization, technical progress is irreversible. (2) Technical progress tends to act, not according to an arithmetic, but according to a geometric progression."[9] The progress is irreversible because the result of this progress is the maximization of efficiency. Any method becomes defunct when a superior method is discovered. Since technology is always a means, the technique that proves to be the means superior to all

---

8 Ibid., 87.
9 Ibid., 89.

alternatives annihilates these alternatives altogether. It is foolishness to apply an inferior means to a given situation.

We can see this process of "progress" at work not just in the machines of industry, but also in political technique, in athletic technique, in financial technique. Art and literature, those basic arenas of spiritual expression, have become more and more techniques of representation. Since musicians have discovered the technique of appealing to the mean, music no longer expresses anything. The idea of art as expression articulated not long ago by Benedetto Croce and R. G. Collingwood already begins to feel antiquated. As Karl Jaspers says, "All things are interrelated. The technical mastery of space, time, and matter advances irresistibly, and no longer through casual and isolated discoveries, but by organized collaboration, in the course of which discovery itself has been systematized and subjected to purposive endeavor."[10]

Because there is no turning back, and because efficiency replaces independent thought, technique levels humanity. Ellul writes, "Human beings are, indeed, always necessary. But literally anyone can do the job, provided he is trained to it. Henceforth, men will be able to act only in virtue of their commonest and lowest nature, and not in virtue of what they possess of superiority and individuality. The qualities which technique requires for its advance are precisely those characteristics of a technical order which do not represent individual intelligence."[11] Technology leads thought, rather than thought leading technology. Anyone can learn a technique, just as anyone can learn the practice of reflection. Technology is not in any way exclusive. It is not coincidental that the technological world and the democratic world historically arise at the same time. Because *ingenium* is not a technique, it cannot be open to all, but only to a privileged few. Nor is it a means to any particular end. It *can* suggest solutions to problems, but it has no method and its success is rooted in its essentially playful character. World economies, and other serious matters on which so much depends, can no longer wait on philosophical thought. Technique moves in front of thought just as, for Shereshevskii, thought is guided by images. Technology turns us all into Shereshevskiis: not very good at thinking, but with an infinite supply of information at our fingertips. The loss of thought dehumanizes, and the technological society is one of self-alienation. T. S. Eliot captured the changing human condition early in the twentieth century when he wrote,

---

10 Jaspers, *Man in the Modern Age*, 17.
11 Ellul, *Technological Society*, 93.

> We are the hollow men
> We are the stuffed men
> Leaning together
> Headpiece filled with straw. Alas![12]

In 1929, Ortega y Gasset observed, "The characteristic of the hour is that the commonplace mind, knowing itself to be commonplace, has the assurance to proclaim the rights of the commonplace and to impose them wherever it will. ... The mass crushes beneath it everything that is different, everything that is excellent, individual, qualified and select. Anybody who is not like everybody, who does not think like everybody, runs the risk of being eliminated."[13] When technology attains absolute control and becomes a self-augmenting process, rolling ever forward, it forces the individual to adapt. Human things win the ascendancy over human beings. To thrive, one does not need wisdom; one needs only a willingness to play by the rules of technique. Whatever lies outside the control of technique—whatever disdains to embrace method—is the only true "other" in society. All other difference, so long as it follows technique's law of maximum efficiency, can be assimilated. This is why reflection and method have won the day in philosophy. Ernst Cassirer correctly writes, "A new determination of value and meaning is now established for [human] consciousness: the genuine 'purpose' of action is no longer measured by what it brings about and finally achieves; rather, it is the pure form of doing, the type and direction of the productive force as such, that determines this purpose."[14] Technology has no essential ends because its purpose is entirely in its means and action, in the cry of "Excelsior!"

The effect that this state of things has on memory is to cancel its entire purpose. The well-meaning technician will say that, in the techno-

---

12   T. S. Eliot, "The Hollow Men," in *The Complete Plays and Poems: 1909–1950* (New York: Harcourt, Brace & World, 1962), 56.
13   José Ortega y Gasset, *The Revolt of the Masses*, trans. [J.R. Carey] (New York: W.W. Norton, 1957), 18. Karl Jaspers, in *Man in the Modern Age*, reached the same conclusion: "The technical life-order and the masses are closely interrelated. The huge machinery of social provision must be adapted to the peculiarities of the masses; its functioning, to the amount of labour power available; its output, to the demands of the consumers. We infer, therefore, that the masses ought to rule, and yet we find that they cannot rule" (37).
14   Ernst Cassirer, "Form and Technology," trans. Wilson McClelland Dunlavey and John Michael Krois, in *Ernst Cassirer on Form and Technology: Contemporary Readings*, eds. Aud Sissel Hoel and Ingvilo Folkvoro (New York: Macmillan, 2012), 34. C.f. Donald Phillip Verene, *Philosophy and Self-Knowledge*: "Technology is the Promethean gift of Descartes realized as a way of life. In it all is means without ends apart from the means" (143).

logical world, whatever is obsolete is altogether dead. There is no longer a use for the memory of the past because what matters is maximal efficiency. When past techniques are overcome by more efficient techniques, they do not persist in haunting the latter. They are forgotten, and the world moves on. Inefficiency is a death warrant for which there can be no pardon.

In the technological world, *memoria* is supplanted by information storage. *Fantasia* is replaced by the techniques of artistic production and reproduction. *Ingegno*, without its foundation of *memoria* and *fantasia* in their proper senses, is impossible. The power of true genius to give things a new turn is a threat to mass-life. Where it does still flash to life, its yield is immediately appropriated by technology and transformed into a part of the overall technical process. Even philosophy, in order to retain a place for itself in the technical world-apparatus, must turn its gaze toward linguistics and semiotics, or hermeneutics and grammatology, or, worst of all, political rhetoric, all fields in which some method can be articulated. Lovers of wisdom are replaced by "professional philosophers." In this way, philosophy becomes integrated into the technological society.[15] No longer at issue are the perennial questions about the good and the true. There is no transcendent "good" when all is efficiency. Ortega y Gasset writes, "The mass-man is simply without morality, which is always, in essence, a sentiment of submission to something, a consciousness of service and obligation."[16] The "true" is whatever can be subjected to quantitative control. The technological world can accomplish great *things*, things not dreamt of in even the recent past. However, there can no longer be great *souls*; Aristotle's *megalopsuchia* is out of the question.

While the technician tells us that memory is simply useless, the truth is that it is in fact *dangerous* to the technological world. It is the Tartar menace at the boundaries of civilization, the only thing that can truly threaten the technological order. The only way to launch a holistic critique of a prevailing state of things is to position oneself outside of that state of things. This is no longer possible spatially, since technology has overrun every sovereign state in the world. We can only distance ourselves from the technological order temporally. We can only envision a different order by remembering that different orders have prevailed in times gone by. The beliefs, desires, and values of modernity can only be

---

15 C.f. Ellul, *Technological Society*, 426–27. For Ellul, the technological society is completed only through the total integration of all opposition. Its aim is to make philosophy subservient to technique, not to nullify it.

16 Ortega y Gasset, *Revolt*, 189.

called into question if we remember that other peoples have thrived in the past, despite altogether different sets of beliefs, desires, and values. Without our memory of the past, no complete critique is possible. If we cannot escape a standpoint within the technological world, then the most that we can do is critique its various elements.

"Memory as philosophy" stands over and against technique and method. In staking a claim for individual human memory, it defies the computer with its infinite capacity for information storage. In investigating the inner form of things, it rejects the completely external view of things given by reflection, which method promises will lead us to certainty. It concerns itself with what is and what will be and what has been; it seeks the necessary order of things. Such an inquiry in an age of means, in an age when there are no problems that are not particular to a certain time and place, is an aberration. It is an abnormal discourse, abnormal because it entails a familiarity with a world order different than that within which normal discourse occurs.

If we wish to have philosophy in its classical sense—if we wish to have *thought*—if we wish to have true *inventio*, true insight into *rerum natura* and the human condition—most importantly of all, if we wish to have *self-knowledge*, then we must be willing to entertain the idea that technology is not the *deus ex machina* we have been waiting for to solve all of our problems. Self-knowledge is a recollection of oneself. Technology cannot recall us to ourselves. It can tell us what we can become, though not what we ought to become. The art of auto-biography as a speculative narrative is replaced by the memoirs of the famous, which are nothing more than collections of facts and dates. The Socratic search for self-knowledge is not realized in the memoir of a well-known general or guitarist. No one any longer stands naked before the world. Reflection on the past is not recollection; the latter is more than a comprehensive date-book.

This analysis is not intended as a jeremiad. I have only meant to draw out the negative side of the technological world for the sake of showing the context within which memory currently abides. One cannot deny that, in the bacchanalia of the technological world, there is much in which to revel. Whatever its effects on human freedom, industrial society has certainly increased the general standard of living.[17] However, technology is irreconcilable to philosophical thinking. We have forgotten the essential character of philosophy, and technology is the instrument of this

---

17 See Herbert Marcuse, *One-Dimensional Man* (Boston: Beacon Press, 1964), Chapter 2.

amnesia. "Philosophy" is now an entry in a website we consult, just as, in Ellul's words, all "attempts at culture, freedom, and creative endeavor have become mere entries in technique's filing cabinet."[18] I propose that the answer to the technological society lies in a return to the cultivation of memory, in the richest sense of its philosophical tradition. For philosophy to thrive over and against the technological world, it must discover a new *topos*. Method is always allied with technique. A return to a memorial *topos* would prevent philosophy from becoming just another technique.

If we desire autonomy, we must relearn how to pursue self-knowledge through self-recollection. If we desire *ingenium*, we must build up our memories with as much matter as we are able, so that we can survey the whole in a single view. If we can rediscover how to find the inner form of things through recollection, we can once more possess the wisdom of the Muses. Philosophy can only move forward if we once remember where the turn was made that resulted in our present technological *aporia*. Ours is a retrograde amnesia, in which the past can slowly be rediscovered if we are willing to undertake the labor.

This is not a seditious proposal, because it cannot ultimately harm technology.[19] Technique will continue to roll along under its own momentum. Philosophy cannot win the day because it cannot match the unscrupulous efficiency of technique or the standard of living that technology provides. Given the option to embrace new values other than efficiency, there are some who will choose to do so, but in the absence of large-scale catastrophe, most people will always opt to retain the comforts and calculability made possible by technology. The moment philosophy, for its part, adopts efficient techniques, it no longer stands over and against the technological world, but becomes just another cog in the greater mechanism. However, so long as the philosopher remembers to always smile at the technician, it is still possible to carve out a space of one's own outside the authority of technological world. Philosophers must keep in mind T. S. Eliot's two significant questions: "Where is the

---

18   Ellul, *Technological Society*, 418.
19   Herbert Marcuse opposes this claim. He writes, "Remembrance of the past may give rise to dangerous insights, and the established society seems to be apprehensive of the subversive contents of memory." *One-Dimensional Man*, 98. Marcuse has an overconfidence in the power of historical recollection to foment revolutionary change. He underestimates the technological society's capacity to appropriate its own past formations as evidence of the superiority of its present formation. Memory is not anathematic to technology because it is subversive, but because it is inefficient.

wisdom we have lost in knowledge? / Where is the knowledge we have lost in information?"[20]

In the second part of the present work, I will turn from theory to history. I will discuss the history of "memory as philosophy," first as an explicit tradition, and then in its implicit forms. In Montaigne and Hegel, we have two very different figures with very different concerns, but nonetheless two figures who can teach us how "memory as philosophy" can still function in a world given over to the madness for method and certainty.

---

20   Eliot, "Choruses from 'The Rock'," *Complete Plays and Poems*, 96.

PART TWO: HISTORY

Section Two: The Memory Tradition

> Bussoftlhee, mememormee!
>
> James Joyce, Finnegans Wake

Before the technological age, before computers and databases, before the printing press and the great European libraries, the formal training of the memory was of the utmost importance. Frances Yates correctly saw that we can no longer imagine what a classically trained memory was like. The role of the faculty of memory has changed. Previously, it was well understood that education and selfhood depend on memory. Philosophers of the past did not have access to voluminous collections of works to consult. Their learning was internalized. William of Ockham, for instance, lived the last seventeen years of his life at a Franciscan convent in Munich, unofficially exiled from the intellectual centers of Europe because he dared to question pontifical power. At Munich, a papal order ensured that he would not be allowed access to the books he needed for his work. Nonetheless, he was able to compose the *Dialogus*. As Mary Carruthers says, "This incomplete and prefatory work composed from memory fills 551 folio pages with material that is certainly not of an elementary nature."[1]

St. Thomas Aquinas, in composing the *Summa Theologica*, is known to have dictated to three or four secretaries at the same time, on as many different subjects. In the cell of his Dominican monastery, he would discourse from memory, addressing one topic to one secretary and then picking up a different topic with another. It was even said by one of these secretaries that Aquinas, having worked out his arguments beforehand, would occasionally continue his dictation from memory after falling asleep.[2] Much of the learning of both Ockham and Aquinas was the result of their extensive reading, but what they read had been fully assimilated, fully internalized. It could be revisited without returning to the original texts. More significantly, the contents of this complete assimilation could be given new twists and put in different relations. Medieval

---

1 Carruthers, *Book of Memory*, 156–58.
2 Carruthers, *Book of Memory*, 6–7.

philosophy, often practiced as monastic composition, was highly dependent on classically trained memories.

We cannot imagine either the quantity or quality of these trained memories. Although no scholar today would be able to function without constant access to information, this explicit link between memory and philosophy abided throughout the vast majority of the history of philosophy. A complete philosophical history of memory has never been attempted. Paolo Rossi, Frances Yates, and Mary Carruthers have all done a great deal of work toward articulating a coherent memory tradition, but all three approach the matter as historians rather than as philosophers. This section is *not* a complete philosophical history of memory. Such an undertaking lies outside the scope of the present project. My aims are only to articulate a philosophical doctrine of memory and to show that such a doctrine has come down to modernity. However, to fully analyze the role of memory in modern philosophy, much historical context is necessary.

I will describe in this section a *partial* philosophical history of memory, in order to illuminate the background against which these two figures wrote. In addressing the philosophical history of memory, I will adopt a version of Ellul's approach to addressing the history of technology. Ellul writes, "It is scarcely possible to give here a history of technique in its universal aspect. ... My book is not a history. I shall speak in a historical vein only when it is necessary to the understanding of the technological problem in society today."[3] This partial history will address certain major figures from the ancient, medieval, and Renaissance worlds, as necessary for understanding the situation of memory today.[4]

Theory precedes history in the understanding. We must first grasp the idea of memory in order to make sense of its application. However, history precedes theory chronologically. Only through working out the history of memory can we arrive at a full understanding of the concept of memory. Parts I and II of the present work are complimentary, in a relationship of reciprocal determination. Having read these two parts forward, I recommend that the reader also peruse them in reverse.

---

3 Ellul, *Technological Society*, 23.
4 Along with the studies of Rossi, Yates and Carruthers, some of the other general historical works I have consulted for this chapter include Richard Bernheimer's "Theatrum Mundi," Lina Bolzoni's *The Gallery of Memory*, Harry Caplan's "Memoria," Helga Hajdu's *Das mnemotechnische Schrifttum des Mittelalters*, and Nicolas Russell's *Transformations of Memory and Forgetting in Sixteenth-Century France*.

VI: The Speculative Line

Paolo Rossi divides the history of the memory tradition into the speculative line and the technical line. I will follow this dichotomy, understanding "speculative" as that tradition that views memory as a philosophical art in its own right, and "technical" as that tradition that views it as a means to some other end, such as oratory or pedagogy. We must recognize throughout this section that, while the two lines will be examined independently, they are by no means mutually exclusive. Rossi writes, "In Albertus and Aquinas the two lines along which the treatment of memory was developed in the course of the Middle Ages ... appear closely linked for the first time."[1] The independent analysis of these two lines will address only those figures prior in time to this Dominican synthesis. The tradition of memory as taken up in the later Middle Ages and Renaissance will be treated separately, under the heading *"Theatrum Mundi."*

Plato's *anamnesis*

The theory of *anamnesis*, articulated in the *Meno* and *Phaedo*, is central to the early psychology of Plato. For what problem is *anamnesis* meant to be a solution? As Norman Gulley says, "The problem of the *Meno* is primarily the problem of whether knowledge is possible at all, and not the problem of specifying the nature of the objects of knowledge."[2] Meno first suggests this problem, saying, "How will you look for [the definition of virtue], Socrates, when you do not know at all what it is? How will you aim to search for something you do not know at all? If you should meet with it, how will you know that this is the thing that you did not know?" (*Meno*, 80d). If we do not know something, how can we set about discovering that thing, and should we discover it, how can we know that this is the thing we sought? Beginning from ignorance, how can we ever recognize something as true, or distinguish the true from the merely plausible? The paradox of learning is that we cannot know what to look for regarding what we do not know.

Plato introduces his theory of knowledge with an appeal to religious authority, to the "priests and priestesses whose care it is to be able

---

1 Rossi, *Logic and Memory*, 12.
2 Norman Gulley, *Plato's Theory of Knowledge* (London: Metheun & Co., 1962), 5.

to give an account of their practices." These authorities "say that the human soul is immortal; at times it comes to an end, which they call dying; at times, it is reborn, but it is never destroyed" (*Meno*, 81b). This lends the authority of antiquity to Plato's theory, and aligns it with the indisputability of revealed truth. He continues, "As the soul is immortal, has been born often, and has seen all things here and in the underworld, there is nothing which it has not learned; so it is in no way surprising that it can *recollect* the things it knew before, both about virtue and other things. As the whole of nature is akin, and the soul has learned everything, nothing prevents a man, after recalling one thing only—a process men call learning—discovering everything else for himself ... for searching and learning are, as a whole, *recollection*" (*Meno*, 81c–d, emphasis mine).

Recollection, *anamnesis*, is the manner in which the individual learns what he or she does not consciously know. For Plato, "learning" is not the acquisition of completely foreign cognitive material, but the rediscovery of what one has already always known. R. G. Collingwood reaffirmed this principle in the twentieth century: "There is in philosophy no such thing as a transition from sheer ignorance to sheer knowledge, but only a progress in which we come to know better what in some sense we have always known."[3] In recollecting, we bring into consciousness what had been forgotten in the flux of death and rebirth. That we are able to bring into vivid clarity what we had not been aware the memory contained is a discovery repeated by the self-experiments of Francis Galton, and the basic principle of Freudian psychoanalysis.

In one way, knowledge for Plato is *a priori*, and in one way it is not. It is *a priori* in the sense that it is not derived from the experience of this particular life, this manifestation of the immortal soul.[4] Plato does not, however, claim that the soul contains native or innate knowledge prior to *all* experience. Knowledge is still *a posteriori* and depends upon experience, but this experience is not one's own. Because my soul is immortal, I know everything *a priori* in the sense that the knowledge is prior to the personal experience of *this* life, but not prior to experience as such. The soul knows all because it has learned everything at some time in the limitless past. Forgetting ensues because dead souls must drink from the river Lethe (oblivion) before they can be reborn (*Rep.*, 621b–c).

---

3   R. G. Collingwood, *An Essay on Philosophical Method* (Wiltshire: Thoemmes Press, 1995), 105–6.
4   Gulley writes, "[Anamnesis] is a theory that knowledge is *a priori* in the sense that its source is independent of the experience of this life." *Plato's Theory*, 5.

To demonstrate the validity of this theory, Plato offers the reader a dialogue between Socrates and one of Meno's slave boys. The intention of this dialogue is to show that a person without any formal education or previous knowledge is able to recognize the truth or falsity of propositions that he had never previously considered. The boy is ignorant of the principles of geometry. The problem set before the boy is how to construct a square that has double the area of a given square. Through the Socratic *elenchus*, the method of question and answer, Socrates is able to lead this slave to the correct conclusions, which the slave for his part recognizes as correct (*Meno*, 82b–85b). The boy did not previously know how to construct this figure, and yet, relying only on answers that are entirely his own, he is able both to discover the correct construction and to recognize its validity. Socrates asks, "So the man who does not know has within himself true opinions about the things that he does not know? ... And he will know it without having been taught but only questioned, and find the knowledge within himself? ... And is not finding knowledge within oneself recollection?" Meno must assent to all three proposals (*Meno*, 85c–d).

What is meant by "recollection" in this dialogue? Gregory Vlastos writes, "Reduced to its simplest terms ... 'recollection' in the *Meno* is any enlargement of our knowledge which results from the perception of logical relationship."[5] The appeal to empirical data in the case of the slave boy is incidental. Knowing requires that one look inward, rather than toward the outside world; recollection is the discovery of knowledge "within oneself."[6] Apprehending the logical relationships or logical structure of a concept does not depend upon sensory experience, and the *Meno* does not develop the relationship between sense-perception and knowledge. However, in the *Phaedo*, Plato insists that sensory observation is a necessary preliminary stage for the recollection of the Forms [*eidoi*]. Recollection must begin with an outward look. Plato writes, "If we acquired this knowledge before birth, then lost it at birth, and then later by the use of our senses in connection with those objects we mentioned, we recovered the knowledge we had before, would not what we call learning be the recovery of our own knowledge, and we are right to call this recollection?" (*Phaedo*, 75e).

---

5   Gregory Vlastos, "Anamnesis in the *Meno*," *Dialogue: Canadian Philosophical Review* 4 (1965), 156–57.
6   See ibid., 160–61.

The recollection of the Forms requires sense-perception as a prompt for the memory. Plato writes, "Our sense perceptions must surely make us realize that all that we perceive through them is striving to reach that which is Equal but falls short of it" (*Phaedo*, 75b). We are reminded of the universal Form by the particular specimen. The Form is the standard, prior in knowledge, by which we are able to judge the particular sense-object; the shortcomings of the particular refer us back to the universal. But we only begin to think of the universal when we are faced with a particular, of which it is the Form. Sense-perception is always the necessary occasion for *anamnesis*. The particular specimen is the starting point that inspires us to recollect the Form, of which it is a pale copy.[7]

In the *Meno*, the starting point for recollection is *doxa*, opinion, rather than sensation. Socrates' questioning begins by making explicit the opinions of the slave boy, which are shown under interrogation to be untenable (*Meno*, e.g. 82e). Finally, a logically sound belief is reached, which the boy recognizes as the truth. In the *Phaedo*, sensation is this starting point. The difference is that the *Phaedo* is not concerned with knowing as such, but with knowing the Forms, and ultimately knowing the soul. To this end, Plato must give an account that incorporates sense experience, and is not limited to logical propositions. The difference in the two presentations is not, however, radical. Recollection still depends upon the same kind of *a priori* knowledge, that acquired by experience prior to the present life. This always entails, for Plato, the immortality of the soul. In the *Meno*, this immortality is assumed on the authority of the priests, and is a proof of *anamnesis*; in the *Phaedo*, recollection of the Forms is introduced as a proof of immortality. *Anamnesis* is a doctrine that suggests a certain religious view of the soul. Vlastos does not overstate the matter when he writes, "The theory of recollection in the *Meno* is the work of a profoundly religious spirit united with a powerful philosophical mind. Those who come to our text without sympathy for its religious inspiration are apt to look at this union with annoyance."[8]

The question of learning is not fully answered by the *Meno*, and leads us into a troubling paradox. We are able to recognize propositions as true because we have already learned all things in the infinite prior

---

7   C.f. Gulley, *Plato's Theory*: "No form can be recollected without the reminders given by sense-experience. And since reference to an ideal standard, which all perception involves, implies previous knowledge of the standard, then all knowledge, it is argued, must precede the first use of the senses; it must, therefore, have been possessed before birth" (38).
8   Vlastos, "Anamnesis," 166.

embodiments of the soul. However, each thing must have been learned at some point in this infinite process. How was this learning possible, if it depended on the recollection of some previous instance of learning? An infinite regression ensues. There must be some first moment of learning, but the recollective theory of learning never admits this first moment. The *Phaedrus* excises both the language of the *Meno* and the implication that the soul knows all things. However, the same problem obtains with regard to the Forms: at what stage did the soul first behold the Forms, and what was its condition prior to this? Plato gives a likely story that is ultimately a description of recollection rather than an explanation.

In his later works, Plato considers memory in a different light, likely because he realized this weakness in the theory of *anamnesis*. In working out his own analysis of memory, the Platonic dialogues in which Aristotle is most interested are not the *Meno* and *Phaedo*, but the *Theaetetus* and *Philebus*. In these late dialogues, the nature of memory is considered in relation to a more complete psychology. The possibility of knowledge is no longer at issue, and memory is no longer bound up with religious doctrines concerning the immortality of the soul.

In the *Theaetetus*, Plato says, "I want you to suppose, for the sake of argument, that we have in our souls a block of wax, larger in one person, smaller in another ... in some men rather hard, in others rather soft, while in some it is of the proper consistency" (*Theae.*, 191c). This wax analogy was to become a commonplace for future philosophers concerned with memory.[9] Plato continues, "We may look upon it, then, as a gift of Memory [Mnemosyne], the mother of the Muses. We make impressions upon this of everything we wish to remember among the things we have seen or heard or thought of ourselves; we hold the wax under our perceptions and thoughts and take a stamp from them, in the way in which we take the imprints of signet rings. Whatever is impressed upon the wax we remember and know so long as the image remains on the wax; whatever is obliterated or cannot be impressed, we forget and do not know" (*Theae.*, 191d). Memory is here thought of in terms of an *impression*. Aristotle inherits this idea and this terminology. However, Plato ultimately rejects this model as being too corporeal and admitting of errors in judgment. Impressions may be mistaken (*Theae.*, 195e–196e). The wax model is a solely negative analogy. Socrates chides, "Don't you

---

9   The wax tablet remained a prominent analogy for memory well into modernity. Even Freud employs a version of the wax tablet analogy in his short essay, "A Note Upon the 'Mystic Writing-Pad'," in *On Metapsychology: The Theory of Psychoanalysis*.

think it is a shameless thing that we, who don't know what knowledge is, should pronounce on what knowing is like?" (*Theae.*, 196e).

In the *Philebus*, a dialogue concerning the nature of pleasure, Plato writes, "If someone were to call memory the 'preservation of perception', he would be speaking correctly as far as I am concerned" (*Phil.*, 34a). He distinguishes this from recollection: "Do we not call it 'recollection' when the soul recalls as much as possible by itself, without the aid of the body, what she had once experienced together with the body? ... When, after the loss of memory of either a perception or again a piece of knowledge, the soul calls up this memory for itself, we also call these events recollection" (*Phil.*, 34b–c). Recollection is, as Helen Lang says, "soul in and by itself, apart from body, recapturing what soul has experienced in common with body."[10] Recollection performs the same act as memory, but free of conjunction with the body. Only independently of body can memory discover what is desirable and move the organism toward the desirable.

Plato writes, "By pointing out that it is this memory that directs it towards the objects of its desires, our argument has established that every impulse, and desire, and the rule over the whole animal is the domain of the soul" (*Phil.*, 35d). Sensation is the soul's interpretation, through memory, of bodily irritation. Memory is the seat of this interpretation and the faculty that directs all pursuit and aversion. This is the positive version of the negative account given in the *Theaetetus*. It is more successful than that of the *Theaetetus* because it separates mind and body rather than collapsing the two as the wax analogy does.[11]

In Plato's earlier dialogues, *anamnesis* is the wellspring of all knowledge and all education. The individual need only look inward, with or without an external prompt, to discover the truth. Man is a type of micro-cosmos. Because of the problematical metaphysical commitments involved in this doctrine, Plato's later dialogues consider recollection as one faculty of the soul amongst others, and attempt to relate these faculties to one another. This line of investigation, not the earlier, is what sets the stage for Aristotle's work on memory.

---

10   Helen S. Lang, "On Memory: Aristotle's Corrections of Plato," *Journal of the History of Philosophy* 18 (1980): 382.
11   See ibid., 383.

Aristotle's *De memoria*

Aristotle gives two related accounts of the role of memory in relation to the other faculties of the soul, and in relation to wisdom. The location of these two accounts demonstrates their centrality in his philosophical project: one appears in the final chapter of the *Posterior Analytics*, and the second in the first chapter of the *Metaphysics*. In the former, Aristotle writes: "From perception, there comes memory, as we call it, and from memory (when it occurs often in connection with the same thing), experience; for memories that are many in number form a single experience. And from experience, or from the whole universal that has come to rest in the soul ... there comes a principle of skill and of understanding—of skill if it deals with how things come about, of understanding if it deals with what is the case" (*Post. Anal.*, II.17, 100a3–9). In the latter, he writes: "From memory experience is produced in men; for many memories of the same thing produce finally the capacity for a single experience. ... And art arises, when from many notions gained by experience one universal judgment about similar objects is produced" (*Meta.*, I.1, 980b27–981a7).

How does Aristotle understand "memory"? His most extensive analysis of memory is his *De memoria et reminiscientia*, a work that was originally composed as one of several appendices to his work on the soul, *De anima*. These appendices are all short treatises on various natural phenomena, such as sleep and dreams. They are collectively called the *Parva naturalia*, a name first coined by Giles of Rome.[12] Over two thousand years later after their composition, Hegel would assert: "The books of Aristotle on the Soul, along with the discussions on its special aspects and states, are for this reason still by far the most admirable, perhaps even the sole, work of philosophical value on this topic" (*PM*, §378).

In *De memoria*, Aristotle distinguishes between two faculties: memory (*mnēmoneuein* or *memnēsthai*) and recollection (*anamimnēskesthai*). Regarding the psychological mechanism of "memory", he delineates a fourfold schema. Memory always refers to images and objects apprehended by perception and, in particular, to those that have been perceived in the past. Either corporeal objects or intellectual objects (thoughts) may be the proper matter of memory; in both cases, there is a basis in primary sensation. (1) The external object is the first term of

---

[12] On the parts of the *Parva naturalia* and the periods in which they were written, see W. D. Ross' translator's introduction to Aristotle, *Parva Naturalia* (New York: Oxford University Press, 1959), 1–18.

memory. (2) This is followed by immediate perception on the part of the sentient creature. (3) Incorporated with this perception, as a necessary condition, is the imagination. It is as *phantasma* that the external object is transformed into an image. This is the first level at which error is able to enter into memory: the image may or may not properly represent the external object. (4) The final step is memory itself; this is a copy or likeness of the initial perception, separated from it by a factor of time. The actual memory "is only an object of contemplation, or an image; but when considered as relative to something else, e.g., as its likeness, it is also a reminder" (*De Mem.*, 1, 449a1–451a3).

Each of these terms requires further commentary. (1 and 2) The object of memory is an *impression* [*tupos*] insofar as it is related to an object. This term is used literally by Aristotle, to indicate a pressing-down: "The process of movement stamps in, as it were, a sort of impression of the percept, just as persons do who make an impression with a seal" (*De Mem.*, 1, 450a34–450b1). The actual content of a memory is an image impressed or stamped onto the soul through sensation. How does sensation work? In *De anima*, Aristotle writes, "A sense is what has the power of receiving into itself the sensible forms of things without the matter, in the way in which a piece of wax takes on the impress of a signet-ring without the iron or gold; what produces the impression is a signet of bronze or gold, but not *qua* bronze or gold" (*De An.*, II.12, 424a17–22). Aristotle appropriates the image of the soul as a wax tablet that Plato had suggested in the *Theaetetus*. Aristotle is not bothered by the physical nature of this image. Further, he develops an analogy of the soul's surface to other surfaces which are better or worse at holding impressions due to texture and fray, moisture and dryness: the mnemonic portion of the human soul is like a textured and contoured area capable of holding these imprints with more or less success (*De Mem.*, 1, 450b1–11).

(3) Because sensation is the basis of memory, Aristotle's account must incorporate *phantasma* as a middle term. At the stage of imagination, the object is converted into a symbolic image. Imagination is that stage of the process in which error can enter. The symbolic image may be a true or false representation, whereas perception is always simply true. Aristotle writes, "Perception ... is always free from error, and is found in all animals, while it is possible to think falsely as well as truly, and thought is found only where there is discourse of reason. For imagination is different from either perceiving or discursive thinking, though it is not found without sensation, or judgment without it" (*De An.*, III.3, 427b11–

15). However, one cannot ascend to thought without the help of imagination: "Without an image, thinking is impossible" (*De Mem.*, 1, 450a1; c.f. *De An.*, III.8, 432a4–9). There is no way to retain an impression without the imagination as a middle term between sensation and memory.[13]

(4) Aristotle emphasizes, "To remember what is future is not possible ... nor is there memory of what is present, but only sense-perception. For by the latter we do not know what is future or past, but what is present only. But memory relates to what is past" (*De Mem.*, 1, 449b10–14; c.f. *Top.*, 111b27–30).[14] Nonetheless, memory remains integral to the rational inferences made by thought, and the grasp of universals through experience. Memory is the starting point for the ascent to wisdom, and wisdom concerns not just the past, but the present and future also. As this starting point, Aristotle's view of memory is not contrary to the philosophical sense I have proposed. Memory is still the faculty by which the causes of all things are grasped, even though a different faculty is necessary to project this knowledge into the future. Lang correctly understands this emphasis on the past as a direct engagement with Plato. She writes, "[On Plato's view], memory belongs to soul independently of body, is prior to temporal distinctions, and is properly associated with intelligence. Aristotle denies each of these points. He intends to separate memory from intelligence. In order to do this, he first denies that memory applies equally to all experience past, present, and future; memory is limited to past experience alone."[15]

Perception of the immediate object is the beginning of the ascent to wisdom. Memory is the first spiritual faculty involved in thinking, but

---

13 In the sixteenth century, Gianfrancesco Pico della Mirandola (nephew of Giovanni) reported on a "question which troubles a great many: Is imagination different from memory, the common sense, and the estimative or cognitive faculty?" Aristotle's psychology leaves in question whether imagination and memory are identical or distinct faculties. Both sides found ample support amongst scholars. See *On the Imagination*, trans. Harry Caplan (New Haven, CT: Yale University Press, 1930), 35. For a good case study of the interdependence of memory and the poetic imagination, see John Livingston Lowes' *The Road to Xanadu*. The best critique of the idea that memory requires images is Norman Malcolm, "Memory and Representation," *Nôus* 4 (1970): 59–70. Malcolm and I hold fundamentally different ideas concerning what is meant by "memory." I have followed Vico and Joyce in my earlier claims that the two faculties as inseparable.
14 Richard Sorabji writes, "Aristotle is not in a position to defend his view that the thing remembered belongs to the past. For in several of the examples which he actually discusses ... the view is not true." *Aristotle on Memory* (Providence, RI: Brown University Press, 1972), 13. I do not know which examples Sorabji has in mind; none of Aristotle's examples, given throughout the text, *clearly* violate the dictum that memory relates only to things past.
15 Lang, "Of Memory," 389.

memory relies upon sensation. This is a denial of the argument of the *Philebus*, in which Plato asserts that the soul constitutes all sensation through memory. For Aristotle, the actual object comes first, and memory follows. When repeated memories, or repeated impressions, are conjoined, we arrive at experience. Experience is a contemplative condition, two levels removed from raw sensation. It is the grasp of universals, derived from the particular impressions stored in memory. This is the initial movement of inductive thinking. Beginning from the universals grasped by experience, one is able to continue on to *technē*, a complete field of knowledge. For example, one might have a number of particular instances of movement in falling bodies imprinted on the memory. Transforming these particulars into "experience" would involve abstracting a universal claim about motion in *all* falling bodies, arrived at through an inductive inference. From several such experiences, we might arrive at the general axioms of a *technē* such as mechanics, and from this ascend upward, to a more general science, and so on. All knowing relies on experience, but experience relies on initial impressions. The impression is the most primordial internal ground of all knowledge, the objects themselves being the external ground. Memory is the spiritual starting point and foundation of wisdom.

In contrast to memory, Aristotle understands "recollection" (*anamimnēskesthai*) as a willful act that requires reason because it is a mode of inference. When recollecting, "we are experiencing one of the antecedent movements until finally we experience the one after which customarily comes that which we seek" (*De Mem.*, 2, 451b17–18). Memory is common to all animals with the capacity for sense-perception, but recollection is the privilege of humans, as the only rational and inferring animals. Recollection depends entirely on memory as its foundation, but it is more than memory. It is a manner of reasoning, and thus a mode of thought. To recollect is to undertake a search for knowledge, to deliberate with oneself. Aristotle writes, "He who endeavors to recollect infers that he formerly saw or heard, or had some such experience, and the process is, as it were, a sort of investigation. But to investigate in this way belongs naturally to those animals alone which are also endowed with the faculty of deliberation; for deliberation is a form of inference" (*De Mem.*, 2, 453a10–13).[16] Since recollection is memory joined to thought, it is the

---

16 Aristotle's doctrine of recollection is sometimes credited with introducing the laws of association of ideas, most completely formulated by David Hume in the eighteenth century. See Sorabji, *Aristotle on Memory*, 42–46. This is probably correct, but recol-

philosophical element of Aristotle's doctrine, and it is what is at issue for "memory as philosophy." The philosopher recollects when investigating any problem.

While Aristotle's discussion of memory takes the *Theaetetus* and *Philebus* as its starting point, his discussion of recollection is more indebted to the *Meno* and *Phaedo*. In general, Plato's doctrine of memory, though rejected by Aristotle, is the speculative theory with which Aristotle is most actively engaged. There is no question that it is through Plato that Aristotle inherits his interest in memory. However, *De memoria* attempts to give a purely psychological account of the faculty of memory that avoids the spiritual speculations of the Platonic dialogues while retaining the centrality of memory as an instrument of knowing. Logical inference is Aristotle's replacement for Plato's religious *a priori* knowledge.

One tangential point requires consideration. In the second chapter of *De memoria*, Aristotle writes, "One must get hold of a starting-point. This explains why it is that persons are supposed to recollect sometimes by starting from 'places' [*topoi*]. The cause is that they pass swiftly from one point to another, e.g. from milk to white, from white to mist, and thence to moist, from which one remembers autumn if this be the season he is trying to recollect" (*De Mem.*, 452a12–16). A similar passage appears in the *Topics*: "In arguments it is a great advantage to be well up in regard to first principles, and to have a thorough knowledge of propositions by heart. For just as in a person with a trained memory, a memory of things themselves is immediately caused by the mere mention of their 'places' [*topoi*], so these habits too will make a man readier in reasoning" (*Top.*, VIII.14, 163b26–31). There are several other allusions to a mnemonic "place-system" elsewhere in Aristotle's corpus.[17] Scholastic writers like St. Albertus Magnus and St. Thomas Aquinas believed that the art suggested by Aristotle was the same as that described later by "Cicero" in the *Rhetorica ad Herennium*.

These passages enjoin the student to practice some version of the mnemonic art that I have referred to as the "technical line" of the memory tradition. Because of the foundational role memory has within

---

lection for Aristotle is not merely a passive activity. The investigator remains in control of the search.

17 See *De An.*, III.3, 427b18–22 and *De Ins.*, 1, 458b20–22. These two passages do not advocate the mnemonic art, but merely mention its existence. For a longer commentary on Aristotle's allusions to *ars memoriae*, see Sorabji, *Aristotle on Memory*, 22–34, and Yates, *Art of Memory*, 31–35.

Aristotle's psychology, any technique that improves the memory is to be encouraged. We do not know what mnemonic techniques were contemporary in Aristotle's times; no Greek treatises on the art have survived. Three points are noteworthy: that Aristotle was well aware of the "place-system" of mnemonics; that it was a system famous enough in Athens to mention without further explanation, as a means of illuminating other points; and that Aristotle believed it to have a practical utility for those who set out to reason or argue well.

Plutarch and Plotinus

Between the ages of Aristotle and St. Augustine of Hippo, there is little speculative consideration of memory that is truly original or interesting. Plutarch (46–120 CE) accepts the Platonic idea of the immortality of the soul. In the *Consolatio ad Uxorem*, he writes, "Consider then that the soul, which is imperishable, is affected like a captive bird: if it has long been reared in the body and has become tamed to this life by many activities and long familiarity, it alights again and re-enters the body, and does not leave off or cease from becoming entangled in the passions and fortunes of this world through repeated births." Along with the immortality of the soul, Plutarch also accepts Plato's doctrine of *anamnesis*. He continues, "For do not fancy that old age is vilified and ill spoken of because of the wrinkles, the grey hairs, and the debility of the body; no, its most grievous fault is to render the soul stale in its memories of the other world and make it cling tenaciously to this one" (*Cons.*, 10, 611E). The soul retains the memory of that which is prior to its personal experience, though this memory tends to become obfuscated.

In *De liberis educandis*, Plutarch enjoins the cultivation of a trained memory. He writes, "Above all, the memory of children should be trained and exercised; for this is, as it were, a storehouse of learning; and it is for this reason that the mythologists have made Memory the mother of the Muses, thereby intimating by an allegory that there is nothing in the world like memory for creating and fostering. This, then, is to be trained in either case, whether one's children be naturally gifted with a good memory, or, on the contrary, forgetful. For we shall thus strengthen nature's generous endowment, and thus fill out her deficiency" (*Educ.*, 13, 9E). This passage emphasizes the creative role of memory, as well as its connection with education. Memory is education and the key to selfhood. It also connects Plutarch, like Aristotle, to the technical line of the memory tradition.

Plotinus (204/5–270 CE), the late Neoplatonist, incorporates the Platonic doctrine of *anamnesis* in his fourth *Ennead*, but ultimately finds it an insufficient ground for grasping the eternal "intellectual objects." He writes, "When we seize anything in the direct intellectual act there is room for nothing else than to know and to contemplate the object; ... there is not included any previous knowledge; all such assertion of stage and progress belongs to the lower and is a sign of the altered; this means that, once purely in the intellectual, no one of us can have any memory of our experience here. Further, if all intellection is timeless ... there can be no memory in the intellectual world, not merely none of the earthly things but none whatever: all is presence there."[18] The intellectual objects, Plotinus' version of the Platonic Forms, exist in a transcendental spiritual realm as pure, unchanging presence. Plotinus accepts Aristotle's claim that memory relates only to what is past. The intellectual objects, as eternally stable, are atemporal, and therefore admit no past. Memory only occurs "after the soul has left the higher spheres; it is first known in the celestial period."[19] Memory implies banishment from the kingdom.

The memory of the intellectual objects has a practical utility for Plotinus in that it uplifts the fallen soul toward the intellectual realm. "At any time when we have not been in direct vision of that sphere, memory is the source of its activity within us; when we have possessed that vision, its presence is due to the principle by which we enjoyed it."[20] However, the soul, when recollecting the intellectual things, does not at that time have an immediate grasp of these things. This is a response to Plato's argument in the *Phaedo* that the Forms are stored within the unconscious memory of the immortal soul. Memory of the intellectual things sets one to pursuing these things, but they cannot be attained by the recollection. Intellection of these things is immediate. Plotinus cannot fully incorporate the doctrine of *anamnesis* for this reason. Even though memory is the impetus toward knowing, memory and knowing are two separate and irreconcilable acts.[21]

For Plotinus, the soul also contains the memory of earthly things, which draw it back down into the finite world. These are memories that are only potential while the soul is in immediate contemplation of the intellectual realm. Spiritual contemplation of the intellectuals is an act that

---

18   Plotinus, *The Six Enneads*, trans. Stephen MacKenna and B. S. Page (Chicago: Encyclopaedia Britannica, 1955), IV. 4.1.
19   Ibid., IV. 4.5.
20   Ibid.
21   See also ibid., IV. 7.12 and IV. 8.4.

precludes all other cognitive acts. Because Plotinus cannot allow memories of the finite to arise while one is thinking in the intellectual realm, he rejects the analogy of impressions stamped on a wax tablet as an "absurdity."[22] Elsewhere, he writes, "If memory were a matter of seal-impressions retained, the multiplicity of objects would have no weakening effect on memory. Further, on the same hypothesis, we would have no need of thinking back to revive remembrance." Memory is not a passive receptivity, but an active "power" of the soul. The mind is a unity not subordinate to the external object.[23]

What of the divine memory? Plotinus asks, "Would it not seem inevitable that ... Zeus should have memory of all the periods, their number and their differing qualities?" If memory and knowing are separate acts, how are we to understand the divine cognition? It would seem that the divine wisdom would recollect all that has been. "The answer is that he will know all to be one thing existing in virtue of one life for ever: it is in this sense that the All is unlimited, and thus Zeus' knowledge of it will not be as of something seen from outside but as something embraced in true knowledge, for this unlimited thing is an eternal indweller within himself ... and is seen by indwelling knowledge."[24] Plotinus' conception of the divine wisdom entails the whole of time existing in a single perceptual glance. He denies that this knowledge is memory. Nonetheless, this idea of past, present and future coalescing in one view is a notion central to the Renaissance idea of the theater of memory.

St. Augustine's *Confessions*

St. Augustine (354–430 CE) encountered the works of the Neoplatonists, including Plotinus, in early adulthood, "through a man puffed up with monstrous pride." He admits to having been enamored at first with these works, before discovering their weaknesses.[25] One inheritance from the Platonists is Augustine's interest in memory and its power to elevate one to the realm of the purely intellectual things. However, while Plotinus was a pagan philosopher, Augustine was a Christian bishop and theologi-

---

22 Ibid., IV. 4.4.
23 Ibid., IV. 6.3. C.f. Kate Gordon Moore, "Theory of Imagination in Plotinus," *The Journal of Psychology* 22 (1946): 48.
24 Plotinus, *Enneads*, IV. 4.9.
25 St. Augustine, *Confessions*, trans. Henry Chadwick (New York: Oxford University Press, 2008), VII.ix, 13–14. It is significant that this encounter occurs in the middle paragraphs of the middle book of the *Confessions*.

an. As such, the Christian God is the only intellectual object with which Augustine is concerned.

The central question of Augustine's *Confessions* is, "How then am I to seek for you, Lord?"[26] Memory is the key to this seeking. Because God is not an external object, one must look inward to discover God's presence. Augustine writes, "I will therefore rise above that natural capacity in a step by step ascent to him that made me. I come to the fields and vast palaces of memory [*memoria*], where are the treasuries of innumerable images of all kinds of objects brought in by sense-perception."[27] He follows this with a long panegyric on the various powers and contents of memory. Memory contains in its treasury a host of sensations, skills, ideas and emotions. The greatest thing found in memory is God, but God is not reducible to any of these other contents of memory. It is by the grace of God that sensations, emotions, and ideas abide in memory, but God Himself is none of these. "See how widely I have ranged, Lord, searching for you in my memory. I have not found you outside it. For I have found nothing coming from you which I have not stored in my memory since the time I first learnt of you."[28]

In what sense is God an object of recollection? Augustine writes, "But where in my consciousness, Lord, do you dwell? ... You conferred this honor on my memory that you should dwell in it. ... You remain immutable above all things, and yet have deigned to dwell in my memory since the time I learnt about you."[29] The best way to make sense of this claim is to consider Augustine's discussion of the memory of happiness. He writes, "Where and when, then, have I experienced the happy life for myself, so that I can remember and love and long for it? The desire for happiness is not in myself or in a few friends, but is found in everybody. If we did not know this with a certain knowledge, we would not want it with determination in our will." Each individual has a different notion of the happy life, but "since no one can say it is a matter outside experience, the happy life is found in the memory and is recognized when the words are uttered."[30] This claim entails a universal sense of something irreducible to sensation. "Happiness" is an *a priori* concept understood and pur-

---

26 Ibid., X.xx, 29.
27 Ibid., X.viii, 12. Dave Tell interprets this passage as articulating "the first premise of the mnemotechnic tradition, *memoria ex locis*." See Tell, "Beyond Mnemotechnics: Confession and Memory in Augustine," *Philosophy and Rhetoric* 39 (2006): 233. C.f. Yates, "Ciceronian Art," 880.
28 Augustine, *Confessions*, X.xxiv, 35.
29 Ibid., X.xxv, 36.
30 Ibid., X.xxi, 31.

sued by all. It exists as an idea in the soul's memory. Similarly, sensory experience alone could never bring one to an understanding of God. It must be that God is likewise a universal concept, known to the memory of all. This is a version of Plato's theory of *anamnesis* and its doctrine of knowledge in the soul that predates the particular life.

Ultimately, God transcends memory; one does not directly reach the presence of God through memory. Augustine asks, "What then ought I to do, my God? You are my true life. I will transcend even this my power which is called memory. I will rise beyond it to move towards you, sweet light." Memory gives the impetus to the ascent to the divine. However, this transcendence of memory is problematic: "As I rise above memory, where am I to find you? ... If I find you outside my memory, I am not mindful of you. And how shall I find you if I am not mindful of you?"[31] Thought alone is unable to capture the divine. This is a denial of Plotinus' doctrine of the intellectual sphere. For Augustine, the communication between the human and divine always depends upon the mediation of Christ. We desire God in remembering Him, but this desire requires Christ for its satisfaction.[32]

---

31   Ibid., X.xvii, 26.
32   See ibid., X.xlii, 68–70. For a longer discussion of Augustine in the context of the memory tradition, see Yates, *Art of Memory*, 46–49.

VII: The Technical Line

At a banquet in Thessaly, the poet Simonides of Ceos (c. 556–468 BCE) recited a lyric poem he had composed in honor of his host, a wealthy noble named Scopas. As was customary, the poem contained a long passage celebrating the Dioscuri, Castor and Pollux. After the performance, Scopas informed Simonides that he would only pay half the agreed fee for the poem, and that Simonides should apply for the rest to Castor and Pollux. Shortly thereafter, Simonides was told that two gentlemen on horseback wished to speak with him outside the building. He found nobody, but as soon as he left, the roof of the banquet hall collapsed, killing all those inside. The bodies were so mangled as to be unrecognizable, even to the relatives of the deceased. Simonides realized that he was able to recall the places at which each of the revelers had been seated, and he could thereby identify the remains. This suggested to him that the best means of attaining a clear memory was an orderly arrangement of places [*topoi*]. This is the fundamental principle of the art of memory, of which Simonides is credited as the inventor.[1]

The technical line of the memory tradition, which begins with Simonides, predates Plato by a century or more. The existence of the art of memory was widely known in ancient Greece, though no treatises have survived.[2] We have seen that Aristotle and Plutarch were both advocates of memory training. There was also a prominent art of memory in Rome, which was considered a part of rhetoric. Augustine, who was a trained rhetorician and teacher of rhetoric, was aware of this classical art and likely employed it himself. Frances Yates suggests, "Possibly, therefore, the passage on memory in the *Confessions* may reflect in its frame-work memories of the memory-training of a rhetor, with its carefully instilled

---

1   See Cicero, *De Or.*, II. lxxxvi.352–53; Quintilian, *Inst. Orat.*, XI. ii.11–13; Yates, *Art of Memory*, 1–2, and "Ciceronian Art," 873–74; and Helga Hajdu, *Das Mnemotechnische Schrifttum des Mittelalters* (Amsterdam: E.J. Bonset, 1967), 14. In Quintilian's version, the banquet was in honor of a boxer who had just won a victory. This better explains the praise of the Dioscuri, as Pollux was a legendary boxer. Quintilian admits that there is disagreement over whom the banquet honored (*Inst. Orat.*, XI. ii.15–16), though it is agreed that Scopas the Thessalian was in attendance. These variations suggest that this was an oral story that Simonides never committed to writing.
2   There does survive a short section on memory in a fragment called the *Dialexis*, which suggests that the subject "place on what you know," e.g. "for courage (place it) on Mars and Achilles." This is an art of simple association of ideas. See Yates, *Art of Memory*, 29–30 for a translation. The fragment appears in H. Diels, *Die Fragmente der Vorsokratiker*.

habit of storing material to be remembered through mnemonic systems of *places* and *images*."[3] In many of the memory treatises of the Middle Ages, Augustine was considered an authority and advocate of *ars memorativa*.[4]

The Latin tradition of mnemotechnics, as it was received and appropriated by the thought of the Middle Ages and Renaissance, derives from three primary sources: Cicero's *De oratore*, the anonymous *Rhetorica ad Herennium*, and the eleventh book of Quintilian's *Institutio oratoria*. The *Ad Herennium* was thought to have been composed by Cicero, until the philological research of Lorenzo Valla and Raphael Regius in the middle and late fifteenth century disproved this attribution. Quintilian's *Institutio* was lost and forgotten until it was discovered in 1416 by Poggio Bracciolini in the monastery of St. Gall. The *Institutio* is significant as the most extensive Latin treatment of the rules of the art of memory. It also expresses the author's doubts about the efficacy of this art. Along with Cicero, the Pseudo-Cicero, and Quintilian, I will also consider the Aristotelian commentaries of St. Albertus Magnus and St. Thomas Aquinas, in which the mnemotechnic is recommended to Christians as a part of morality.

We must keep in mind throughout this chapter that ancient mnemotechnics were always encouraged for the sake of some other practice. Usually this practice was oratory, and it is easy to see why having an artificially enhanced memory would be an advantage to the orator, especially for long or complex speeches. As Quintilian points out, there were countless other practical fields in which increased retention would have its benefits. For Aristotle, memory training is of *use* to philosophical investigation. Nonetheless, the technical line of the memory tradition, taken by itself, is *not* inherently philosophical. Any technique is anathematic to "Memory as philosophy." We must, however, consider this line thoroughly, because the tendency in the later Middle Ages and Renaissance was to combine the technical with the speculative line. To understand this, we return once more to Vico: *ingegno* depends on *memoria* and *fantasia*. Mnemotechnics are a training in *memoria*, necessary but not sufficient to ascend to *ingegno*.

---

3   Yates, "Ciceronian Art," 881. In *The Art of Memory*, Yates writes: "Augustine is not discussing or recommending the artificial memory in those passages which we have quoted. It is merely almost unconsciously implied in his explorations in a memorywhich is not like our own in its extraordinary capacity and organisation" (48).
4   See Rossi, *Logic and Memory*, 11.

Cicero and Pseudo-Cicero

We saw above that Cicero, in *De inventione*, considered *memoria* one of the three parts of *prudentia*, along with *intelligentia* and *providentia* (*De Inv.*, II. liii.160). He takes prudence to be one of the four human virtues, along with *iustitiam, fortitudinem*, and *temperantiam* (*De Inv.*, II. liii.159). *Memoria*, therefore, is an ethical matter, not just a rhetorical issue. As such, its cultivation and perfection are ethical obligations; complete virtue depends upon the excellence of its parts and their right relations. Prior to the philological work of the Renaissance, *De inventione* was considered the "First Rhetoric" of Cicero and the *Ad Herennium* the "Second Rhetoric."[5] While the First Rhetoric emphasized the importance of a trained memory, its focus on the topic was limited to its role in *inventio*, the composition of the subject matter of a speech. The Second Rhetoric articulated the rules by which the memory could be artificially improved. Further suggesting that the *Ad Herennium* was a Ciceronian composition is the fact that Cicero had already given an account of the art of memory and advocated its use in *De oratore* and, in the *Tusculanae disputationes*, had called memory a proof of the soul's divinity and one of the "divine attributes" of the soul (*Tusc. Disp.*, I. xxiv.60; I. xxvi.65).[6]

What are the principles of the art of memory recommended in *De oratore*? After relating the story of Simonides and the Dioscuri, Cicero writes, "Persons desiring to train this faculty must select locations [*locos*] and form mental images [*effingenda*] of the facts they wish to remember and store those images in the localities, with the result that the arrangement of the localities will preserve the order of the facts, and the images of the facts will designate the facts themselves, and we shall employ the localities and images respectively as a wax writing tablet and the letters written on it" (*De Or.*, II. lxxxvi.353–54).[7] The rules for the application of locations and images are central to the classical art of memory. We fix in our minds an arrangement of locations, and then we superimpose images representing the things we wish to remember upon these locations. By surveying the order of the images, we are able to recollect the proper order of that which we desired to commit to memory. The utility of such an art for the orator is obvious: the order of an entire speech can be kept

---

5   See Yates, *Art of Memory*, 21.
6   Yates suggests that these passages from the *Tusculan Disputations* were an influence on Book X of Augustine's *Confessions*. See *Art of Memory*, 48.
7   Aristotle's image of the wax writing table as an analogy for memory is here appropriated, even though Cicero rejects this model in *Tusc. Disp.*, I. xxv.61.

in mind through the fixing of representative images onto mental locations. Nothing debases the merit of an oration as much as forgetfulness and uncertain grasping for words. For Cicero, a good memory is essentially an endowment from nature. The artificial memory is a supplement to this natural faculty, but without the blessings of nature, there is no remedy.

Though *De oratore* is the earliest surviving work to describe the Latin art of memory, Cicero says that the art is already "well known and familiar," and that he has no intention of subjecting the reader to the tedium of a full description of something so familiar (*De Or.*, II. lxxxvii.358). Because of its wide dissemination, he articulates only a few of the rules of the art. Regarding the "memory of things", he writes, "One must employ a large number of localities which must be clear and defined and at moderate intervals apart, and images that are effective and sharply outlined and distinctive ... the ability to use these will be supplied by practice, which engenders habit, and by marking off similar words with an inversion and alteration of their cases or a transference from species to genus, and by representing the whole concept by the image of a single word" (*De Or.*, II. lxxxvii.358). Cicero also mentions an art for the "memory of words," less useful for the orator, which requires a much larger store of images (*De Or.*, II. lxxxviii.359). The different application of the two concerns whether one intends to memorize an order of ideas on which to speak, or the verbatim phrasing of a speech.[8] From this brief discussion, it is clear that locations must be well-defined and images distinct and striking, to keep these images from blending into one another, so that the orator can keep to the right path.

A more detailed account of the Latin art of memory is given in the *Ad Herennium*, believed for so long to be Cicero's completion of the discussion. Like *De inventione*, this is a textbook on rhetoric, but one that treats of all aspects of rhetoric, not just *inventio*. Memory is one of the five divisions of classical rhetoric. The rhetor, who I will call Pseudo-Cicero, writes, "should possess the faculties of invention [*inventionem*], arrangement [*dispositionem*], style [*elocutionem*], memory [*memoriam*], and delivery [*pronuntiationem*]. ... Memory is the firm retention in the mind of the matter, words, and arrangement" (I. ii.3). Elsewhere, the au-

---

8   Any professional orator (politician, pastor, or pedagogue) will see at once that the memory for things is much more important and useful than the memory for words. A good speech requires orderly topics, but not the rote memorization of text.

thor calls memory "the treasure-house of the ideas supplied by invention" and "the guardian of all the parts of rhetoric" (III. xvi.28).

Mirroring the approach of *De oratore*, Pseudo-Cicero distinguishes between natural and artificial memory, and says that the role of the latter is the strengthening of the former, so that it may become exceptional (III. xvi.28–29). What are the rules of the art of memory recommended by this text? Pseudo-Cicero writes, "The artificial memory includes backgrounds and images. By backgrounds I mean such scenes as are naturally or artificially set off on a small scale, complete and conspicuous, so that we can grasp and embrace them easily … for example, a house, an intercolumnar space, a recess, an arch, or the like. An image is, as it were, a figure, mark, or portrait of the object we wish to remember; for example, if we wish to recall a horse, a lion, or an eagle, we must place the image in a definite background" (III. xvi.29).

Committing a large number of things to memory requires a large number of locations and images. The locations must be arranged in an orderly fashion, so that one can move from one to another in either direction. Locations are fixed, while images change. Every fifth location should be distinctly marked in some way. The locations should be in deserted regions, in solitude. They should be of moderate size and neither too bright nor too dim. These locations may be either representations of real places, or inventions of the imagination. Regarding the images, these ought to be likenesses of the things they represent, either in terms of subject-matter or of words. The images should be striking and novel, exceptionally base, excellent, or laughable, bloody or disfigured, because common images are easily forgotten. They should represent action, and amongst actions the violent or comic are most easily recalled. Finally, the author enjoins that each individual create his or her own collection of images (*Ad Her.*, III. xvii.30–xxiii.39).[9]

These rules illuminate what is entailed in the system of places and images. The orator must train himself to convert the various elements of a speech into visual images, and to fix these images onto distinct locations, in a clear order. The longest example the author gives is curious, but worth considering: "The prosecutor has said that the defendant killed a man by poison, has charged that the motive for the crime was an inheritance, and declared that there are many witnesses and accessories to the

---

9   C.f. Luria's description of Shereshevskii's "eidotechnique," which employed locations and images in a similar manner. The Russian mnemonist developed this technique without any knowledge of the European memory tradition. Luria, *Mind of a Mnemonist*, 41–66.

act." How is the counselor for the defense to hold this all in memory? "We shall picture the man in question as lying ill in bed, if we know his person. If we do not know him, we shall yet take someone to be our invalid, but not a man of the lowest class, so that he may come to mind at once. And we shall place the defendant at the bedside, holding in his right hand a cup, and in his left tablets, and on the fourth finger a ram's testicles. In this way we can record the man who was poisoned, the inheritance, and the witnesses" (*Ad Her.*, III. xx.33). We see how striking, bizarre, and grotesque this imagery is. In this single image, the orator has captured all of the relevant facts of the case.

Quintilian

Quintilian (c. 35–100 CE) was an influential teacher of rhetoric, and a Roman consul during the reign of Vespasian. Pliny the Younger was among his students. I have noted above that the existence of Quintilian's *Institutio* was forgotten for centuries until rediscovered in the second decade of the fifteenth century. Its discovery was a major event, primarily because of its role in the humanist revival of classical rhetoric. Quintilian was known as the educator of the western world for centuries after this accidental discovery.

The eleventh book of the *Institutio* gave a more thorough enumeration of the rules of the classical art of memory [*artem autem memoriae*] than had hitherto been available. Yates credits the *Institutio* with having clarified the elements of the process recommended but not elaborated by Cicero. She writes, "Had it not been for [Quintilian's] clear directions about how we are to go through the rooms of a house, or a public building, or along the streets of a city memorising our places, we might never have understood what 'rules for places' were about."[10] By the time of the Renaissance, the art of memory was widely used, having been recommended by the secular authority of Cicero and Aristotle on the one hand and, as I shall explain below, the spiritual authority of the Dominican church fathers on the other. The illumination of the principles of this art offered by the *Institutio* was of the utmost interest to the scholarly element of Europe.

Like Cicero, Quintilian holds that a good memory is a gift of nature, and that the art of memory is only an artificial supplement to nature. Memory's importance is vital: it is the basis of all learning and education.

---

10 Yates, *Art of Memory*, 23.

With regard to rhetoric, memory is the storehouse of the examples, commonplaces, and rules that the orator must keep in mind to employ in speeches when expedient. It is also the faculty by which the facts of any matter are given their arrangement and sense. Quintilian writes, "As thought is going on ahead, it is always seeking something further away, and whatever it finds it commits to the care of memory, which thus acts as a sort of intermediary, and hands on to elocution [*elocutioni*] what it receives from invention [*inventione*]" (*Inst. Orat.*, XI. ii.1–3).

What rules does Quintilian add to those of the art of memory already described in the *Ad Herennium*? He writes, "Students learn places [*loca*] which are as extensive as possible and are marked by a variety of objects, perhaps a large house divided into many separate areas. They carefully fix in their mind everything there which is notable, so that their thoughts can run over all the parts of it without any hesitation or delay" (*Inst. Orat.*, XI. ii.18). The students of the art are to go into the world and make a study of real places, to contemplate these places at length, and to return to them over and over, to ensure that they are properly fixed in the mind. Such places could be a building, or "a long road, a town perambulation, or pictures. One can even invent these settings for oneself" (*Inst. Orat.*, XI. ii.21). One imagines students walking through ancient Rome—the ideal city for the practice—noting the architecture of the city, memorizing the series of buildings and statues that they pass, and then walking the same streets backwards, over and over, to ensure that these places are fixed in the right order. This architectural model of memory would be used as a dramatic philosophical device by such Renaissance authors as Giordano Bruno, in his *Cena de la ceneri*, and Tommaso Campanella, in his *Città del Sole*. Yates has demonstrated that the philosophical content of both texts is organized and recalled through copious descriptions of the architectural layout of their respective cities.[11] This process of seeking out and studying actual places in the city is the part of the classical art that Cicero left out of his account, as too well-known and "tedious" to discuss.

Having chosen a site that is well-studied, the student is to arrange striking images such that they are mentally fixed to the various places of this site. As to what these images should be, Quintilian repeats verbatim the advice of Cicero: "effective, sharp, distinctive, and such as can come

---

11 See Yates, *Art of Memory*, 297–99 and 309–13. I suspect that a similar device is used by many twentieth century works, such as Joyce's *Finnegans Wake*, Italo Calvino's *Castle of Crossed Destinies* and Harold Bloom's *Genius*.

to mind and make a quick impression" (*Inst. Orat.*, XI. ii.22; c.f. Cicero, *De Or.*, II. lxxxvii.358). With images fixed upon these locations, students are then able to mentally "go over the sites from the beginning, calling in whatever they deposited with each of them, as the images remind them. Thus, however many things have to be remembered, they become a single item, held together as it were by a sort of outer shell, so that speakers do not make mistakes by trying to connect what follows with what goes before by the sole effort of learning by heart" (*Inst. Orat.*, XI. ii.20).

Quintilian is not, however, ultimately convinced that the art of memory is a useful technique. His position on the matter is equivocal. He writes, "I do not wish to deny that these processes are useful for some purposes, for example if we have to recall many names of things in the same order as we have heard them. ... This may well have been an aid to those who, at the end of a sale, reported what they sold to each buyer." Though he admits a practical utility of the art for some professions, he warns, "The technique will be less useful for learning by heart what is to be a continuous speech. For on the one hand, *ideas* do not have the same images as objects, since we always have to invent a separate sign for them, but a site may none the less somehow remind us of them ... on the other hand, how can a verbal structure be grasped by this art? ... How can we produce a distinct flow of words if we have to refer to a distinct symbol for every individual word?" (*Inst. Orat.*, XI. ii.23–26).

The practical advice that Quintilian offers for training the memory is much simpler than the statutes of *ars memoriae*. He suggests that long speeches be divided into shorter sections, following their specific topics. One should speak softly to oneself when one is attempting to memorize. One should practice the technique of division and composition, finding the fixed points of a speech in the orderly development of its ideas, and the threads by which its entire structure hangs together (*Inst. Orat.*, XI. ii.27–39). Quintilian writes, "If I am asked what is the one great art of memory [*artem memoriae*], the answer is 'practice and effort': the most important thing is to learn a lot by heart and think a lot out without writing, if possible every day. No other faculty is so much developed by practice or so much impaired by neglect. ... [Students] should be willing to swallow the initially wearisome business of repeating over and over again what they have written or read, and as it were chewing over the same old food" (*Inst. Orat.*, XI. ii.40–41).

For Quintilian, the formal art of memory and the intensive labor of developing and fixing images and places that it entails are not worth the trouble, save in special venues like the auction-house. His alternative is the tedious work of memorizing by heart, without appeal to an artificial architecture. Nonetheless, he devotes a good deal of discussion to the principle of *ars memoria*, as a received practice. Quintilian's account of the art is impartially critical and rational. His position is not an outright rejection of the art, but an open skepticism as to its efficacy. As a teacher, he was not interested in encouraging the intensive labor of the mnemotechnic for such small gains. Despite this skepticism, his articulation of the "rules for places" was a major influence on Renaissance thought.[12]

The Middle Ages and the Church fathers

Paolo Rossi writes, "All the great works of mediaeval rhetoric took their primary impetus from the texts of Cicero. ... In Albertus and Aquinas the two lines along which the treatment of memory was to be developed in the course of the Middle Ages (the 'speculative' line and the 'technical' line) appear closely linked for the first time."[13] In the work of these two authoritative Church fathers, the Platonic-Aristotelian-Augustinian tradition becomes merged and often conflated with the Ciceronian tradition. Both Dominican writers advocate the cultivation of the formal art of memory on ethical and religious grounds, and read this art into the speculative psychology of Aristotle. Because of the weight of their spiritual authority, their approval of the art of memory gave it sanction and credibility in the later Middle Ages and Renaissance.

St. Albert (c. 1200–1280) and St. Thomas (1225–1274) lived well over a thousand years after Cicero and Quintilian had outlined the principles of art of memory. In between, this art was widely disseminated, and had already been suggested as a means of religious study. Augustine's "fields and vast palaces of memory" and its "treasuries" were early justifications for aligning the memory arts with Christianity. Later, the Saxon canon Hugh of St. Victor (c. 1096–1141), in his *De Tribus Maximus Circumstantiis Gestorum*, enjoined the student to "artificially" memorize Scripture. Biblical history is learned in outline, in "single units," and the content of the verse is then filled in around these units so that the entire text can be retained in memory. The basic *loci* of this study method are

---

12 Regarding Quintilian's skepticism about the art of memory, see Harry Caplan, *Of Eloquence* (Ithaca, NY: Cornell University Press, 1970), 233–35; Carruthers, *Book of Memory*, 73–75; and Yates, *Art of Memory*, Chapter 2.
13 Rossi, *Logic and Memory*, 12.

the persons, places and times related in the stories of Scripture.[14] Using Hugh's model, Alan of Lille (1116/7–1202/3), a French theologian, arranged penitential concepts into "compartments" or locations.[15]

Another direct influence on Albert and Thomas was the Arabic philosopher Averroës (1126–1198), whose commentaries on Aristotle, translated into Latin during the thirteenth century, were largely responsible for reintroducing Aristotelian philosophy to Europe. His commentary on the *Parva naturalia* was the most widely read predecessor to the commentaries of Albert and Thomas. Albert begins his own commentary with a gloss on Averroës. Averroës' most significant addition to Aristotle is his division of memory into five faculties, each with its own distinct location in the head: the physical senses, the common sense, the imaginative faculty, the estimative faculty, and finally the memorative faculty.[16] Albert considered this division a part of the true Aristotelian philosophy, despite its much later origin.[17]

Why were these two church fathers so interested in memory? In *De bono*, Albert considers the objection: "To recollect things that have occurred is the action of a cognitive power; prudence, however, is a characteristic of ethical judgments; therefore again memory is not a part of the virtue of prudence." He replies, "Memory has two functions, that is, it is a condition for what we know rationally [*habitus cognitivorum*], and a condition for making ethical judgments [*habitus moralium*], and here it is discussed as a condition of making moral judgments."[18] Memory's importance in Albert's philosophy is twofold. It is a necessary condition for rational knowledge and metaphysics; it is also a necessary condition for ethical knowledge and morality. Memory is the faculty by which the soul asks the two central philosophical questions, "What is the true?" and "What is the good?"

Thomas introduces his commentary on *De memoria* by writing, "It is in the nature of prudence that prudent people are directed through

---

14 See Hugh of St. Victor, *The Three Best Memory Aids for Learning History*, trans. Mary Carruthers, in *The Medieval Craft of Memory*, ed. Mary Carruthers and Jan M. Ziolkowski (Philadelphia: University of Pennsylvania Press, 2002), 33–40. This is a revision of a translation that appears as Appendix A of *The Book of Memory*.

15 Alan of Lille, *On the Six Wings of the Seraph*, trans. Bridgit Balint, in *Medieval Craft of Memory*, 87–102.

16 See Averroës, *Epitome of Parva Naturalia*, trans. Harry Blumberg (Cambridge, MA: The Mediaeval Academy of America, 1961), 26–27.

17 Albertus Magnus, *Commentary* on Aristotle, *On Memory and Recollection*, trans. Jan M. Ziolkowski, in *Medieval Craft of Memory*, 125.

18 Albertus Magnus, *De bono*, trans. Mary Carruthers, in *The Book of Memory*, IV.ii, Article 1.

those courses of action which are at hand by a consideration not only of the present circumstances but also of past events. For this reason, Cicero, in his *Rhetoric* [*De inventione*], proposes as the parts of prudence not only foresight, by which the future is planned, but also understanding, by which the present is comprehended, and memory by which the past is perceived." The importance of memory is its role in *prudentia*, which makes it ethical. Thomas continues, "Therefore, the Philosopher [Aristotle], in the beginning of his *Metaphysics*, says that in certain animals memory is formed out of the senses, and on this account they are prudent."[19] Cicero's union of memory and the ethical is read into Aristotle as the starting point of the latter's discussion of memory and recollection. Here is the point at which the two lines of the memory tradition become one.

Both Albert and Thomas, within their discussions of the Aristotelian treatment of memory, recommend the use of the Ciceronian technique of memory. Albert draws heavily on the method of the *Ad Herennium*, especially his favorite example from this text. He writes, "Tully, in the art of memory that he sets forth in his second *Rhetoric* [*Ad Herennium*], prescribes that when forming images we seek out dark places containing little light. ... He prescribes ... that we figure it in many images, and that we assemble the images. For example, if we wish to recall the person who opposes us in a court case, we should imagine some ram in the dark with great horns and great testicles coming against us; for the horns prompt us to recall our opponent and the testicles prompt us to recall the arrangement of those testifying."[20] He stresses that one ought to acquire appropriate starting places, and then follow "a sequential order which originates in necessity." The recollecting person passes from one thing to another, from one place to another.[21] This is the method of places suggested by Cicero and Quintilian. As an example of this method, Albert uses a strange image used by Aristotle in *De memoria*: "It is as when from the memory of milk one recollects the white that is like milk in color. By white one is led to air, for the reason that white and air are in part alike. ... By air one is led to moist. ... By moist one is reminded of

---

19 Thomas Aquinas, *Commentary* on Aristotle, *On Memory and Recollection*, trans. John Burchill, in *Medieval Craft of Memory*, 156.
20 Albertus Magnus, *Commentary*, 138. This example of the ram is an incomprehensible rendering of the example in the *Ad Herennium*. On Albert's misinterpretation, see Carruthers, *Book of Memory*, 139–40, and Yates, *Art of Memory*, 11–12.
21 Ibid., 141–43. Aquinas gives a similar account of the starting points and natural order of recollection in his *Commentary*, 175.

spring, which is a warm and moist season."[22] Albert assumes Aristotle to have been a practitioner of the Ciceronian art as well as an advocate.

In the *Summa Theologica*, Aquinas also recommends the Ciceronian art in relation to prudence. In an article titled, "Whether memory is a part of prudence?" he answers in the affirmative, on the authority of both Aristotle and Cicero's *De inventione*. He writes, "Just as aptitude for prudence is in our nature, while its perfection comes through practice or grace, so too, as Tully says in his *Rhetoric* [*Ad Herennium*], memory not only arises from nature, but is also aided by art and diligence." He proceeds to articulate the ways in which one perfects one's memory, drawing from both *De memoria* and *Ad Herennium* but conflating the two. One must create corporeal images and place these in an orderly arrangement. Thomas even recommends that these images be "suitable yet somewhat unwonted," shocking or grotesque.[23]

The credibility granted to the Ciceronian art by the Church fathers Albert and Thomas, and their syntheses of Aristotle with Cicero, and of both with the demands of Christian piety, had an enormous influence on medieval culture. One sphere of influence was the literary and visual arts. Carruthers writes, "Albertus's stress upon the mnemonic *usefulness* of what is marvelous and unusual gives a crucial ethical justification for using even fantastical or salacious or violent images. Albertus makes it clear that the criterion for creating mnemonic images is not decorum but utility. ... It may well be that much of what we suppose to be 'allegory,' and thus to have a specifically iconographic meaning (if only we knew what it was) is simply a mnemonic heuristic."[24]

It has been suggested by Yates that Dante's *Inferno* is a memory system, using images and places, for memorizing the punishments of Hell.[25] The graphic depiction of the tortures of the Inferno, and the orderly *ratio* of the different circles of Hell make it easy for the reader to remember the catalogue of sins and punishments. The writings and authority of St. Albert and St. Thomas also gave theological sanction for

---

22 Ibid., 144. Aristotle's example terminates in a memory of autumn rather than spring. It is likely that Albert's slight deviations in this example and that of the ram, above, are the result of a monastic method of composition that relies heavily on memory rather than textual reference, similar to that of Thomas.
23 Thomas Aquinas, *Summa Theologica*, trans. Fathers of the English Dominican Province (Westminster, MD: Christian Classics, 1981), II.ii.49, Article 1.
24 Carruthers, *Book of Memory*, 142. See Lina Bolzoni's *The Gallery of Memory*, E. H. Gombrich's *Symbolic Images*, and Lu Beery Wenneker's "*L'Idea del Theatro* of Giulio Camillo" (Ph.D. diss.), on the connection between iconography and memory images.
25 Yates, *Art of Memory*, 95.

memory to ascend to a prominent position in philosophical speculation.[26] As European thought became increasingly syncretistic in the fifteenth century, the classical memory arts grew to embrace other sources of wisdom. *Ars memoria* promised not just a reproduction of reality, but access to the magical, creative *source* of reality. In the Renaissance idea of *theatrum mundi*, memory and divine wisdom are identical.

---

26 The role of Albert and Thomas as forefathers of later developments is acknowledged by Giordano Bruno, who calls the two Dominicans, along with Cicero and Ramon Lull, the great teachers of the memory arts. Bruno, *De umbris idearum*, 16.

VIII: Theatrum Mundi

After Albert and Thomas called all Christians to cultivate their memories, the memory treatise became a ubiquitous literary genre in medieval Europe. Most of these treatises recycled the same suggestions and rules, adding little or nothing but a bit of exposition on some familiar formula. They were taken seriously, however, in most spheres of European culture, recommending themselves to theologians, preachers, professors, judges, and merchants. Among those who composed such works were writers like Bartolomeo da San Concordio, Giovanni da San Gimignano, and Iacopo Ragone da Vicenza. I mention these men because are all utterly unknown today, though they were quite famous in their own times.

The best-known treatise of this type was Peter of Ravenna's (c. 1448–1508) *Phoenix seu artificiosa memoria.* Peter was famous throughout Europe for his excellent trained memory. He claimed to have developed over a hundred thousand memory-places for the retention of Scripture and law. This work explained the function of memory-images rather than the rules for selecting places.[1] Another well-known treatise was the Dominican Johann Host von Romberch's (c. 1480–1532/3) *Congestorium*, interesting for its elaborate drawings of the place-system. The mnemotechnic was so widely disseminated that it found its way as far as China. A Jesuit missionary named Matteo Ricci (1552–1610), following St. Ignatius of Loyola's doctrine that reflection on sin requires a balance of memory, will, and reason, developed a memory palace by which the major stories of the Gospels could be recalled. Ricci taught this system to his Chinese disciples.[2]

Not all Renaissance philosophers shared the same idea of memory or the same interest in mnemotechnics. Petrus Ramus, for example, was famously hostile toward the system of Giordano Bruno and the prominence of the imagination in the classical art of memory. For Ramus, memory was absorbed into categorical logic. The idea of *theatrum mundi* and the corresponding predominance of memory was one strand of Renaissance thought amongst others, but it was not a minor strand. In this section, I will limit my discussion to the work of a few of the major figures of the memory tradition between the time of Aquinas and modernity. Each brings something new to the classical art. Ramon Lull is the most

---

1   See Rossi, *Logic and Memory*, 20–22.
2   See Jonathan D. Spence's *The Memory Palace of Matteo Ricci*.

original figure in the late medieval period. His esoteric *ars combinatoria* was a major influence on later thinkers. Several centuries after Lull, the two figures to epitomize the Renaissance fascination with memory were Giordano Bruno and Giulio Camillo. I will consider their works out of chronological order, because Bruno is more closely linked to Lull, whereas Camillo draws from all lines of the memory tradition and represents a sort of wild, dynamic apex in the tradition. Through considering these writers, we will see what was at issue in *ars memorativa* of the sixteenth century, to which Montaigne was responding.

Ramon Lull

Ramon Lull (or Llull, 1232–1316) was a Majorcan logician and Franciscan tertiary. Nonetheless, he was influenced by the Dominican tradition. His biographer, J. N. Hillgarth, writes, "Lull met, probably in Barcelona, St. Ramon de Penyafort, former General of the Dominican Order, then (in about 1265) aged about ninety but still very active. The influence of Ramon de Penyafort on Lull seems to have been decisive. ... [Penyafort] set him to work, once back in Majorca, to acquire the fundamental grounding he needed, both in Latin and also, even more important, in Arabic."[3] Lull's interest in memory was likely influenced by this early encounter with Dominican thought.

Lull's art of memory is famously obtuse. What sense can we make of the mysterious Lullian art? "In one of its aspects," Yates writes, "the Lullian Art is an art of memory. The divine attributes which are its foundation form themselves into a Trinitarian structure through which it became, in Lull's eyes, a reflection of the Trinity, and he intended that it should be used by all those powers of the soul that Augustine defined as the reflection of the Trinity in man. ... As *memoria*, it was an art of memory for remembering truth."[4] The Lullian art begins from the knowledge of the names or attributes of God: *Bonitas, Magnitudo, Eternitas, Potestas, Sapientia, Voluntas, Virtus, Veritas,* and *Gloria*. Each of these concepts is designated by a letter, respectively B, C, D, E, F, G, H, I, and K.[5] The art functions with regard to every level of being, from God

---

3 J. N. Hillgarth, *Ramon Lull and Lullism in Fourteenth-Century France* (New York: Oxford University Press, 1971), 5.
4 Yates, *Art of Memory*, 174. C.f. Augustine, *De Trinitate*, X: 17–19.
5 This is the case in Lull's later work, particularly his most influential text, *Ars brevis*. In earlier versions of the art, there are twenty-three letters. See Anthony Bonner's introduction to *Ars brevis* in Lull, *Doctor Illuminatus: A Ramon Llull Reader*, ed. Anthony Bonner (Princeton, NJ: Princeton University Press, 1985), 291–92.

to the created world, by finding the divine attributes on each level. The meanings of the letter notations change on each level of being.

The attributes are treated in various ways. In one figure of the *Ars brevis*, the nine letters are each presented on three concentric circles or wheels, one fixed and the other two mobile. By spinning the inner two wheels, the letters can be combined and recombined in various permutations. On another figure, the letters are placed on a wheel that surrounds three triangles that connect the attributes. These triangles each relate to a different modality of the attributes. On yet another figure, the letters are paired together in a table of boxes: BC, CD, DE, and so on.[6] "*Ars combinatoria*" is Lull's name for the mechanical methods by which the letters are combined in each figure.

The Lullian art is best understood as a systematic approach to the classical *ars topica* and *ars critica*. Regarding the figure of the table of letter pairs, Lull writes, "Each compartment contains two letters, and these represent subject and predicate, between which the artist seeks the middle term that will join them, like goodness and greatness that are joined through concordance. ... With this middle term the artist tries to reach a conclusion and state a proposition. This figure is meant to show that any principle can be attributed to any of the others. ... This is so that the intellect may know each principle in terms of all the others, and be enabled to deduce many arguments from a single proposition."[7] The combinations of attributes give the *topoi* to the artist. With each spin of the concentric wheels, we discover a new *topos*. Goodness, for instance, is greatness. From these *topoi*, the artist can then proceed to logical deductions. Lull's definitions give the basic *topoi* with which to begin, while their combinations in subject-predicate relationships suggest the basic deductions.[8] *Ars brevis* does not illustrate these deductions, but they make up the content of the speeches of the sages in *The Book of the Gentile and the Three Wise Men*. Each speech is a deduction from certain combinatory *topoi*. For instance, Lull writes, "It is clear to the human understanding that good and greatness accord with being; for the greater the good, the more it accords with essence, or with virtue, or with both together," and so on.[9]

---

[6] Lull, *Ars brevis*, trans. Anthony Bonner, in *Doctor Illuminatis*, 300–08.
[7] Ibid., 305.
[8] See ibid., 309–15 for the definitions and the rules for moving from *topoi* to propositions. This method may have been an influence on Hegel's notion of the *spekulativer Satz*.
[9] Lull, *The Book of the Gentile and the Three Wise Men*, in *Selected Works of Ramon Lull*, ed. and trans. Anthony Bonner (Princeton, NJ: Princeton University Press, 1985), 119.

How is Lull's *ars combinatoria* an art of memory? In the *Ars brevis*, Lull articulates a hundred forms, writing that "by means of the definitions of the forms, the intellect will be conditioned to examining them by the principles and rules." These forms are given in logically connected sets, such as quantity, quality and relation, or genus, species and individuality. The hundredth figure, which stands alone, is memory: "Memory is that thing with which things can be recalled."[10] That this form is freestanding and terminates the series suggests its importance to Lull. Later, he writes, "The first part [of the art] states that the artist should know the Alphabet by heart, as well as the figures, definitions, and rules, along with the arrangement of the Table."[11] The basis of the entire art is the recollection of its principles. With these principles cemented in the memory, the topical combinations and critical deductions easily follow. As Yates suggests, Lull's is an art of memory for remembering truth, for remembering the first causes from which all else can be deduced. This view is close to Augustine's use of memory to discover God within. In Lull's work, *ars memorativa* is crucial as the means of remembering *ars combinatoria*. The object of Lullian memory is the Lullian art itself.

Lull's influence in medieval and Renaissance culture was enormous. Yates writes, "Lullism is no unimportant side-issue in the history of Western civilization. Its influence over five centuries was incalculably great. Lull was much in Italy and manuscripts of his work were early disseminated there and may have been known to Dante. ... The Renaissance seized on Lullism with intense enthusiasm; in fact, it is hardly an exaggeration to say that Lullism is one of the major forces in the Renaissance."[12] Giovanni Pico della Mirandola acknowledged an intellectual debt to Lull's *ars combinatoria*. The German philosopher Nicholas of Cusa is known to have copied Lull's manuscripts. However, the philosopher who did the most to join Lullism to the classical art of memory, and to disseminate Lull's teachings in all of the major intellectual centers of sixteenth-century Europe, was Giordano Bruno.[13]

---

10   Lull, *Ars brevis*, 336–43.
11   Ibid., 363.
12   Frances A. Yates, "The Art of Raymond Lull: An Approach to It Through Lull's Theory of the Elements," *Journal of the Warburg and Courtland Institutes* 17 (1954): 166.
13   For much more comprehensive treatments of Lull and the influence of Lullism, see Anthony Bonner's introduction to the *Selected Works of Ramon Lull*, Hillgarth's *Lull and Lullism*, and Yates' "Art of Raymond Lull" and "Ramon Lull and John Scotus Erigena," *Journal of the Warburg and Courtland Institutes* 23 (1960): 1–44.

Giordano Bruno the *magus*

By the time of Giordano Bruno of Nola (1548–1600), the memory tradition had undergone several major upheavals. In 1416, the *Institutio* of Quintilian had been rediscovered. Later in the fifteenth century, the Florentine Academy, Marsilio Ficino (1433–1499) and Pico della Mirandola (1463–1494) in particular, had introduced a doctrine of syncretism that interpreted all wisdom traditions as essentially expressing the same basic truths. Ficino had translated the *Corpus Hermetica* into Latin; Hermes Trismegistus, as we saw in the third chapter, taught that man is a microcosm and that memory is a divine faculty. Pico was the first European Christian to master the esoteric Jewish theology of Kabbalah. He was also an admitted student of the Lullian arts. The Ciceronian art of memory became merged Plato's doctrine of *anamnesis*, as well as Hermeticism, Lullism, Kabbalah, and even the occult. The new magical memory art that arose was called *ars notoria* and its origin was often attributed to Solomon. Magicians of *ars notoria* would chant magical prayers while looking at esoteric diagrams. Cornelius Agrippa (1486–1535), the German *magus*, was the most notorious practitioner of this occult art of memory.

Bruno was born with this syncretistic culture of memory as a background. As a young man, he was an initiate in the Dominican Order in Naples. In 1572, he was ordained a Dominican priest. It is certain that while in the Dominican Order, Bruno was trained in some version of the classical mnemotechnic so vigorously recommended by Albert and Thomas. Bruno's interest in banned books created a controversy in the Order, which compelled him to give up the habit and flee from Naples in 1576. His biographer, Dorothea Singer, observes that Bruno's "tempestuous personality, fed to fever with omnivorous reading," was bound to eventually land him in trouble. She expresses surprise only that he was able to remain a member of the order for as long as he did, eleven years in all.[14]

In his wanderings, Bruno was able to rely for support on one particular skill he had learned from the Dominicans. Yates writes, "When Bruno fled from his convent in Naples and began his life of wanderings through France, England, Germany, he had in his possession an asset. An ex-friar who was willing to impart the artificial memory of the friars

---

14 Dorothea Waley Singer, *Giordano Bruno: His Life and Thought* (New York: Henry Schuman, 1950), 12.

would arouse interest, and particularly if it was the art in its Renaissance or occult form of which he knew the secret."[15] Bruno set out to become a teacher of this art, and a self-proclaimed *magus*. He wrote and published *De umbris idearum*, his esoteric textbook on the art of memory, in 1582. The title itself situated Bruno in the realm of the dark arts, mirroring the *Liber de umbris idearum*, attributed to Solomon, which had been cited by the necromancer Cecco d'Ascoli, who had been burned at the stake two centuries prior.[16]

Bruno's art of memory owes much to the Hermetic tradition and to the occult and Kabbalistic arts of his time. It owes even more to the Lullian *ars combinatoria*. Bruno spent much of his life fleeing from Inquisitors because of the pagan and magical elements of his teachings. Eventually, this led to his seven-year imprisonment and execution under the authority of the Inquisition. Zuane Mocenigo, Bruno's host during the latter's time in Venice and a high officer likely attached to the Venice Inquisition, was directly responsible for Bruno's persecution. Mocenigo's primary complaint against his guest was that Bruno had not initiated him "into the secrets of [his] memory system," and he feared that Bruno would teach this system to others.[17] One of the charges of which Bruno was accused was the heretical practicing of magic and divination. He was burned at the stake in the Campo de' Fiori in February of 1600. In the words of Joyce's Stephen Dedalus: "He said Bruno was a terrible heretic. I said he was terribly burned."[18]

What was so scandalous about the art of memory that Bruno taught? In *De umbris idearum*, he promises a true "solar art" that is not dependent on natural capacity.[19] Bruno denies the notion that the art of memory is only a supplement for those already possessed of good natural memories. This is a rejection of the first principle suggested by both Cicero and Quintilian, that the art is nothing more than an artificial aid to the natural memory. Bruno's art claims to be altogether independent of one's natural faculties. For him, the natural memory is always a weaker foundation than the artificial. In a sense, the art is an early attempt at discovering the sort of scientific method or technique that can be taught to anyone. It is a precursor of the method of Descartes. Bruno laments, "There

---

15 Yates, *Art of Memory*, 200.
16 See Yates, *Giordano Bruno*, 197.
17 Singer, *Giordano Bruno*, 160.
18 James Joyce, *A Portrait of the Artist as a Young Man* (Ware, Hertfordshire: Wordsworth, 1992), 193.
19 Bruno, *De umbris idearum*, 12.

exist many published works regarding the art of memory, all of which offer the same canon of lessons, and which present us with the same difficulties."[20]

Bruno's art claims to be something new, not just a revision of the common mnemotechnic of Peter of Ravenna and other treatise writers. What he promises is access to the divine mind. The "shadows of ideas," *umbris idearum*, are the shadows of the divine intelligence. "An act of the divine mind happens at the same time and place as the thought. In the intelligences, acts and thoughts are discrete. In heaven, in the multiple active powers, successive. In nature, by means of footsteps, almost as if by impression. In intentions and rationality, by the means of shadows."[21]

Bruno's secret art promises the ascent to divine knowledge by means of these shadows. Human reason is a shadow of the divine mind; man is a microcosm of God. Memory is the key to this ascent, the idea of which is appropriated from Hermeticism. Through recollection, the *magus* can reconstruct the entire universe within his mind.

In the dialogue that Bruno wrote to precede *De umbris idearum*, Hermes Trismegistus is the interlocutor who describes this new art of memory. The Hermetic element is intertwined with the classical mnemotechnic recommended by Cicero. In large part, despite promising to do so, Bruno does *not* move beyond the traditional advice of *ars memoriae*. He recommends that striking images be used, particularly the monstrous and grotesque, which is an inheritance from Bruno's time in the Dominican Order. He suggests rules for the arrangement of images and their proper distance from the subject. He advocates "repeated excursions" into the memory palace, and gives rules for the size and quality of images.[22] All of this is a repetition of the stale advice of the medieval memory treatises that Bruno promised to surpass. His most significant contribution to the technical line is more suggestive than explanatory. He suggests that images alone are inadequate, and that other guises of representation are necessary. He writes, "You have, in the *Clavis magna*, twelve ways of clothing your subjects: Species, Forms, Simulacra, Images, Specters, Models, Vestigia, Indications, Signs, Figures, Characters and Seals."[23] Unfortunately, because the *Clavis magna* does not exist, what Bruno understands by these twelve terms is just as veiled as the master key of the art.

---

20 Ibid., 17.
21 Ibid., 41.
22 Ibid., 67–85.
23 Ibid., 66.

The strong influence of Ramon Lull on Bruno's system can be seen in Bruno's "wheels." He writes, "We form in ourselves the shadows of ideas, when such an opportunity presents itself through adaptability and malleability to all such forms. We form them of such similitudes, through the rotation of the wheels. If you can try this any other way, then try."[24] These wheels are concentric, one rotating within another. On the wheels are thirty characters, mostly from the Latin alphabet, but also from the Greek and Hebrew alphabets, Bruno's thirty "seals". In his *Cena de le ceneri*, Bruno addresses "Thou, my Mnemosine, who art hidden under thirty seals and shut up in the bleak prison of the shadows of Ideas."[25] These wheels are a more complex version of the combinatory wheels of Lull, but they follow the same basic principles.

The secret art of employing these combinatory wheels was either never committed to writing by Bruno or has been lost. He refers several times to a work called *Clavis magna*, the master key of the art, but, as noted above, no record of this work exists. I suspect that the *Clavis magna* was Bruno's own mind. Yates writes, "The Great Key might have explained how to use Lullian wheels as conjuring for summoning the spirits of the air. For that is, I believe, a secret of the use of the Lullian wheels in *Shadows*. Just as he converts the images of the classical art of memory into magical images of the stars to be used for reaching the celestial world, so the Lullian wheels are turned into 'practical Cabala', or conjuring for reaching the demons, or angels, beyond the stars."[26] The wheels are the means of communication with the divine, but also with the demonic. For example, Bruno claims, with no more explanation than an appeal once again to the *Clavis magna*, that "Using [signs, figures, characters and seals], one can act in nature, *above* nature, and if the situation requires it, *contrary to* nature."[27]

Bruno's esoteric style, his great ambiguities, and his incompletely presented system make it exceedingly difficult to unravel the mystery of his art. He writes with the secrecy of a *magus*. Of course, he was a dealer in mysteries, and mysteries require initiation under the guidance of a master. He could not have committed the key to his art to writing. Be-

---

24 Ibid., 55. Yates has attempted to "excavate" the secret of the shadows by sketching a possible model of concentric wheels with the one hundred fifty divisions of images Bruno uses overlaid onto them. She admits that this system will never be understood in detail. See *Art of Memory*, Plate 11 (between pp. 208 and 209).
25 Bruno, *The Ash Wednesday Supper*, trans. Edward A. Gosselin and Lawrence S. Lerner (Toronto: University of Toronto Pressm 1995), 85.
26 Yates, *Art of Memory*, 211.
27 Bruno, *De umbris idearum*, 67 (emphasis mine).

cause his memory images are mostly celestial, it is likely that he intended to align memory with the sidereal world. It is also likely that, as *magus*, he believed that through this sidereal connection, the student would acquire the wisdom and powers of the celestial bodies.[28] This conjurer's art, though a version of the art of Lull, is intended to be much more efficacious and diabolical. It promises not just understanding, but power. Lull's art teaches a sort of memory as *ars topica*. Bruno teaches a cosmic communication with the divine and a mysterious link to occult powers. He was not content to create artificial memory places, but sought to discover the memory places of nature. His faith, as Yates says, is "that of a Renaissance Neoplatonic Hermeticist."[29] It is no surprise that the grand inquisitor would not let such lessons pass unpunished.

The divine Camillo

Giulio Camillo (c. 1480–1544) was one of the most famous men of the sixteenth century, and his fame was as great in France as it was in his native Italy. He was considered "divine" because of an incident that occurred in Paris. Camillo himself relates this story: "To the author of this *Theatre* it happened that, finding himself in Paris, at the place called 'La Tournelle,' in a room with many windows looking out over a garden, a lion, who had escaped from his cage, came into that room. Drawing near to him from behind, with its paws, took him without harm by the thighs, and with his tongue, proceeded to lick him. And at that touch and at that breath ... all the others having fled, some here and some there, the lion humbled himself to him, almost in the sense of asking forgiveness."[30] This event was taken as evidence of Camillo's "solar power," the same power that Bruno later claimed was at work in his art. Because the lion had humbled itself before Camillo, it was clear that Camillo was divine.[31]

The idea that was the source of Camillo's great fame was the construction of an actual physical theater of memory. Camillo was not able

---

28 See Yates, *Art of Memory*, 215–17.
29 Yates, *Giordano Bruno*, 350.
30 Giulio Camillo, *L'Idea del Theatro*, trans. Lu Beery Wenneker, in "An Examination of *L'Idea del Theatro* of Giulio Camillo, Including an Annotated Translation, with Special Attention to His Influence on Emblem Literature and Iconography," Ph.D. dissertation, University of Pittsburgh, 1970, 39. Appearing as part of Wenneker's dissertation, this is the only English translation of Camillo's *L'Idea*. In citing this work, I have used the sub-pagination that Wenneker gives for his translation.
31 Giuseppe Bertussi wrote that Camillo stayed where he was "not to give proof of himself, but because the weight of his body made him slower in his movements than the others." See Yates, *Art of Memory*, 133.

to ultimately complete this project, though he did produce a wooden model of the theater on a small scale. The secret of how the theater worked was only communicated to one person: Francis I, the King of France. Francis became for a time Camillo's patron, though the king's promises of funding exceeded his actual liberality.[32] What was the unfinished theater that so consumed this man's life? Like Bruno, and like another *magus*, Cornelius Agrippa, Camillo believed *ars memoriae* could potentially extend far beyond its utility in rhetoric. Richard Bernheimer writes, "Camillo was a victim, not a charlatan—victim of an idea so grand and so demanding that it exceeded a lifetime's devotion and impeded secondary accomplishment. That idea was, as the reader will have guessed, that of a heavenly theater or, in more concrete terms, of a theater of the world."[33] Reading Camillo's essay, *L'Idea del Theatro*, we encounter the confused thinking of a mind that does not fully grasp its own large ideas. Nonetheless, we can appreciate the boldness of the project, and recognize the good intentions of the man.

Camillo's theater of memory is *theatrum mundi*, a theater of the world. The great fame of Camillo was largely due to his timely seizure of the notion of *theatrum mundi* in his idea of the memory theater, which captured the spirit of the times. The idea of *theatrum mundi* likely has its source in Marcus Aurelius. In his *Meditations*, Aurelius suggests that the utility of tragedies is to inoculate us from those evils that might otherwise surprise and distress us "on the greater stage of life," or stage of the world.[34] Aurelius also compares life to a performance, and death to the actor's dismissal from the stage. "'But I haven't played all five acts, only three!' Very well; but in life three can make up a full play."[35] *Theatrum mundi* was also embraced by Pico, whose *Oration on the Dignity of Man* begins, "Most esteemed fathers, I have read in the ancient writings of the Arabians that Abdala the Saracen on being asked what, on this stage, so to say, of the world, seemed to him most evocative of wonder, replied that there was nothing to be seen more marvelous than man."[36] This was taken as a central passage of the humanist movement partially inspired

---

32 Ibid., 130–32.
33 Richard Bernheimer, "Theatrum Mundi," *The Art Bulletin* 38 (1956): 226.
34 Marcus Aurelius, *Meditations*, trans. Robin Hard (New York: Oxford University Press, 2011), XI.6.
35 Ibid., XII.36.
36 Giovanni Pico della Mirandola, *Oration on the Dignity of Man*, trans. A. Robert Caponigri (Washington, DC: Regnery, 1956), 3.

by Pico. The theater of the world was also an image taken up in the drama of Shakespeare.

Camillo writes, "We, wishing eternally to perpetuate the eternal nature of all things, which may be clothed from the oration with the eternals of the oration itself, find them in their eternal places. Therefore, our great labor has been of finding order in these seven measures, which is capacious, sufficient, clear and which will jog the memory." The influence of the classical mnemotechnic is clear: the theater presents its images as memory cues following a necessary order. Camillo continues, "This great and incomparable arrangement not only performs the service of conserving for us the things, words and art entrusted to it, which are with impunity, shaped to our every need before we can find them, but gives us also true wisdom in whose sources comes to us knowledge of things from their causes and not from their effects. ... In order to understand these things of the Inferior world, it is necessary to climb to the Superior, and looking down from on high, we shall be able to have a surer knowledge of these things."[37] The theater is an attempt to replicate the absolute and simultaneous knowledge of God by attaining the divine perspective.[38] The whole of the cosmos is presented through an arrangement of first causes. All of God's creation can be witnessed in a single field of vision: God's field of vision.

How did Camillo's theater work? It was actually a wooden amphitheater, in which the spectator stood upon the stage and faced outward. The theater had seven divisions, each with seven levels. In the front level of each division, where the orchestra is usually situated, were images representing those things created first, and the levels progressed to the human arts furthest removed from these first things. In this way, one could survey the necessary order of the whole, by way of its initial and subsequent causes. The first levels of each division had doors of some sort, upon which the various celestial bodies were painted. These first sidereal paintings—the Moon, Mercury, Venus, and so on—were intended to represent the first causes for those things that followed in their respective divisions, as the levels progressed. The source of the "celestial sev-

---

37 Camillo, *L'Idea*, 10–12.
38 That God's perception took the form of *theatrum mundi*, in which past, present, and future were laid out on a single stage, was an idea that was credible even to as rational a thinker as Locke. Locke describes God's knowledge of "all things, past, present, and to come," as constantly in view, "as in one picture." See Locke, *Essay*, vol. 1, 199–200.

en" is Ramon Lull.[39] The second level was the banquet of the gods, in which the various Greek deities and myths were represented. The third level, the cave, portrayed the basic elements of the world. On the seventh and final level, the "Prometheus" level, all of the derived human arts were represented.[40] What phenomena fell under each division appears arbitrary at times, though Camillo was likely influenced by contemporary astrological schemas. The necessary connection from one cause to the next may have been a part of the secret he imparted to the king of France.

We are also told, though not by Camillo himself, that beneath each image there were boxes containing the speeches of Cicero, which related to the subjects associated with the images. Camillo's contemporary, Bernardino Partenio, writes, "I remember having seen in Venice, when he himself showed it to me, such a multitude and variety of words gathered and positioned in his great tomes that I was amazed that one man alone could adorn his work with such riches and decoration."[41] Partenio makes no mention of the actual theater; it is possible Camillo showed him only the speeches of Cicero. Another contemporary, Viglius Zuichemus, had been allowed to enter the theater. In a letter to Erasmus, he writes, "The work is of wood, marked with many images, and full of little boxes; there are various orders and grades in it. He gives a place to each individual figure and ornament, and he showed me such a mass of papers that, though I always heard that Cicero was the fountain of richest eloquence, scarcely would I have thought that one author could contain so much or that so many volumes could be pieced together out of his writings." Regarding the theater's general plan, Viglius says, "He pretends that all things that the human mind can conceive and which we cannot see with the corporeal eye, after being collected together by diligent meditation may be expressed by certain corporeal signs in such a way that the beholder may at once perceive with his eyes everything that is otherwise hidden in the depths of the human mind."[42]

We find an influence on the theater from every quarter of the memory tradition. Clearly, this is a place system of memory. It employs places and images according for the most part to the classical rules,

---

39 See Yates, *Art of Memory*, 196.
40 Frances Yates' sister, R. W. Yates, has attempted to draw a blueprint of what this memory theater might have looked like. See *Art of Memory*, insert between pp. 144 and 145.
41 From Partenio's *Pro lingua latina oratio*, quoted by Lina Bolzoni in *The Gallery of Memory: Literary and Iconographic Models in the Age of the Printing Press*, trans. Jeremy Parzen (Toronto: University of Toronto Press, 2001), 30.
42 Quoted and translated in Yates, *Art of Memory*, 131–32.

though, as Bernheimer notes, it does violate some of these rules, such as the prohibition on similar shapes and circularity in the images employed.[43] It is unclear what the connection is between the speeches of Cicero and the images, or what use was to be made of the "mass of papers" beneath each image; perhaps the images were to help the spectator recall the speeches. Whatever the function of this element of the theater, it is certain that Camillo considered Cicero, the advocate of the classical mnemotechnic, a great authority on all things human and divine. However, as Bernheimer says, "Camillo's scheme, unlike those of the ancient orators, was more than a method only, since it was directed toward the presentation of universal truth, and that therefore it must take its place not only in the history of the mnemotechnic arts, but also of philosophy and cosmology."[44] The theater was not merely a method for recollecting, but an attempt at attaining the divine apprehension of truth.

In this respect, the theater is influenced by the Hermetic tradition. Camillo, with the *Imago Dei* of Scripture in mind, calls the "inner man" the "last and most noble creature made by God in His likeness." He quotes as evidence the *Asclepius* of Hermes: "'Man is a marvel. ... Asclepius, honour and reverence to such a thing! Man takes on him the attributes of a god, as though he were himself a god ...'" He supports this view of the likeness between man and God with the testimony of "other Cabalistic writers," the epistles of St. Paul, and the *Alcibiades* of Plato.[45] Later, he credits Prometheus with the gift of divine knowledge: "By that theft, therefore, man alone among the animals acquainted with the divine force, had knowledge of the gods from the beginning."[46] Camillo's syncretistic thought has no problem moving between sacred and profane sources. The mainspring of the theater is the idea that man is a microcosm of God, an image of God, and that because of this, man has always possessed divine wisdom in his inner being. The human memory is a memory essentially in tune with the cosmos.[47] In the theater, the technical line meets the speculative line, especially Plato's theory of *anamnesis* and Augustine's doctrine of searching for God through memory. These two lines in turn intersect with Hermeticism, Kabbalah, and Lullism.

---

43 Bernheimer, "Theatrum Mundi," 230.
44 Ibid., 230.
45 Camillo, *L'Idea*, 53–54.
46 Ibid., 80.
47 C.f. Yates, *Art of Memory*, 145–48.

The theater was never finished; its idea alone was the source of the great fame of Camillo. His short treatise on the theater, published posthumously, is rushed and veiled in mystery. It engages with great, powerful ideas, but it is unfortunately neither a great nor powerful piece of literature. As with Bruno, the secret of the art seems to have died with the man. However, Verene has suggested that there actually is no esoteric secret, that the vital thing for the theater was its proportions. He writes, "The proportion of the images is crucial—in fact, it is everything. The architecture of the image, each image, and the system of images that is the theater must be precise or it will not function."[48] This is a plausible interpretation. The proper order, the proper *ratio*, the proper dimensions are the needful thing. Their necessity mirrors the necessity of the architecture of the created universe. Camillo suppressed neither the inventory of his materials nor their serial order. He took these materials to be the natural *loci* of the cosmos, not the artificial *loci* of *ars memoriae*. The mastery of these natural *loci* enables one to call to mind not merely a complete oration, but the complete speech of the cosmos. The only thing he left unsaid was the relations in which they stood to one another. Presumably, if one could discover or invent the correct proportions between his *loci*, one could attain cosmic knowledge or solar power.

The theater of Camillo is a perfect representation of the Renaissance strain of the memory tradition. This strain moves far beyond the simple arts of recollection and views memory as the *clavis magna* for unlocking the secrets of the cosmos, attaining the celestial powers, and communicating with the divine. As Umberto Eco's character Jacopo Belbo says, "O Raimundo, O Camillo, you had only to cast your mind back to your visions and immediately you could reconstruct the great chain of being, in love and joy, because all that was disjoined in the universe was joined in a single volume in your mind, and Proust would have made you smile."[49] By holding the whole in a single view, *theatrum mundi*, one mimetically becomes God.

---

48 Verene, *Speculative Philosophy*, 74.
49 Umberto Eco, *Foucault's Pendulum*, trans. William Weaver (New York: Harcourt Brace, 1989), 23.

Section Three: Memory in Modernity

> At Kithairon
> Lay Eleutherae, the city of Mnemosyne. There, too, when
> God's mantel was cast off, the one like night then parted
> Her locks.
>
> Friedrich Hölderlin, "Mnemosyne"

> There is no man who has less business talking about memory. For I recognize almost no trace
> of it in me, and I do not think there is another one in the world so monstrously deficient.
>
> Montaigne, *Essays*, I: 9

In this the final section, I will discuss the "modern" period of European philosophy. I hesitate to remove the quotation marks from "modern" because I am skeptical of all attempts to label philosophical "ages." No two commentators agree on the boundaries of the "modern period," or "early modern period," or whether there is a distinction between the two. When I speak of a "modern" age, I most often use it as shorthand for the philosophical period beginning with Descartes and continuing through Kant.

In this "modern" age, memory fell out of favor amongst philosophers. In the third chapter, above, I argued that "reflection" has replaced memory as the central faculty of philosophical contemplation. In Chapters Eleven and Twelve, I will explore the reasons that this occurred. There were many socio-political currents of culture that unconsciously undermined recollection. The general tendency of the age was to reject authority and tradition in favor of egalitarian individualism. As this tendency developed, memory simply became less significant a part of everyday life than it had once been. Memory was also consciously undermined by Descartes, who considered it to be a mechanical process of the body rather than a spiritual faculty. This view had far-reaching effects throughout modernity. However, both the cultural and philosophical neglect of memory result from certain worldviews and assumptions that failed to embrace the full significance of memory. Once we bring these assumptions to light, we will be able to better judge whether history was right to reject the memory tradition, or whether we have gone astray.

To that end, I will also discuss Montaigne and Hegel at length. I have suggested that each exemplifies "memory as philosophy" in his own way. Montaigne uses memory as the basis of an ethical doctrine of prudence, and Hegel uses memory as the foundation of his metaphysics. My purpose is to show that even in the modern age—the age of science, of reason, of technology—a philosophical doctrine of memory may still shine forth.

IX: Montaigne's Monstrous Memory

Michel Eyquem de Montaigne was born in the Aquitaine region of France, near Bourdeaux, in 1533. The Eyquem family was wealthy and politically prominent. His father, Pierre Eyquem, had been mayor of Bourdeaux, as Montaigne himself would be in adulthood. The Montaigne title is taken from the name of the family's estate, Château de Montaigne, in a French commune now called Saint-Michel-de-Montaigne.[1]

Giulio Camillo had remained in Paris, one of the most well-known men in France, working on his theater under the patronage of Francis I until 1537. He died in Italy in 1544. Montaigne never mentions Camillo, but given the latter's great fame in Paris, and the worldliness of the Eyquem family, it is likely that Pierre Eyquem had heard of the man and his theater, and that the young Montaigne had at least some notion of who Camillo was. Giordano Bruno arrived in France with his secret memory arts in 1580, living first in Toulouse and later in Paris. He dedicated *De umbris idearum*, published in 1582, to another French king, Henry III, who had taken a personal interest in Bruno. He remained in France until he migrated to England in 1583. Montaigne's *Essays* had been presented to Henry III in 1580, and had been well-received by the king. In 1581, Montaigne was elected to his first term as mayor of Bourdeaux, in part because he was, according to Donald Frame, "the one man of judgment acceptable to all four princely parties most concerned: Henry III, Catherine de' Medici, Henry of Navarre [later Henry IV], and his wife, the king's sister, Margaret of Valois."[2] In the ensuing turbulent years, Montaigne served as a mediator between the parties. It is highly likely that, being familiar in the same circles, Montaigne had some knowledge of Bruno at this time. However, as with Camillo, Montaigne never mentions Bruno in the *Essays*, nor do the works of either author appear in his extensive library.[3]

---

1   For comprehensive biographies of Montaigne, see Sarah Bakewell's *How to Live or, a Life of Montaigne*, Donald M. Frame's *Montaigne: A Biography*, and Stefan Zweig's *Montaigne*. An "autobiography" of Montaigne was compiled by Marvin Lowenthal, who reassembled autobiographical excerpts from Montaigne's writings into a linear narrative. See Lowenthal, *The Autobiography of Michel de Montaigne*.
2   Frame, *Montaigne's* Essais, 13–14.
3   The contents of Montaigne's library are listed in *V*, xlii–lxvi. Many of the volumes in Montaigne's collection were willed to him by his friend Étienne de la Boétie. See *CW*, 1280.

Whether or not he had Camillo and Bruno specifically in mind, Montaigne was certainly familiar with the memory treatises of the sixteenth century, and with the standard Renaissance pedagogy in which the cultivation of memory was elevated to supreme importance. His own early education had taught him as much. In the first section of this chapter, I will consider Montaigne's challenge to the memory tradition, in particular to the classical mnemotechnic. In the second section, I will articulate why I nonetheless see Montaigne's philosophy as memorial; this will require an analysis of his thought as dialectical, and a consideration of the role of self-knowledge in the *Essays*. In the following chapter, I will discuss Montaigne's artificial supplement for his weak memory: his writing.

Criticism of *ars memoria*

By the sixteenth century, there was already amongst many writers a suspicion that the memory arts were not all they claimed to be. Erasmus, for one, followed Quintilian in suggesting that the utility of the mnemotechnic was limited, and that ordinary methods of memorization were superior. He also regarded the Hermetic strain of the memory tradition as laughable and superstitious.[4] In Rabelais' *Gargantua*, the sophist and tutor Holofernes teaches the titular hero to memorize his learning forward and backward. As a result, there is not a single young person who "doesn't have better judgment, better command of words, better speech … and better bearing and civility in society" than poor Gargantua.[5] Cornelius Agrippa, though a devotee of the magical element of the memory arts, thought that the monstrous images advocated by the Dominicans "caused madness and frenzy instead of profound and sure memory."[6]

Of all sixteenth-century criticisms of *ars memoriae*, Montaigne's was the most nuanced. Sarah Bakewell writes, "Montaigne's admission of such failings [of his memory] was a direct challenge to the Renaissance ideal of oratory and rhetoric, which held that being able to think well was the same as being able to speak well, and being able to speak well depended upon remembering your flow of argument together with sparkling quotations and examples to adorn it. Devotees of the art of memory, or *ars memoriae*, learned techniques for stringing together

---

4 See Yates, *Art of Memory*, 132–33.
5 François Rabelais, *Gargantua and Pantagruel*, in *The Complete Works of François Rabelais*, trans. Donald M. Frame (Los Angeles: University of California Press, 1999), 39.
6 Jonathan D. Spence, *The Memory Palace of Matteo Ricci* (New York: Penguin, 1984), 12.

hours' worth of rhetoric, and even developed these techniques into a whole program of philosophical self-improvement. This had no appeal for Montaigne."[7]

Paolo Rossi likewise treats Montaigne as one of the great critics of the mnemotechnic in the first pages of his *Clavis universalis*. He writes, "In a more ironic vein [than Erasmus], Montaigne (another critic of humanist pedantry) attacked mnemotechnical literature by emphasizing the deficiency of his own memory (with a coarseness which derives from the particular cultural situation in which he was writing). ... Montaigne, like Erasmus, questioned the Renaissance pedagogical assumption that memory and knowledge were incidental: 'knowledge in the memory is not knowledge,' he says, 'it is simply the conservation of the knowledge of others.'"[8] In the ellipsis of this passage, Rossi quotes the second epigraph of this section. He takes this to be a direct response to mnemotechnics, in particular to those employed by the pedagogical methods of the Renaissance. Rossi continues, "Montaigne criticized the pedagogical use of artificial memory in favor of a more spontaneous and organic form of learning: pupils should not be required to learn the words of their class texts by rote, but rather to give an account of their meaning or substance. The effects of education should be visible in a pupil's conduct, he argued, rather than in their aptitude for memory."[9]

Rossi is referring to Montaigne's early essay, "Of pedantry." In this essay, Montaigne claims that the pedagogical emphasis on memory is deleterious to the student's soul. He writes, "We labor only to fill our memory, and leave the understanding and the conscience empty. ... We are, I believe, learned only with present knowledge, not with past, any more than with future" (*CE*, I: 25, 100; *V*, 136). Later, he writes of students educated in such a manner that "most of the time they understand neither themselves nor others, and that they have a full enough memory but an entirely hollow judgment, unless their nature has of itself fashioned it otherwise" (*CE*, I: 25, 102; *V*, 139). Montaigne happens to be one of those whose judgment nature has fashioned well. How can it be that Montaigne's memory, "so monstrously deficient," is able to serve as the basis for his judgment?

The main problem that Montaigne finds with the mnemotechnic is that it does not encourage a good character. It is a technique, but tech-

---

7   Bakewell, *How to Live*, 70.
8   Rossi, *Logic and Memory*, 2–3.
9   Ibid., 3.

nique, as we have seen, is not good in itself. Technique expands outward and absorbs everything into itself, but technique as such has no sense of good or bad, right or wrong. It is amoral; it is concerned only with efficiency. It is always a means to an end, but the end is irrelevant. Extensive learning is nothing without right action and decent behavior. A pedagogy that stresses the classical technique of memory is a pedagogy that imbues the student with a vast quantum of facts and dates—a wealth of *information*—but no wisdom for overseeing the correct application of these facts. The thought and character of the *memorioso* student are as hollow as that of Borges' Ireneo Funes. Rousseau, strongly influenced by Montaigne, would repeat this sort of critique two centuries later in *Émile*: "A preceptor thinks of his own interest more than of his disciple's. He is devoted to proving that he is not wasting his time and that he is earning the money he is paid. He provides the child with some easily displayed attainments that can be showed off when wanted. It is not important whether what he teaches the child is useful, provided that it is easily seen. He accumulates, without distinction or discernment, a rubbish heap in the child's memory."[10]

In "Of liars," Montaigne writes, "If in my part of the country they want to say that a man has no sense, they say he has no memory. And when I complain of the defectiveness of mine, they argue with me and do not believe me, as if I were accusing myself of witlessness. They see no distinction between memory and understanding. This makes me look a lot worse than I am. But they do me wrong. For rather the opposite is seen by experience: that excellent memories are prone to be joined to feeble judgments" (*CE*, I: 9, 22; *V*, 34).

Many critics have questioned Montaigne's honesty in downplaying his own memory. The *Essays* deal with hundreds or thousands of characters drawn from Montaigne's reading. Such a massive work, appealing constantly to obscure examples from classical literature, must surely have been composed by a man with an exceptional power of retention. Malebranche, for example, writes: "Can he forget the French names of his domestics? Can he not know, as he says, 'most of our coins,' [etc.] ... and at the same time have a mind full of the names of the ancient philosophers and their principles, 'of the ideas of Plato, the atoms of Epicurus,' [etc.]? ... A man who, in three or four pages of his book, relates more than fifty names of different authors together with their opinions, who

---

10 Jean-Jacques Rousseau, *Emile, or On Education*, trans. Allan Bloom (New York: Basic Books, 1979), 162.

has filled all his work with historical poetry and his meat in the manner of books ... should this man brag about having more judgment than memory?"[11] The poet Dominique Baudier said that Montaigne's claims about his memory drove him to "nausea and laughter."[12] It has even been suggested recently that Montaigne was in fact a secret practitioner of *ars memoriae*.[13] This is a claim I will consider in the following chapter.

Setting these critics aside, we ought to take Montaigne at his word and try to make sense of the ethical element of his claim, that excellent memories are prone to be joined to feeble judgments. In the following section, I will discuss in what way this claim of a poor memory is to be taken. For the moment, I will appeal to a letter written around 1563 by Montaigne to his father, narrating the final days and death of Étienne La Boétie. Given that La Boétie was Montaigne's most intimate friend and the subject of the essay "Of friendship," and that the recipient of this private epistle was his father, a man whom he deeply respected, it is unlikely that Montaigne was writing in a flippant or insincere manner. He writes, "It is true, sir, that since my memory is very short and was further disturbed by the confusion that my mind was to suffer from so heavy and important a loss, it is impossible that I have not forgotten many things that I would like to be known. But those I have remembered I shall report to you as truthfully as I can" (*L*, 1276–77). By his own report, Montaigne's memory was unable to retain even the final moments of his dearest friend to an appropriate degree.

Why is good memory aligned with feeble judgment? What is the ethical element of forgetfulness? In "Of liars," Montaigne writes, "[Lack of memory] is an evil that has shown me the way to correct a worse evil which could easily have developed in me—to wit, ambition; for lack of memory is intolerable in anyone who is involved in public negotiations" (*CE*, I: 9, 22; *V*, 34–35). Again, "Anyone who does not feel sufficiently strong in memory should not meddle with lying" (ibid., 23; *V*, 35). A strong memory is necessary for ambition; one cannot advance in the world if one cannot remember a watchword given a few hours before or a commission recently received (*CE*, II: 17, 494; *V*, 651). It is also the pre-

---

11   Nicolas Malebranche, *The Search After Truth*, trans. Thomas M. Lennon and Paul J. Olscamp (New York: Cambridge University Press, 1997), 188.
12   Quoted in Bakewell, *How to Live*, 71.
13   See, e.g., William E. Engel, "The Art of Memory and Montaigne's Scene of Writing," in *The Order of Montaigne's Essays*, ed. Daniel Martin (Amherst, MA: Hestia, 1989), Cynthia Israel, "Montaigne and Proust: Architects of Memory," *Romance Languages Annual* 6 (1994): 105–9, and Daniel Martin, *L'Architecture des Essais de Montaigne: mémoire artificielle et mythologique* (Paris: Librairie A.-G. Nizet, 1992).

condition for lying. A liar must be able to hold in mind an entire web of deceits, so as not to accidentally speak the truth. This requires constant care and constant application. Deception and ambition are the provinces of those gifted with strong memories either by nature or art. Montaigne considers lying an "accursed vice," and writes, "I am not sure that I could bring myself to ward off even an evident and extreme danger by a shameless and solemn lie" (*CE*, I: 9, 23–24; *V*, 36–37). Luckily, his poor memory precludes this possibility.[14]

The account Montaigne reports having given of himself upon being recalled to serve as mayor of Bourdeaux is deliberately worded. He writes, "On my arrival I deciphered myself to them faithfully and conscientiously, exactly as I feel myself to be: without memory, without vigilance, without experience, and without vigor; also without hate, without ambition, without avarice, and without violence" (*CE*, III: 10, 768; *V*, 1005). The first set of predicates names the faculties or temperaments that Montaigne lacks (excepting experience, which is an accidental circumstance), and the second set names the vices to which he is not subject. There is a correlation between the two sets. *Because* the first set is lacking, the second is lacking also. Montaigne's poor memory is the efficient cause of his lack of vigilance and vigor. The absence of these conditions is a proof that the correlated vices are also absent. The forgetful man is not very good at hating or plotting or harming.

This is a direct challenge to the position of Cicero, widely accepted in Renaissance thought. Memory is ethical for Cicero, for whom *memoria* is a part of *prudentia*. Albert and Thomas had confirmed this claim, and extolled memory as a Christian virtue. For Montaigne, however, there is a reverse side to memory: it is also a necessary condition for the most "accursed vices." A strong and full memory brings with it a sort of power over the less learned. It is always conjoined with the temptation to deceive, or to harbor ambition, avarice, and hatred. It does not necessarily lead to vice, but these vices cannot arise where memory is lacking. Forgetfulness, in this sense, is the lesser evil. Nietzsche offers a similar argument for the link between memory and vice centuries later. Montaigne's confession to the citizens of Bourdeaux is in one sense an admission of fault: his weak memory will make him a poor politician (though

---

14 A similar manner of thinking appears in Henry More, who was perhaps influenced by Montaigne. More writes, "As a strong and retentive *Memory*, which holds all fast, how many an honest Man is there that has it not? For ... those Noble and Divine Things, wherein Happiness did consist, were very few." More, *Enchiridion Ethicum*, trans. Edward Southwell (New York: Facsimile Text Society, 1930), 162.

this proved to be untrue). On the other hand, it is an appeal to his strength: his inability to remember will prevent him from harming his own citizens for personal gain. In the tumultuous political climate of Montaigne's France, such a mayor must have seemed a godsend.

The educational side of memory is also an ethical issue for Montaigne. As Ann Hartle writes, "The distinctions that [Montaigne] makes between memory and understanding and between memory and invention suggest that memory holds thought in its power by the unrecognized authority of remembered or 'borrowed' opinions. Montaigne's deficiency of memory is his freedom from subjection to unexamined presuppositions. His intellect is not dominated by either philosophical or common authoritative opinion and is not a mere storehouse or collection of received opinions."[15] The consecutive essays "Of pedantry" and "Of the education of children" are complementary. In the former, Montaigne is critical of the pedagogical practice of compelling the student to memorize large quanta of information. Learning, he thinks, is not wisdom, and philosophical thought is not identical with good judgment (*CE*, I: 25, 98; *V*, 134). Goodness, judgment, and wisdom are the proper objects of education, not "learning" (ibid., 100; *V*, 136). The problem with traditional pedagogy is that it merely sets down as given what authorities have decreed: "We take the opinions and the knowledge of others into our keeping, and that is all. We must make them our own. ... What good does it do us to have our belly full of meat if it is not digested, if it is not transformed into us, if it does not make us bigger and stronger?" (ibid., 101; *V*, 137).

Montaigne's own early education, which largely consisted of the grammatical study of Cicero, nearly turned him off from the *belles lettres* altogether. We saw in the introduction that Hegel classifies Montaigne as a writer of "Ciceronian popular philosophy." However, Montaigne was never a devotee of the Ciceronian style. Though admitting a respect for Cicero's moral philosophy, Montaigne writes, "To confess the truth boldly (for once you have crossed over the barriers of impudence there is no more curb), [Cicero's] way of writing, and every other similar way, seems to me boring. ... If I have spent an hour reading him, which is a lot for me, and I remember what juice and substance I have derived, most of the time I find nothing but wind" (*CE*, II: 10, 301; *V*, 413–14). It was only his discovery of Ovid's *Metamorphoses* that sparked Montaigne's liter-

---

15 Ann Hartle, *Michel de Montaigne: Accidental Philosopher* (New York: Cambridge University Press, 2003), 109.

ary interests (*CE*, I: 26, 130; *V*, 175).[16] What most aided Montaigne's own education was a peculiar personal trait, not anything taught to him by his preceptors: "For all that, my mind was not lacking in strong stirrings of its own, and certain and open-minded judgments about the things it understood; and it digested them alone, without communication" (ibid., 131; *V*, 176).

Education ought to cultivate the goodness of the student, and to inform the student's habits and judgment. Montaigne argues that this is altogether lacking in the usual Ciceronian education of the sixteenth century. According to Montaigne, the pedagogy of the time, influenced by the classical enjoinders to practice *ars memoriae*, was more concerned with filling the mind with clutter than teaching the student to exercise good judgment. Teachers tended to emphasize quantity of learning at the expense of quality, breadth over depth.[17] The student's development of his or her own judgment was compromised by the authority of others. Montaigne writes, "To know by heart is not to know; it is to retain what we have given our memory to keep. What we know rightly we dispose of, without looking at the model, without turning our eyes toward our book" (*CE*, I: 26, 112; *V*, 152). For Montaigne, rote memorization is actively hostile to judgment. The unsuspecting student is imprinted with a set of pre-formed opinions and prejudices. These prejudices preclude the student's own judgments, and annul the possibility of open-minded discourse. The student develops the character of a recording device, able to play back programmed speeches but not generate new ones. Without judgment, the student cannot develop ethical standards. Memorization of stories of virtuous action is not internalization; the student can recite these stories verbatim even while performing great villainy.

Montaigne writes, "The surest sign of wisdom is constant cheerfulness ... you can get there, if you know the way, by shady, grassy, sweetly flowering roads, pleasantly, by an easy smooth slope, like that of the celestial vaults" (*CE*, I: 26, 119; *V*, 161). He then claims that he has only one new lesson to offer to educators: "This new lesson, that the value and height of true virtue lies in the ease, utility, and pleasure of its practice, which is so far from being difficult that children can master it as well as men, the simple as well as the subtle. Virtue's tool is moderation, not

---

16 On the role of Cicero in Montaigne's early education, see Bakewell, *How to Live*, 64.
17 Peter Kanelos writes, "A memory enhanced through artifice in the tradition of Simonides ... gets wider and wider but not deeper. Looking for answers, rather than information, one becomes lost in its chambers and passages." Kanelos, "Montaigne and the Grotto of Memory," *Proteus: A Journal of Ideas* 19, no. 2 (2002): 15.

strength" (ibid., 120; *V*, 162). Virtue is easy and natural, whereas the cultivation of a trained memory is a laborious task that does *not* lead to virtue. Virtue, being tied to forgetfulness, is easy and cheerful. It is free from the tension entailed by the life of the inveterate liar. A pupil inclined toward forgetfulness and virtue will not know many things, but, like Rousseau's Émile, will know well those few things he has learned. He will have internalized these things and made them his own. He will not be inclined to cruelty or avarice. His judgment will give him the rule of action rather than authority, and he will be open to novelty, since he will not be bound to received presuppositions.[18]

Montaigne's critique of the classical art of memory is aimed at its original *raison d'être*: the inclusion of memory in Cicero's schema of virtue. By arguing that the mnemotechnic in fact encourages, on the one hand, avarice and deception, and on the other, a blind and vapid educational program, Montaigne shows the spuriousness of the connection between *ars memoriae* and the ethical. This opposition applies not just to Cicero, but also to the authority of the Dominican fathers, and to the reading of Aristotle suggested by Albert and Thomas. *Nota bene*, however, that Montaigne never suggests that memory is not closely tied to the ethical. The object of his critique is always the mnemotechnic. For Montaigne also, the ethical depends on memory, but in a very different sense from that suggested by Cicero.

How can a figure with so "monstrously deficient" and unsystematic a memory still have a philosophical doctrine of memory? To understand this, we must understand Montaigne's dialectic of judgment, as well as the importance of self-knowledge in his philosophical thinking. As a means of entering into Montaigne's thought on these topics, we will begin by considering his creative inversion of Aristotle.

Aristotle reversed

Aristotle is often the antagonist in Montaigne's writing. Though the range of ancient and contemporary thinkers commented upon in the *Essays* is enormous,[19] Aristotle time and again appears as the philosopher with whom Montaigne is most closely engaged. This is clear as early as the

---

18 On the influence of Montaigne on European pedagogy in the ensuing centuries, see Pierre Villey, *L'influence de Montaigne sur les idées pédagogiques de Locke et de Rousseau*.

19 On the many sources of Montaigne's *Essays*, see Pierre Villey, *Les sources & l'évolution des essays de Montaigne*, and the second chapter of Hugo Friedrich, *Montaigne*.

note "To the Reader," with which the *Essays* begin. Here, Montaigne appropriates the four Aristotelian causes to justify the writing of his book, devoting a paragraph each to the final, formal, and material causes of the book (and thereby implying that the efficient cause is Montaigne himself) (*CE*, 2; *V*, 3). This engagement with Aristotle is not arbitrary. Though it is true that the philosophy of the Florentine Academy and the Neoplatonism of the Italian Renaissance had shaken the unquestioned acceptance of Aristotle's authority so characteristic of Scholastic thought, the philological research into antiquity and new editions of his work had, on the other hand, helped to give new life to Aristotle. Academic philosophy remained predominantly Aristotelian even at the time of the Florentine Academy.[20] On the whole, Aristotle remained The Philosopher, whose every word "overturned the image of the world."[21]

In *De memoria et reminiscientia*, the external object is stamped into the mind, impressed by way of perception. This psychic impression [*tupos*] becomes the actual object of memory. In the analogy that Aristotle borrows from Plato, the soul is like a wax tablet. The "impression" plays an equally foundational role in the *Essays*. In "Of cruelty," Montaigne writes, "I hold [most vices] in horror, I say, from an attitude so natural and so much my own that the same instinct and impression (*instinct et impression*) that I brought away from my nurse I have still retained. Nothing has been able to make me alter it, not even my own reasonings, which, having in some things broken away from the common road, would easily give me license for actions which this natural inclination makes me hate" (*CE*, II: 11, 312; *V*, 429, emphasis mine). The word "impression" is the same in French and English, and has the same etymology: it always literally means a pressing or stamping down.

In this passage, impressions stand over and against reason, as a check on the power of ratiocination. It is the retention of first impressions that guides and informs Montaigne's later judgments. In a shallow reading of the *Essays*, this claim might suggest that philosophy for Montaigne depends upon the Proustian, psychological form of recollection. The *petites madeleines* set off a flood of childhood impressions, which act as a

---

20 On the Renaissance revitalization of Aristotle and Plato, see Bouwsma, *Waning of the Renaissance*, 156–58. Paul Oskar Kristeller argues that Aristotelianism remained the dominant paradigm of thought in academic philosophy departments during the Renaissance, despite the resistance of humanism. See "The Aristotelian Tradition" (chap. 2), in *Renaissance Thought: The Classic, Scholastic, and Humanist Strains* (New York: Harper & Row, 1961), 24–47.
21 Umberto Eco, *The Name of the Rose*, trans. William Weaver (Orlando, FL: Harcourt Brace, 1994), 473.

standard by which to weigh novel experiences. Right judgment, on this model, would be a product of the power of the simplest form of memory, and knowledge would be a *recherche du temps perdu*.²² However, if first impressions are the only ethical standard for Montaigne, then this would be a memorial ethics that does not develop with experience, an ethics in which everything is pre-judged. One's first impressions are a poor standard for thinking, as arbitrary and conducive to closed-mindedness as the teaching of the pedants.

Are the "impressions" of Montaigne actually the same as those Aristotle discusses? For the latter, the impression is the basic unit of memory, preceding all knowledge; in order to arrive at any inferential conclusion, one must begin by making comparisons between a number of impressions ready at hand. The upward progress of thought leaves these particular impressions behind. In the passage cited above from "Of cruelty," it seems that Montaigne shares this understanding of impressions. However, an underlying thread in the *Essays* is the notion that an inversion of Aristotle is both possible and necessary.

For example, in Aristotle's *Metaphysics*, experience is the beginning of philosophy. He writes, "Experience [*empeiria*] seems to be very similar to science and art [*epistēmē kai technē*], but really science and art come to men *through* experience; for 'experience made art,' as Polus says, 'but inexperience luck'" (*Meta.*, I.1, 981a1–5). Experience is the foundation and starting point of all knowledge and art. In Montaigne's *Essays*, experience is the *end* of knowledge, not its beginning. "Of experience" is the title of the final essay in the book. Here, Montaigne writes, "It is an absolute perfection and virtually divine to know how to enjoy our being rightfully" (*CE*, III: 13, 857; *V*, 1115). A proper orientation to experience is the goal that knowledge and art seek, not their source.²³ Just such an inversion is involved with Montaigne's notion of memory. He does not return to pre-rational first impressions as such, but rather constitutes these impressions anew through thought, with the assistance

---

22 Sarah Bakewell has suggested that Montaigne's memory is Proustian: "Montaigne was attuned to the kind of 'involuntary' memory that would one day fascinate Proust: those blasts from the past that irrupt unexpectedly into the present, perhaps in response to a long-forgotten taste or smell." *How to Live*, 71–72. While he may have been "attuned" to such a form of memory, my reading will stress the ingenious element of his memory.

23 For a discussion of Montaigne's inversions of Aristotle, in relation to Montaigne's presentation of the "new figure" of the philosopher, see the chapter, "Reversing Aristotle," in Ann Hartle, *Montaigne and the Origins of Modern Philosophy* (Evanston, IL: Northwestern University Press, 2013), 5–28.

of the imagination. For Aristotle, the impressions give shape to thought. For Montaigne, thought gives shape to impressions, and continues to do so as spirit develops.

In the "Apology for Raymond Sebond," Montaigne writes, "The reason why we doubt hardly anything is that we never *test* [*essaye*] our common impressions. We do not *probe the base*, where the fault and weakness lies; we dispute only about the branches. We do not ask whether this is true, but whether it has been understood this way or that. We do not ask whether Galen said anything worth saying, but whether he said thus or otherwise. Indeed it was very right that that bridle and constraint on the liberty of our judgments [*jugements*], and that tyranny over our beliefs, extended even to the schools and to the arts" (*CE*, II: 12, 403; *V*, 539, emphasis mine). This passage turns any philosophical project in which impressions are to serve as a basis for wisdom into a problem.

For Montaigne, there is no pre-Adamite, innocent and immediate cognition of the world. The world is never simply given, and its character is never fixed. All is movement, all truths are fleeting. It is not enough to return to the simple first impressions, and to develop knowledge and art from this basis. Instead, these impressions must be *tested*. Psychological memory by itself cannot yield anything worthwhile; it can only reinforce received dogmas. To return to one's earliest impressions is to revisit the pre-philosophical and pre-rational level of consciousness, but this is not *to ontōs on*, the really real. These impressions may offer some value, as they are unsullied by the corrupt concepts and opinions one adopts in polite society, but this is also a return to a condition prior to judgment, in which the images themselves have complete sovereignty. We saw with the example of Shereshevskii what results when images guide thinking. What is needful for Montaigne is judgment, the weighing or assaying of impressions. This is the kind of judgment that pedants never teach.

How are we to measure and test our impressions? What Montaigne has in mind can be glimpsed in his early essay, "Of drunkenness." He begins by relating his initial impressions of drunkenness. It strikes him offhand as "a gross and brutish vice" (*CE*, II: 2, 245; *V*, 340). However, thought does not terminate with this impression; judgment is introduced as a measuring device. Montaigne writes, "My taste and constitution [*Mon goust et ma complexion*] are more inimical to this vice than my reason. ... I find it indeed a loose and stupid vice, but less malicious and harmful than the others, which almost all clash more directly with society in general" (ibid., 247; *V*, 342). By the end of the essay, he has lauded drunkenness as a "celestial rapture" (ibid., 251; *V*, 348). Montaigne's first impression of drunkenness is belied when he proceeds to measure it against other vices and their relationship to the wellbeing of society. The raw impression by itself is inadequate and misleading. "Taste" and "constitution" have the same meaning in this essay that Montaigne gives elsewhere to "nature" and "inclination". Montaigne's "nature" is never the final arbiter; nature is itself always under scrutiny. Judgment always returns to the pre-rational impressions and re-constitutes them, taking into account an entire field of other judgments and experiences. The impression is always inferior and subordinate to reason.

In "Of cripples," Montaigne writes, "I have seen no more evident monstrosity and miracle in the world than myself. We become habituated to anything strange by use and time; but the more I frequent myself and know myself, the more my deformity astonishes me and the less I understand myself" (*CE*, III: 11, 787; *V*, 1029). Montaigne is unique among men only insofar as his own nature and inclinations never strike him as a matter of course. That is, he never fails to hold himself up to the scales of judgment. Likewise, he never fails to hold his most familiar and comforting impressions up to the same scales. This self-evaluation is what makes Montaigne both monstrous and miraculous.

We find from his account of drunkenness that the "impressions" Montaigne has in mind are not immediate, neutral sense-data. They always include some element of feeling. Drunkenness is initially experienced as *bad*, not as a mere collection of sensory inputs. The subject is never fully disinterested. Montaigne's first impressions always entail evaluations of the thing as good or bad, weak or strong, right or wrong. All things present themselves as either benign or malignant, prior to any process of reasoning.[24] His first impression of cruelty, for example, is an impression of horror (*CE*, II: 11, 312; *V*, 428). This is Montaigne's appropriation of *phantasia*, imagination, as it pertains to the Aristotelian schema in *De memoria*. It is on the level of *phantasia* that error first becomes possible. Because it is the evaluative element of memory, it is the

---

24 "Benign" and "malignant" are the two basic, primitive categories of the pre-rational understanding. Ernst Cassirer writes, "Mythical imagination is always impregnated with these emotional qualities. Whatever is seen or felt is surrounded by a special atmosphere—an atmosphere of joy or grief, of anguish, of excitement, of exultation or depression. Here we cannot speak of 'things' as a dead or indifferent stuff. All objects are benignant or malignant, friendly or inimical," and so on. See Cassirer, *An Essay on Man* (New Haven, CT: Yale University Press, 1972), 76–77.

imagination, and not the raw data of sense-experience, that Montaigne subjects to revision.

The passage cited above from the "Apology for Raymond Sebond" is followed by a discussion of Aristotle, "the god of scholastic knowledge" (*CE*, II: 12, 403; *V*, 539). This discussion concludes with a condemnation of the likely stories of the ancient philosophers, which might have been sufficient for our edification if "they had left us in our natural state, receiving external impressions as they present themselves to us through our senses." Instead, they have "taught us to be judges of the world" (ibid., 404; *V*, 541). Aristotle recognized the importance of the impression and the imagination in the ascent to the universal concepts of *technē* and *epistēmē*, but he is also responsible for drawing us away from this level of simple memory and impression. He utilizes these as mere implements, to be discarded once higher orders of thinking are reached. But having taken up this ascent, we err in not turning our judgments back upon ourselves and our original impressions, the starting points of this climb. Because the world is not static, some form of revision must always occur. Montaigne writes, "The impression of certainty is a certain token of folly and extreme uncertainty" (ibid.).

Though Montaigne recognizes the imagination (*fantasie* or *imagination*) to be an "all-important" faculty (*CE*, III: 13, 833; *V*, 1087), he prescribes that "we must help it and flatter it, fool it if we can" (ibid., 836; *V*, 1090). Imagination is powerful, but because it is unruly it is dangerous. It must be taken up intentionally where this is possible, and tricked into obedience. It must be utilized as a tool. Thought must precede and pilot the imagination, whereas in Aristotle, *phantasia* precedes thought. In the early essay "Of idleness," Montaigne advises: "Unless you keep [minds] busy with some definite subject that will bridle and control them, they throw themselves in disorder hither and yon in the vague field of imagination" (*CE*, I: 8, 21; *V*, 32). Lawrence Kritzman correctly observes, "In the process of self-portraiture, the text reveals the consequences of a fevered imagination. Montaigne sees language and himself in its deformed images; the self that he views risks following its own course, uncontrolled as it is by the power of the imagination."[25]

The sober judgment of the dispassionate present is able to employ the imagination in a constitutive manner, that is, to alter the emotive ele-

---

25 Lawrence D. Kritzman, *The Fabulous Imagination: On Montaigne's Essays* (New York: Columbia University Press, 2009), 30. This book explores many of the uses and miscarriages of Montaigne's "fabulous imagination."

ment of past impressions. We must work to impose this constitutive imagination in place of the *phantasia* of Aristotle's psychological description of memory. Montaigne's imagination, the bondsman of reason, is held, as Grahame Castor says, "to have a close concern with the problem of conflicting value-judgments. Imagination is not simply presenting to the higher faculties a 'common image' compounded of separate sense-images, but it is collating different judgments about the same 'common image' and setting them impartially before the mind."[26] This requires controlled forgetting. The impression must *not* be constituted as it initially was, and the original images of *phantasia* must dissolve away into the river Lethe.[27] Thought must not stop at the vacuous actuality of what is merely given.

The circular dialectic

The *Essays*, as I have said, demonstrate Montaigne's engagement with hundreds of thinkers, and a multitude of themes and subtleties taken up time and again. A feat of such scope would have been impossible had its architect not been gifted with an exceptional faculty of recollection. This obvious fact is the ground of the criticisms of Malebranche, Baudier, and others, and the dismissive accusations that Montaigne is simply deceiving the reader. Nevertheless, Montaigne insists that his memory is "monstrous."

This is a theme that recurs throughout the *Essays*. In "Of presumption," Montaigne writes, "If I were to live a long time, I do not doubt that I would forget my own name," and, "Memory is the receptacle and container of knowledge; mine being so defective [*deffaillante*], I can hardly complain if I do not know much. I know in general the names of the arts and what they treat, but nothing beyond that" (II: 17, 494; *V*, 651). In "Of pedantry," he explicitly claims that his memory is not the sort of treasury or storehouse suggested by Augustine: "I go about cadging from books here and there the sayings that please me, not to keep them, for I have no storehouses, but to transport them into this one [the *Essays*]" (*CE*, I: 25, 100; *V*, 136). In "Of the education of children," he lists as his natural faults: "A slow mind, which would go only as far as it was led; a tardy understanding, a weak imagination, and on top of all an incredible lack of

---

26 Grahame Castor, *Pleiade Poetics: A Study in Sixteenth-Century Thought and Terminology* (Cambridge: Cambridge University Press, 1964), 152.
27 This is the "*science de oubly*" to which Montaigne refers in the "Apology to Raymond Sebond."

memory" (*CE*, I: 26, 129; *V*, 174). How can these claims be reconciled with what is immediately apparent: Montaigne's exceptional memory?

One way to answer this question is to ask what Montaigne understands by "monsters". In "Of a monstrous child," he explains his use of this term: "What we call monsters [*monstres*] are not so to God. ... We call contrary to nature what happens contrary to custom; nothing is anything but according to nature, whatever it may be" (*CE*, II: 30, 539; *V*, 713). This definition may be applied to Montaigne's memory. In "Of custom," he writes, "The principle effect of the power of custom is to seize and ensnare us in such a way that it is hardly within our power to get ourselves back out of its grip and return into ourselves to reflect and reason about its ordinances. ... Men receive the advice of truth and its precepts as if addressed to the common people, never to themselves; and each man, instead of incorporating them into his behavior, incorporates them into his memory, very stupidly and uselessly" (*CE*, I: 23, 83; *V*, 116). The student does not receive a true moral education. Instead, his or her memory is filled with useless examples that are never assimilated. This is because custom, like technology, does not stand up to reflexive self-questioning. Custom advocates a hollow, informational memory as a stand-in for critical thinking. Montaigne's memory is monstrous not because it violates nature or God's will. It is monstrous because it violates the norms of *custom*. It is monstrous because it contains the critical component of judgment. In all corrupt ages, sound judgment is a spectacle.[28]

However, Montaigne's memory is not just "monstrous," but also "monstrously deficient." Ann Hartle writes, "Obviously Montaigne has an excellent memory. But before we conclude that this is false modesty, we ought to take him at his word and try to make sense of this passage [the epigraph of this section, above]. What does Montaigne mean by memory in the sense in which he is monstrously deficient? The distinction that must be made is the distinction between memory and understanding."[29] These are the two terms of the dichotomy Montaigne constructs in "Of liars." On the one side is memory, and on the other are judgment and understanding: "Excellent memories are prone to be joined to feeble judgments" (*CE*, I: 9, 22; *V*, 34).

The "monstrous" memory of which Montaigne speaks concerns his memory of the initial evaluations of his impressions. Judgment challeng-

---

[28] This is the insight of Ovid in exile: "Barbarus hic ego sum, qui non intellegor ulli" ("Here I am the barbarian, for they do not understand me") (*Trist.*, V. x.37). This was also the epigraph for Rousseau's first *Discourse*.

[29] Hartle, *Michel de Montaigne*, 108.

es the immediate benignity or malignance of the event or thing, which occurs at the level of Aristotle's *phantasia*. For Montaigne, this level is not fixed, but is instead subject to perpetual revaluation. Because he is unable to recollect his original evaluations, he is not subject to predetermined dogmas or received *doxes*. His opinions are always new, always the product of his present understanding. The openness to experience intervenes and reconstitutes the object in a new sense. A model of this is Montaigne's reconstitution of his impressions of drunkenness. The percepts remain the same, but his evaluation of them changes. Imagination still plays its constitutive role in memory, as in Aristotle's schema, but it is a backward-looking imagination subject to present judgment and reason, an imagination helped, flattered and fooled by reason. The imagination is guided by thought. It is *not* the unrestrained *phantasia* of the frail individual's initial, pre-reflective encounters with phenomena. In this way, Montaigne's terrible memory is the condition of his freedom from the idols of the marketplace and of the theater. He is always able to creatively reconstitute his first impressions, rather than bowing to them in bondage. This science of forgetting is the basis for developing open ethical relationships with the world, and for approaching the question, "What is the good?" without a pre-scripted answer.

We find another example of this process in "Of experience." Here, Montaigne writes: "He who calls back to mind the excess of his past anger, and how far this fever carried him away, sees the ugliness of this passion better than in Aristotle, and conceives a more justified hatred for it. ... The slips that my memory has made so often, even when it reassures me most about itself, are not vainly lost on me; there is no use in her swearing to me now and assuring me, I shake my ears" (III: 13, 822; *V*, 1073–4). Recollection is unquestionably essential to learning, and yet Montaigne quickly reaffirms his own lack of memory. The meaning of this reversal is clear. The immediate phenomenon of anger is *not* actually experienced as either excessive or ugly. The free imagination delights in anger when it is at hand. It is only after careful thought and judgment that we are able to recognize such anger to be excessive and harmful to social order. Therefore, we must actively *forget* the pleasure actually experienced along with this passion. Thought must not be forever enslaved to pre-rational emotions. We must be able to revaluate from a position of distance and engage our past impressions by this act of creative reconstitution. Reason sets imagination the hermeneutical task of reinterpretation. Only in this manner do we arrive at worldly wisdom.

This idea owes much to the final chapter of St. Augustine's *De civitate Dei*. Writing of the saints who have attained the kingdom of God, Augustine says, "The saints will have no memory of past evils. They will be set free from them all, and they will be completely deleted from their feelings. Yet the power of knowledge will be so great in the saints that they will be aware not only of their own past suffering, but also of the everlasting misery of the damned. For if they were not to know that they had been miserable, how could they, as the psalm says, for ever sing the mercies of God?"[30] For Augustine, this is the character of eternal blessedness: memory of all the events of one's life, but forgetfulness of the emotions with which they were colored, the pain and suffering and misery that they carried.

What emerges in Montaigne's ethical thinking is a circular dialectic that begins and ends in memory. Cognition begins with impressions, but transforms these through thinking and judgment. Later, it returns to these impressions, which are now conditioned and mediated by reason. They are the same, yet not the same. On the one hand, the impression is the starting point for judgment, and on the other, judgment returns to this origin and invests the impression with new meanings. This is speculative philosophy.

Hartle has rightly called Montaigne's "accidental" philosophy "a circular movement in which thought returns to its beginnings and thus possesses those beginnings in a new way."[31] Montaigne's dialectic is a process that never ends, since life and experience are always in movement. Each time we return to our impressions, the intervening period of experience conditions anew what we behold. We then use this new judgment as a platform for action in the world, and at a later time we again return to evaluate our starting point, armed with that much more experience. There is a perpetual chain of travelling and homecoming. This eternal movement of thought is one of the themes of Jean Starobinski's *Montaigne in Motion*. He writes, "One can point to innumerable pages in the *Essays* in which the inner knowledge is the always elusive goal of an interminable pursuit. Rather than deliver itself up at first blush,

---

30 St. Augustine, *The City of God against the Pagans*, trans. R.W. Dyson (New York: Cambridge University Press, 2003), XXII.xxx, 1181.
31 Hartle, *Michel de Montaigne*, 91. Hartle was the first person to use the term "circular dialectic" in reference to Montaigne. This section is indebted to her discussion in ibid., 91–120.

the true self evades the introspective gaze. The quest is lured away into remote distances."[32]

Read in this sense, the *Essays* are a kind of *Bildungsroman*,[33] in which the hero always moves closer to knowledge but is never quite able to pin it down. Maurice Merleau-Ponty observes, "Montaigne does not know that resting place, that self-possession, which Cartesian understanding is to be."[34] Because the world is always in motion, thought must always be in motion as well. It can never rest on its laurels at the first clear and distinct ideas it stumbles upon. The complete picture of the changing subject requires the perspectives of as many vantage points as possible, but this picture is never complete, never settled.[35] Both the subject and the object are forever off-balance. For Montaigne, first impressions are not just the starting line for investigation. They must also be revisited over and over again, revaluated and constituted anew, in a process that does not terminate. This is the truth Adorno expresses when he writes, "The essay is more dialectical than the [Hegelian] dialectic as it articulates itself. ... Neither may the truth of the totality be played off immediately against individual judgments, nor may truth be reduced to individual judgments; rather, the claim of the particular to truth is taken literally to the point where there is evidence of its untruth. The risked, anticipatory, and incompletely redeemed aspect of every essayistic detail draws in other details as negation; the untruth in which the essay knowingly entangles itself is the element of its truth."[36]

This circular dialectic is the motor that carries one toward wisdom, but at no point does it ever attain its goal of objective truth. In the words of Merleau-Ponty, "Destroying dogmatic, partial, or abstract truth, it insinuates the idea of a total truth with all the necessary facets and mediations." Montaigne's dialectic takes up all positions and both sides of all contradictions. Merleau-Ponty continues, "Perhaps in the end he finds in this ambiguous *self*—which is offered to everything, and which he never finished exploring—the place of all obscurities, the mystery of all mysteries, and something like an ultimate truth."[37] Only at the level of absolute knowing could the motion of this dialectic of memory terminate, but

---

32 Starobinski, *Montaigne in Motion*, 68.
33 The view of the *Essays* as a *Bildungsroman* is supported by Marvin Lowenthal's edition of Montaigne's writings, the so-called *Autobiography of Michel de Montaigne*.
34 Maurice Merleau-Ponty, "Reading Montaigne," in *Signs*, trans. Richard McCleary (Evanston, IL: Northwestern University Press, 1964), 199.
35 C.f. Auerbach, *Mimesis*, 292.
36 Adorno, "Essay as Form," 166, partially quoted in the introduction.
37 Merleau-Ponty, "Reading Montaigne," 198.

the *Essays* never claim to achieve absolute knowing. Adorno, with Hegel in mind, calls the essay the "polar opposite" of a philosophy of absolute knowledge.[38] *If* the absolute, for Hegel, is a transcendent mode of thinking somehow qualitatively disconnected from other modes, this is a true claim. If the absolute is a view from nowhere, then the essay form does stand in an irreconcilable opposition to the philosophy of the absolute, as a view always deeply and consciously imbedded within a spatio-temporal context. Adorno's claim, however, misunderstands Hegel's absolute. I will argue in the following section that the Hegelian absolute *is* recollection. The dialectic of the *Essays* raises us to a position from which we can recollect our own self-measurements, our successes and failures. The Hegelian absolute, which is the product of a totalizing *Erinnerung*, is much closer to the final, open position of the *Essays* than Adorno realized.

My theoretical claim has been that the aspect of memory that is truly philosophical is *ingenium*. Where does this come into Montaigne's dialectic? György Lukács has best articulated the connection between *ingenium* and the essay. He writes, "The essay is always concerned with something already formed, or at best, with something that has been; it is part of its essence that it does not draw something new out of an empty vacuum, but only gives a new order to such things as once lived. And because he only newly orders them, not forming something new out of the formless, he is bound to them; he must speak 'the truth' about them, find, that is, the expression for their essence."[39] The subject of the *Essays* is always Montaigne himself. Contained in the book is the complete speech about its subject, the complete lived experience of its author. Montaigne stands naked before the reader, and he comes as close as anyone ever has to bringing the knower and the known, the I and I, into harmony. Holding the entirety of his subject matter in one view, the author is able to reconsider and reorganize its various parts. The book is the theater of his life, his *theatrum mundi*. The memorial dialectic produces nothing new, but it gives all things a new twist, a new order. It places things in new relationships and tests them against one another. The dialectic of the *Essays* cannot give us certainty, which is why Descartes set himself against this form of playful inquiry. However, certainty is static and impotent in a world of perpetual motion.

---

38 Adorno, "Essay as Form," 166.
39 George Lukács, *Soul and Form*, trans. Anna Bostock (Cambridge, MA: MIT Press, 1974), 10.

Self-knowledge and *l'humaine condition*

I have suggested in the third chapter that the project of self-knowledge in the *Essays* is at the same time a project of illuminating *l'humaine condition* through the model of a single representative. Tzvetan Todorov writes, "[Montaigne] is opposed to the tyranny of memory, in which the fragment of the past—the knowledge of the Ancients—is transmitted intact from generation to generation, always prompting the same pious attitude. The *Essays* are, after all, a work of memory as well, since in them their author seeks to define his own identity and the results of his experience; but memory, here, is in the service of a larger goal: meditation on the human condition. If literal and repetitive memory is devalued, exemplary and instrumental memory, which leads to wisdom, is held in high esteem."[40] Meditation on the human condition must take the form of meditation on the individual specimen, who is a microcosm, not of the cosmos, but of the *human as such*. This is the reason that Montaigne, praising Socrates in "Of practice," writes, "Whoever knows himself thus, let him boldly make himself known by his own mouth" (*CE*, II: 6, 275; *V*, 380).[41]

The problem of human existence is that it floats downstream in an unnavigated river. Consciousness itself is a function of change, a function of the needs and desires that arise with the flow of existence. The theologians tell us that the absolute, unchanging One must lack consciousness. Thought does not arise without the flux of being. The world changes around us, and the individual changes along with the world. We find ourselves always de-centered in a struggle between the individual and the world.

In "Of the inconsistency of our actions," Montaigne writes, "Nothing is harder for me than to believe in men's consistency, nothing easier than to believe in their inconsistency" (II: 1, 239; *V*, 332). Because human beings are so inconsistent, the multitude of actions that make up a life require an equal multitude of judgments (ibid., 241; *V*, 334). The *Essays* is such a long book because its subject is constantly changing, and

---

40   Tzvetan Todorov, *Imperfect Garden: The Legacy of Humanism*, trans. Carol Cosman (Princeton, NJ: Princeton University Press, 2002), 50.
41   The praise of Stefan Zweig, himself a great man of letters, is worth noting here. Zweig writes, "A hundred times, page after page, I have the impression when I turn to Montaigne that *nostra res agitur*, the sense that here has been thought, with far more clarity than I could ever muster, all that occupies the most profound recesses of my soul at this moment. Here is a 'you', in which my 'I' is reflected." Zweig, *Montaigne*, trans. Will Stone (London: Pushkin Press, 2015), 52.

each transformation requires a wholesale revision of judgment. For Montaigne, there is no fixed essence of the human species and nothing of the "human nature" that many of his contemporaries appealed to. Each member of the species is a Proteus. Man is an animal who wears a thousand masks. Erich Auerbach writes, "To [Montaigne's] mind, the essence is lost as soon as one detaches it from its momentary accidents. For this reason he must renounce an ultimate definition of himself or of man, for such a definition would of necessity have to be abstract."[42]

The claim that there is no essence of mankind is a direct rejection of the Hermetic doctrine that every individual carries the whole of the cosmos within himself or herself. This view of human changeableness shares much with that of Montaigne's near-contemporary, the Spanish humanist Juan Luis Vives (1493–1540). In Vives' "A Fable about Man", the human being is a performer on stage at the banquet of the gods. He is able to take on any semblance, that of plants or animals or even the gods themselves. The mask is what the gods most honor about man.[43] Shakespeare was voicing an idea prevalent in his time when he had his Jacque say, "All the world's a stage / And all the men and women merely players."[44] Even Descartes embraced the image of the mask when he wrote, "So far, I have been a spectator in this theatre which is the world, but I am now about to mount the stage, and I come forward masked."[45]

Although this changeability is a basic fact about the human species, it is also true that every individual exists within the same flux and has access to the same masks.[46] For Montaigne, as we have seen, "Each man bears the entire form of man's estate [*l'humaine condition*]" (*CE*, III: 2, 611; *V*, 805). Self-knowledge is knowledge of the human condition in general. It cannot shed light on the particular circumstances and experiences of another, but it can reveal much about the shared *form* of human existence, the framework within which we all live. In one sense, this view owes something to Augustine's *Confessions*. Augustine's question,

---

42 Auerbach, "L'humaine condition," 299.
43 Juan Luis Vives, "A Fable about Man," trans. Nancy Lenkeith. In *The Renaissance Philosophy of Man*, ed. Ernst Cassirer, Paul Oskar Kristeller and John Herman Randall, Jr. (Chicago: University of Chicago Press, 1948), 393.
44 William Shakespeare, *As You Like It*, II.vii.139–40.
45 René Descartes, "Early Writings," in *The Philosophical Writings of Descartes*, 1: 2. This is from a partial translation of Descartes' *Cogitationes privatae*.
46 Merleau-Ponty observes, "This man who wrote so well against reason, and showed that we can in no case get beyond opinion to see an idea face to face, has recourse to the *seed of universal reason embedded in every man who is not perverted*." "Reading Montaigne," 203.

"How then am I to seek for you, Lord?" is a universal question, not a question particular to himself. In recording how he turned inward and searched his memory in an attempt to discover God, Augustine is recommending the same procedure to all other inquirers. The *Confessions* is a universal autobiography, and as such a clear precedent for the *Essays*, though Montaigne never mentions the book.[47] In another sense, the *Essays* go far beyond the guiding question of the *Confessions*. It is not just the problem of the basis of individual faith that Montaigne addresses, but the question of the condition of humanity. The *Essays* of Montaigne are what Vico would call a *storia ideale eterna*, an ideal eternal history. Ideal because in its particulars it is a life not actually lived by any but Montaigne. It is nonetheless the blueprint for the eternal history of us all.

Because each individual bears the whole of mankind's estate, every woman and man is mankind in brief. Knowledge of the human condition requires only self-knowledge. Auerbach credits Montaigne with being the first to make this idea explicit: "In the study of his own random life Montaigne's sole aim is an investigation of the *humaine condition* in general; and with that he reveals the heuristic principle which we constantly employ—consciously or unconsciously, reasonably or unreasonably—when we endeavor to understand and judge the acts of others. ... We apply criteria to them which we have derived from our own lives and our own inner experience—so that the depth of our knowledge of men and of history depends upon the depth of our self-knowledge and the extent of our moral horizon."[48] Self-knowledge depends on a deep wealth of autobiographical memory. This requires an open sensitivity to oneself and a stark self-honesty; the hollow retention of information taught by the mnemotechnic can never be an instrument of self-knowledge. Vives writes, "Of little good would all these inventions have been if there had not been added, as the treasury of all things and for the safekeeping of these divine riches, a memory, the storehouse of all that we have enumerated. From religion and memory, foreknowledge is almost obtained, with the prophecy of the future, evidently a spark of that divine and immense science which perceives all future events as if they were present."[49] Montaigne's memory is just such a storehouse.

The memory of Montaigne is attuned to the inner form of personal experience, rather than to accidental superfluities like the proper names

---

47 Auerbach suggests that this may be because he "shrank from the comparison" to the great Church father. See "L'humaine condition," 300.
48 Ibid., 301–2.
49 Vives, "Fable," 392.

of his servants (*CE*, II: 17, 494; *V*, 650). His "nudity" in the *Essays* is effectual only because he does not stop at the accidental, cosmetic view of situations. This is the master key to self-knowledge. Sarah Bakewell observes, "Where Montaigne's memory did seem to work well, if he wanted it to, was in reconstructing personal experiences such as the riding accident [*CE*, II: 6, 268–72; *V*, 373–77]. Instead of resolving them into neat, superficial anecdotes, he could recover feelings from the inside—not perfectly, because the Heraclitean stream kept carrying him away, but very closely."[50] This reconstruction requires that the evaluative element of initial experience added by the imagination be annulled through forgetfulness, so that the core of the experience may be retained in a pure form.[51] Personal experience is then subject to the dialectic of judgment. This is the process we unraveled in the previous sub-section. This entirely inner knowledge then becomes the source of *universal* knowledge, but this is different from *cosmic* knowledge.

In Montaigne's application of memory, Camillo's theater is inverted. No longer does the single individual stand on the stage and look out. There are no sidereal signs, and no bundles of the speeches of Cicero. The idea is not that the person can attain a perfect recollection of the whole of the universe through the prompting of a few memory cues. It is true that the individual still stands on stage, but in Montaigne's version of the theater, all eyes gaze upon him or her. The inquirer is the object of inquiry, and the many disparate elements of his or her life as a whole, in all of its fluctuations, are laid out for the audience to behold. The more the individual can recollect, the more material appears on stage when the curtain is drawn back. This material can be reworked into new arrangements or realigned in a new order. In this ingenious process of transformation, we begin to glimpse something of the human condition, which we have known all along because it has already been *lived* by each and every human being.

In reference to Christophoro Giarda and the art of the Italian Renaissance, E. H. Gombrich writes, "Christianity debarred the philosopher from fully accepting this central view of Platonism according to which all knowledge is reminiscence; since God creates every soul on concep-

---

50 Bakewell, *How to Live*, 71. The story Montaigne tells of his horse-riding accident is noteworthy as perhaps the first phenomenological description of the experience of retrograde amnesia. See *CE*, 272; *V*, 377: "The last thing I was able to recover was the memory of the accident. ..."
51 The French word *oubly* (or *oubli*, in modern French) carries a much stronger sense of oblivion or complete annihilation than the English word "forgetting."

tion there is no place in its world picture for the *anamnese* of former states. Those who wanted to remain Platonists, therefore, were more or less driven to replace the memory of the individual by a theory of the memory of mankind."[52] Montaigne was not a dogmatic Platonist, though he does demonstrate a great admiration for Socrates. Nor was his Christianity entirely orthodox. The Vatican censor objected to a number of elements of the first edition of the *Essays*, though these were minor points like Montaigne's use of the word "fortune", his appeal to pagan poets, and his views on torture (*TJ*, 1166).[53] Montaigne did not amend his book. Nonetheless, Gombrich's claim speaks to the *Zeitgeist* within which Montaigne was writing. Montaigne's memory is not that of the Platonic soul, imbued *a priori* with knowledge of all things human and divine. It is instead a memory shared by all mankind, insofar as all mankind confronts the same general condition. It discovers knowledge *a posteriori*, but this knowledge is nonetheless universal because all humans partake of *l'humaine condition*. Because memory puts us in a relation of kinship to the whole of mankind, it is always ethical. Because experience never terminates, and is always subject to revisions, the ethical form of memory is *prudentia*.

---

52   E. H. Gombrich, *Symbolic Images: Studies in the Art of the Renaissance* (London: Phaidon, 1972), 150.
53   For a discussion of this censorship, see Frame, *Montaigne*, 217–18.

X: Writing and Memory

Before moving on from Montaigne, there remains another aspect of his philosophy that we must consider. Montaigne claims to use writing as an artificial memory, a supplement for the weakness of his natural memory. In this chapter, I will explore the relationship between writing and memory in the *Essays*.

Plato on writing

In the *Phaedrus*, Socrates tells a likely story about the origins of writing. The Egyptian god Theuth (understood by the Greek mind as Hermes) went before Thamus, king of the gods, to exhibit the many great arts he had invented. Theuth explained to Thamus the utility of each art, and Thamus either praised or criticized its invention. When Theuth arrived at the art of writing, he boasted that this would improve the memory of its practitioners: "I have discovered a potion for memory and for wisdom." Thamus responded, "Your affection for it has made you describe its effects as the opposite of what they are. In fact, it will introduce forgetfulness into the soul of those who learn it: they will not practice using their memory because they will put their trust in writing, which is external and depends on signs belonging to others, instead of trying to remember from the inside, completely on their own. You have not discovered a potion for remembering, but for reminding; you provide your students with the appearance of wisdom, not with its reality" (*Phaedr.*, 274d–275a).

For Plato, writing stands over and against memory. It is worth remembering that Plato claims to have never put down his true philosophy in writing.[1] The act of writing removes the matter from its temporality and makes it eternal. Whatever is once written down is preserved as it is for all time. Once the thing is eternal, there is no need to retain it in one's memory. We can return to it whenever we will, for it is always there outside of us, waiting to be taken up. For Plato, writing is a technique, and we have seen that technique and memory are always hostile to one another. In one sense, the externalized written word is mere *information*, which we considered in the fifth chapter.

---

1 "There does not exist, nor will there ever exist, any treatise of mine dealing therewith. For it does not at all admit of verbal expression like other studies, but, as a result of continued application to the subject itself and communion therewith, it is brought to birth in the soul on a sudden, as light that is kindled by a leaping spark, and thereafter it nourishes itself" (*Epist. VII*, 341c–d).

In another sense, however, writing can be a supplement for memory. Let us assume that the memory of the modern human, like the imagination, is not as finely developed as it was for past ages. There is a natural fragility to memory, a tendency to slip and stagger at times, even when *ars memoria* is deliberately cultivated. There is a natural chasm between the present moment and the desired recollection, and memory is not always able to bridge this gap with due haste and accuracy. When this is the case, writing may serve as a cue for the memory. The written word is the occasion for thought to adequately rediscover what it seeks and overcome failures of recollection. In this sense, writing is not a replacement for thought, as the computer is. It is instead a tool for amending the unfortunate lapses and failures of thought. All studies on the correlation between note-taking and retention support this.

The idea that memory requires supplementation is the foundational notion behind *ars memoriae*. Mnemotechnic systems are attempts to bridge the chasm between the present moment and memory with maximum ease and rapidity. The *loci* and imagery of these systems are a shorthand language, an inscripting of symbolism onto the mind itself. The cues that stand out when one mentally traverses one's memory place are of the same type as the brief notations an orator might write down to remember the thread of a speech. The only difference is that writing is symbolically one degree further removed from the ideas themselves. The graphic memory images suggested by the classical mnemotechnic bear some natural relationship to the thing to be recalled, whereas the characters of the written word do not.

It would be folly, as Plato saw, to substitute writing for memory, just as we should not mistake the art of memory for meaningful philosophical thought. He is also correct that the very existence of the practice of writing tends to debilitate memory. Nevertheless, we live in a world of writing and every new technique prohibits the thought of going back. If we are faithfully committed to "memory as philosophy," there is no contradiction in admitting writing as a tool for aiding and abetting the faultiness of memory. Let us consider Montaigne.

Montaigne's artificial memory

In "Of experience," Montaigne writes, "For lack of a natural memory I make one of paper, and as some new symptom occurs in my disease, I write it down. Whence it comes that at the present moment, when I have passed through virtually every sort of experience, if some grave stroke threatens me, by glancing through these little notes, disconnected like the Sibyl's leaves, I never fail to find grounds for comfort in some favorable prognostic from my past experience" (*CE*, III: 13, 837–38; *V*, 1092). This passage ostensibly refers to Montaigne's record of his medical ailments, but could refer to the *Essays* as a whole. Writing is Montaigne's supplement for his terrible memory. One of the purposes of the *Essays* is to function as an artificial memory of Montaigne's personal experiences, a treasury in which Montaigne can find some curative for whatever should ail him.

The "Sibyl's leaves" is an image taken from Virgil's *Aeneid*. The Cumaean Sibyl is the prophetess through whom Apollo reveals the future (*Aen.*, VI.9–12). Her leaves relate the complete wisdom of the god, but their order is random and chaotic. Virgil writes, "Whatever verses the maid has traced on leaves she arranges in order and stores away in the cave. These remain unmoved in their places and quit not their rank; but when at the turn of a hinge a light breeze has stirred them, and the open door scattered the tender foliage, never does she thereafter care to catch them, as they flutter in the rocky cave, nor to recover their places, nor to unite their verses; uncounselled, men depart, and loathe the Sibyl's seat" (*Aen.*, III.445–51).[2] If there is truly nothing new under the sun, then somewhere amongst Montaigne's many sibylline leaves—built up through the experience of a lifetime—is everything. Combing through these leaves of paper is the externalized act of combing through one's memory. One can imagine Montaigne referring, on the occasion of every cramp or stone, to a bundle of papers on the topic. The image is similar to that of the bundles of Cicero in Camillo's theater. However, in Montaigne's case, the leaves only concern the most personal elements of the spectator himself.

Nicolas Russell writes, "Montaigne constructs relationships between writing and another kind of memory: the author's own subjective memory of past experience. Cognitive scientists call this episodic memory, a kind of memory that allows an individual to travel mentally back in time to various moments in his or her own past."[3] This use of writing as a storehouse for episodic memory relates to all aspects of

---

2   The Sibyl's leaves appear at the end of Dante's *Divine Comedy*: "So doth the snow unstamp it to the sun, so to the wind on the light leaves was lost the Sibyl's wisdom." Dante Alighieri, *The Divine Comedy*, trans. John Aitken Carlyle, Thomas Okey, and Philip H. Wicksteed (New York: Vintage, 1959), *Paradiso*, XXXIII.64–66. Joyce responds to Dante at the end of *Finnegans Wake*: "My leaves have drifted from me. All. But one clings still." Joyce, *Finnegans Wake*, 628.
3   Nicolas Russell, *Transformations of Memory and Forgetting in Sixteenth-Century France* (Lanham, MD: University of Delaware Press, 2011), 96.

Montaigne's life, not just his illnesses. In "Of books," Montaigne writes, "To compensate a little for the treachery and weakness of my memory, so extreme that it has happened to me more than once to pick up again, as recent and unknown to me, books which I had read carefully a few years before ... I have adopted the habit for some time now of adding at the end of each book ... the time I finished reading it and the judgment I have derived of it as a whole, so that this may represent to me at least the sense and general idea I had conceived of the author in reading it" (*CE*, II: 10, 305; *V*, 418). He then transcribes some of these notes as examples for the reader. These examples show that what Montaigne records are his personal reactions to each book, rather than its stylistic devices or major arguments. He has little interest in recording what is actually within the book. He is much more concerned to record how the book relates to himself on an emotional level. It is the emotive element, I have argued, that flies at once from Montaigne's memory. His paper memory preserves these emotions and reactions so that they can be revisited at a later time.

Regarding the composition of the *Essays*, Montaigne writes, "I add, but I do not correct" (*CE*, III: 9, 736; *V*, 963) and, "I write my book for few men and for few years" (ibid., 751; *V*, 982). Montaigne's writing is sedimentary in a way that his memory is not. In the *Essays*, he piles judgment upon judgment, forever expanding the stock. He does not, however, correct or excise what has already been written. His composition exists as an undying record, outside of time. Even when his judgments change, the text is not amended because it would then lose its function as an artificial storehouse of past opinions. The movement of the *Essays* is a dialectic of memory that depends on past errors just as much as it depends on the most contemporary judgments at which Montaigne arrives. The *Essays* always display thought in motion. This is why the book is only meant as a temporary document, "for a few years"; Montaigne has faith that as the world turns, each of his judgments will be superseded.[4] Like Eliot's J. Alfred Prufrock, Montaigne is prepared

> For a hundred indecisions,
> And for a hundred visions and revisions,
> Before the taking of a toast and tea.[5]

---

4   C.f. Starobinski, *Montaigne in Motion*: "[Montaigne] moves away from change only to discover that his task is to recreate it and plunge himself back into it, at each new attempt with heightened awareness of the futility of both change and the hope of escaping it" (221).
5   T. S. Eliot, "The Love Song of J. Alfred Prufrock," in *Complete Poems and Plays*, 4.

This conscious self-revisionism is the mark of the philosophical character, and the most striking feature of the essay as a literary form. What is not philosophical in any meaningful sense is the habit of many professional philosophers of today to stand firm in their self-certainty. This is particularly true of those scholars who concern themselves primarily with political matters. In philosophical discourse, the limited applications of social justice tend to replace rich and open inquiries into the foundations moral philosophy. The sense of justice of these scholars, which is usually a product of deeply subjective reasons, tolerates no opposition. Matthew Arnold said in 1880 that poetry is the criticism of life. This is an interesting claim, but ultimately far too general to be of much use. Nonetheless, small thinkers continue to see philosophy as the criticism of life. What we learn implicitly from reading Montaigne is a lesson of the utmost value. There is no question that philosophy requires a preliminary stage in which all received opinions are subjected to criticism. However, it is not enough to stop at that point. The second preliminary stage requires that the critic then turn inward and criticize also his or her own most deeply help dogmas and opinions. This is the stage that most people never bother to reach. Actual philosophical thinking can only take place after both of these stages have been undertaken and exhausted.

To return to Montaigne's self-report of his artificial paper memory, several writers have recently seized this to argue that his writing project mirrors the architectural memory systems of the classical mnemonic. In "Three kinds of association," Montaigne describes his private library, in which he composed the *Essays*: "It is on the third floor of a tower; the first is my chapel, the second a bedroom and dressing room. ... The shape of my library is round, the only flat side being the part needed for my table and chair; and curving round me it presents at a glance all my books, arranged in five rows of shelves on all sides. It offers rich and free views in three directions, and sixteen paces of free space in diameter" (*CE*, III: 3, 629; *V*, 828). Most of the joists in this room were inscribed with Greek and Latin *sententiae*, citations that Montaigne liked to have in view as he walked about.[6] Prominent among these was a quotation from Terence: *Homo sum, humani a me nil alienum puto*.[7] Describing his method of composition in this library, Montaigne writes, "There I leaf through now one book, now another, without order and without plan, by

---

6   These *sententiae* are listed in *V*, lxvii–lxxii. The originals have been effaced, but replicas can be seen in the library today.
7   Frame, *Montaigne*, 120.

disconnected fragments. One moment I muse, another moment I set down or dictate, walking back and forth, these fancies of mine that you see here" (ibid.).

William Engel understands these passages as evidence that Montaigne "displays a well-developed sense of being able to create imaginary places within his own home."[8] His books, which rest on five rows of shelves (five being the key number for groupings in the *Ad Herennium*), can all be taken in at one glance. The three-windowed room is an architectural model of the three books of the *Essays*. The *sententiae* served as the spur for further invention by Montaigne. Engel views the entire tower library as a "memory palace," but he never develops the implications of this idea, or how this architectural basis manifests itself in the *Essays*, except to suggest that Montaigne "had in mind a symmetric arrangement for the order of his book."[9] Cynthia Israel suggests that the *Essays* depend on a "visual mnemonic plan" that "preceded the writing of the text. The discernment of these hidden structures requires that, while reading the text, the reader also construct a blueprint of the visual images or parallels which ... convey meaning not immediately evident without attempting to create such a blueprint."[10] She calls this blueprint a "hypertext." She also considers Montaigne's *Travel Journal* to be a series of memory places. In particular, she seizes on a grotto that he discovered between Scarperia and Florence (*TJ*, 1132), which she argues is a mental model for the *Essays*.[11]

These claims that Montaigne's composition embraces some version of *ars memoriae* are conjectural and assume an order and master plan of the *Essays* that is not apparent. Donald Frame has pointed out that, "In Book III the nearest thing to a pattern is that the chapters seem arranged in the order of their composition. The only one whose place appears unchangeable is the last, 'Of Experience,' whose final pages form a triumphant conclusion to Book III and the entire *Essais*."[12] I will go further than basing my counter-argument on the apparent lack of order in the *Essays*. While Montaigne's writing is tied closely to memory, it *cannot*, by

---

8   Engel, "Art of Memory," 43.
9   Ibid., 44–49. Engel does not take into account Montaigne's claim that his best thoughts occur to him spontaneously, "on horseback, at table, in bed, but mostly on horseback, where my thoughts range most widely" (*CE*, III: 5, 668; *V*, 876).
10 Israel, "Montaigne and Proust," 106.
11 Ibid., 105–7.
12 Frame, *Montaigne's* Essais, 76.

the very nature of Montaigne's literary project, be an expression of *ars memoria*.

We will recall that originally, the primary utility of the mnemotechnic was its efficacy for holding together the thread of an oration. The classical texts that recommend the art of memory—*De oratore, Rhetorica ad Herennium*, and the *Institutio oratoria*—are all textbooks of rhetoric. The reason the mnemotechnic was theoretically useful for orators is because the complete speech must be composed prior to its delivery. The orator knows what point he wants to reach, and the art of rhetoric is the invention of the most expedient means to that end. The selection of *topoi* is made by considering what commonplaces the judges will accept, and which are most applicable to the desired conclusions. The orator then guides the judges from beginning to end. All of the parts of the complete speech stand in a natural order. If the speech is composed well, the orator need only recollect this order, and the technique of places and images is able to facilitate this recollection.

For Montaigne, it is not a polished speech, but *l'humaine condition* that is at issue. The human condition is not yet finished or complete. It makes its own path through the vicissitudes of change. The myriad relationships in which the individual stands to the outside world are never final; his or her judgments are always open to the influence of new experiences. Nor can we begin from a neat *topos*; we fall into the world pellmell, *in media res*. For Montaigne, there is not a proper order of human institutions. Instead, there are simply human things, human experiences, human situations, and the work of philosophers is to discover or invent the proper arrangements of these phenomena while on the run. In the *Essays*, we find contradictions and frivolities alongside profound observations, because lived experience is at times contradictory and at times frivolous. The mnemotechnic is a technique, and "memory as philosophy" is opposed to technique. The decision to stand naked before the world is a decision to forego all artifice.

Peter Kanelos has suggested that the architectural scene of Montaigne's memory is not his library, or the road from Rome to Loreto, but the Cumaean grotto suggested by the image of the Sibyl's leaves. This is a different grotto than that suggested by Israel. He writes, "In the *Aeneid*, the Sibyl resided in a 'hollow grotto'; it is here as well that Montaigne has decided to store his remembrances. With little faith in his own recollection, he deposits in the *Essais* the fragments of his experience. ... Only by leaving the dissonant parts of his character side by side, without apology, can Montaigne hope to portray himself as he is, in flesh and bone."[13] This is to say that the setting in which Montaigne mentally walks, pasting his memories, is a dimly lit cave, full of irregular crannies and protuberances. The choice of such a *locus* would violate every rule of the classical mnemotechnic. Every gust of wind upsets the order of what is inside. For Kanelos, the *Essays* are not the presentation of the speech recollected by walking through this grotto. The *Essays* are the grotto itself. Montaigne never imagined his work on any sort of locational terms, but the image of the Cumaean grotto is nonetheless *a propos* as a sort of anti-architectural image. Like Montaigne's memory, the grotto is a monstrous product of nature rather than a cultivated and well-organized palace. There is poetic truth to Kanelos' claim, though it lacks existential truth.

Montaigne's final word on his writing reveals how he conceives of his relationship to the origins of western wisdom. He writes, "If anyone tells me that it is degrading to the Muses to use them only as a plaything and a pastime, he does not know, as I do, the value of pleasure, play, and pastime. I would almost say that any other aim is ridiculous. I live from day to day, and, without wishing to be disrespectful, I live only for myself; my purposes go no further" (III: 3, 629; *V*, 829). Montaigne writes under the auspices of the Muses, the daughters of Mnemosyne, but he uses them playfully. His ends are pleasure and pastime. The value of play is a large part of the moral teaching of the essays; it ties in with Montaigne's other lesson, the ease of virtue. The Muses themselves, whose essence is forgetfulness of evils, are prone to speak truly to a writer with such a keen sense of playfulness. Montaigne has no concern for the gaps in his memory; he does not want to remember well. He supplements this lack through a paper memory, but the very gaps in his reminiscence are necessary for his circular dialectic of judgment.

In his *Travel Journal*, Montaigne describes a merchant he met in La Villa, the description of whom could be a description of Montaigne himself: "There came to the baths in these days a merchant from Cremona, living in Rome. He was suffering from many extraordinary infirmities. Nevertheless he talked and walked, and led quite a jolly life, as far as I could see. His principle failing, he said, was a weak head: he had lost his memory so completely that when eating he never remembered what had been put before him at table. If he left the house to go on some business of his, he had to go back to the house ten times to ask where he was to

---

13 Kanelos, "Montaigne and the Grotto," 16.

go" (*TJ*, 1216). This man's weakness of memory is so extreme that he cannot recall the simplest details of his everyday life, just as Montaigne admits that he himself often cannot keep the thread of a speech, remember the names of his servants, or recall where he laid his purse (*CE*, II: 17, 493–94; *V*, 650–51). And yet Montaigne emphasizes that this merchant "led quite a jolly life." Forgetful of evils like the Muses, the poor man must have been blessed by their favor.

XI: Memory versus Modernity

Montaigne's dialectic of memory never leads one to a position of certainty, nor does it claim to do so. His acceptance of incompleteness and his openness to revision stand over and against that scientific approach that promises apodictic truth. In this regard, Montaigne stands very much against the main currents of the intellectual world of the sixteenth century. Montaigne's great virtue is eloquence, which is always tied to *ars topica*. This is the art of finding the middle term in argument, the art of rhetorical invention. *Ars critica*, on the other hand, is the instrument that promises the "true speech," but it nullifies eloquence.

Descartes, whose work is in large part a response to Montaigne, substitutes his critical philosophy for classical eloquence. Certainty becomes the object of philosophical inquiry, and *mathesis universalis* becomes the ideal of modernity.[1] Certainty is always preferable to plausibility for literal-minded thinkers, even though there is a profound difference between certainty and truth. We should remember Vico's distinction between the two: "Truth arises when the mind is in conformity with the order of things; the certain arises when the consciousness is secure from doubt." He also writes, "Falsehood is as far from the doubtful as the certain is from the true. If these two things are not carefully distinguished, given that many true things are doubtful, it might appear that a thing can be certain and doubtful at the same time. On the other hand, since many false things are held to be certain, they might be held to be both false and true."[2] To have one's consciousness free from doubt *may* be a sign that one's mind is also in conformity with the order of things. It may also be a sign that one has given up inquiring into the first principles of things and has left off contemplating at the stage of sense-certainty. The certain is not of the same order as the true.

For Kant, *ars critica* is likewise supreme, and it takes its most complete and systematic form in his three critiques. Kant sees so little value in eloquence or the classical *ars topica* that he writes, "Rhetoric, insofar as by that is understood the art of persuasion, i.e., of deceiving by

---

1   René Descartes, *Rules for the Direction of the Mind*, in *Philosophical Writings*, rule IV: "There must be a general science which explains all the points that can be raised concerning order and measure irrespective of the subject-matter, and that this science should be termed *mathesis universalis*" (1: 19).
2   Giambattista Vico, *Universal Law*, Book 1: *On the One Principle and One End of Universal Law*, trans. John D. Schaeffer, in *New Vico Studies* 21 (2003): 50.

means of beautiful illusion (as an *ars oratoria*), and not merely skill in speaking, is a dialectic, which borrows from the art of poetry only as much as is necessary to win minds over to the advantage of the speaker before they can judge and to rob them of their freedom." In a footnote, he adds, "Eloquence and well-spokenness (together, rhetoric) belong to beautiful art; but the art of the orator (*ars oratoria*), as the art of using the weakness of people for one's own purposes (however well intentioned or even really good these may be) is not worthy of any *respect* at all."[3]

In the philosophical period that begins with Descartes and continues linearly through Kant and his followers, criticism—which subjects all propositions, however commonsensical, to reflective consideration— became the dominant instrument of philosophy. Grappling with the problems articulated by Descartes, and using the method of reflection, Spinoza was led to abolish free will, Malebranche to abolish natural causes, and Berkeley to abolish matter altogether. At the same time, philosophy moved closer to the hard sciences. In Descartes' image of philosophy as a tree, metaphysics is the roots, but physics is the trunk and the branches are the practical sciences, medicine, mechanics, and morals. The utility of philosophy is seated in these practical sciences.[4] An art of memory is no longer necessary if philosophy is concerned only with fact and not eloquence, only with reflection on the matter at hand and not contemplation of what was, is, and shall be. Descartes writes, in his *Cogitationes privatae*, "It is clear there is no need at all for memory in any of the sciences," and he calls *ars memoria* a "*nebulonis arti*," a scoundrel art.[5]

In this chapter, I will investigate some of the intellectual reasons that memory fell into philosophical disfavor in the "modern" period. There were many forces at work even during the height of *ars memoriae* in the Renaissance that would come to undermine the connection between philosophy and memory. The general trend of the era was the rejection of tradition and authority in favor of individualism. The changing tenor of the European intellect, deeply shaken by the Copernican Revolution, the Protestant Reformation, and the overthrow of tradition political forms, was confronted with a host of new problems. It is no surprise that it sought new methods in an attempt to find solutions to these problems. It is incumbent upon us now to bring these solutions under review. In the

---

3   Immanuel Kant, *Critique of Judgment*, trans. Paul Guyer and Eric Matthews (New York: Cambridge University Press, 2000), 204–5.
4   René Descartes, *Principles of Philosophy*, in *Philosophical Writings*, 1: 186.
5   Descartes, *Cogitationes privatae*, 230 (my translation), partially quoted in the introduction.

following chapter, I will examine the particular significance of Descartes and his intellectual children in removing the classical conception of memory from philosophical discourse. Was it right for philosophy to distance itself from memory, or was this based on spurious reasons and misunderstandings? In the final two chapters, I will turn to Hegel as the voice of resistance to modernity's war on the memory tradition.

The intellectual forces of modernity

It would require a work of several volumes to thoroughly analyze the ideas that dominated philosophical and scientific thought in the two hundred year period between Montaigne and Hegel (roughly 1600–1800). Besides this, many others have written such treatises. I will select only a few of the larger revolutions of modernity to consider, those that I believe had the greatest influence in undermining the importance of memory for philosophy.

It is worth noting in advance that part of the reason memory as philosophy fell into disfavor had to do with the synthesis of the speculative and technical lines of the tradition. Only the former was ever truly philosophical, and it was the speculative line that informed all of the earliest and greatest teachers of the west—Plato, Aristotle, Plutarch, and Augustine. The technical line was considered a useful supplement for memory, even by Aristotle. Speculative thought requires a wealth of easily accessed knowledge with which to work. However, even the ancient teachers of the technical art of memory understood it as a tool for making the retention of certain things easier, not the primary cognitive instrument of philosophical speculation. Its main value for Cicero and Quintilian was oratorical, not philosophical, and the Dominican fathers (and Dante as well) viewed it as a useful means of recollecting one's Christian duty.

The Renaissance project of joining the two lines led to obvious excesses and the appearance of charlatanism. Descartes' term, *nebulonis arti*, is not entirely inappropriate when only these excesses are considered. Despite Camillo's great fame, there were few who ever took the divine pretenses of his theater seriously. And Bruno, as great a mind as he had for astronomical and metaphysical contemplation, could never successfully separate his memory arts from black magic. Montaigne was able to separate the two lines in his thinking, and dismiss the technical side while retaining the speculative side. The result was a profound ethical doctrine. However, Montaigne is an aberration. Popular thought could not so readily make this distinction, and after the burning of Bruno the tradition of memory as philosophy seemed at best a quaint Hermetic idea and at worst the darkest sort of devilry, the attempt to make gods out of men through some sort of recollective sorcery. It was a mistake to attempt to make one doctrine out of two separate traditions. However, the monstrosity of the child need not reflect ill on the parents.

With this in mind, let us now proceed to examine the spirit of the "modern" age.

The printing press

Johannes Gutenberg introduced movable type to Europe around 1439, and his printing press changed the face of the world. Access to the written word, whether concerning things divine or human, had always been the privilege of very few Europeans. Monasteries, the primary source of hand-copied texts, were generally well-supplied with books, but, as we have seen in the case of William of Ockham, it was not particularly difficult to deprive even a friar in convent of all reading material. Texts copied by hand, because of the energy needed to produce them, were exceedingly scarce, and usually unreliable. Gutenberg's invention made it possible for a large number of identical texts to be reproduced in a short time and at a much lower cost than previously. This is not to say that the commoners of Europe became literate all at once. It took some time for the effects of the printing press to be felt. However, it did become possible for anyone with adequate means to at least potentially have access to all of the received wisdom of the world. Once this was possible, it was not long before it would have a leveling effect upon both church and state.

I do not want to defend the more extreme conclusions of Marshall McLuhan; it is by no means clear to me that schizophrenia is a consequence of literacy and therefore proliferated by the Gutenberg revolution.[6] However, McLuhan is correct in suggesting that literacy changes our mental processes by altering the ratios between our senses. He writes, "If a technology is introduced either from within or from without a culture, and if it gives new stress or ascendancy to one or another of our senses, the ratio among all of our senses is altered. ... Any sense when stepped up to high intensity can act as an anesthetic for other senses."[7] What he means is that a sudden change in the reception of data from primarily auditory sources to primarily visual sources (that is, the written

---

6 Marshall McLuhan, *The Gutenberg Galaxy* (New York: Signet, 1969), 32–34.
7 Ibid., 35.

word) has substantial effects on human cognition and its faculties. If we consider the first books printed by Gutenberg's press—Aelius Donatus's textbook of rhetoric, *Ars minor*;[8] the famous "Gutenberg Bible"; and Cicero's *De officiis*—it is clear that either Gutenberg valued the teaching of eloquence and religion above all else, or else he thought that his readers would be most likely to value these subjects. What he failed to realize was that spoken eloquence becomes far less relevant in a world dominated by print.

In a certain sense, the effects of the advent of the printing press were only an extension of effects that had begun much earlier with the advent of writing. In the previous chapter, we saw that Plato was highly skeptical of the art of writing, and that he believed it necessarily served to hasten the deterioration of memory. In the time of Plato, very little was written. The astounding thing about his criticism of writing is that it was made prior to the age of the computer, prior to the constant access we have today to a panoply of digital search engines at the touch of a button. The printing press did not instantly transform civilization into the world we live in today. It did, however, accelerate the process of transformation. It made it possible for the everyman to discover the wisdom of the sages without having been born into the right social caste. It also made it possible for the everyman to discover limitless information, and to mistake information for wisdom.

By putting so much information at the disposal of all, the printing press destroyed most of the *raison d'être* of the expansive powers of memory so necessary and so esteemed in the middle ages and earlier times. Vico has asserted, as a philological truth, that the first people always have strong memories.[9] One had to cultivate the power of recollection in order to retain all that was needful for life. If one was not able to recollect something, there was no way to revisit it, no artificial memory in letters. Today, the things we need to know for our respective occupations are contained somewhere in our books or, more vulgarly, on our browser histories. We are not ruined if we cannot recall them on command. For the pre-Gutenberg person, perhaps he or she could write down a few things of the utmost importance if he or she happened to be literate. For the most part, one faced the world with nothing but one's own mind. A cultivated memory was necessary not just for orators and philosophers,

---

8   See Jürgen Leonhardt, *Latin: Story of a World Language*, trans. Kenneth Kronenberg (Cambridge, MA: Belknap Press, 2013), 99.
9   Vico, *New Science*, §819.

but for clergy, for shopkeepers, for artisans and tradesmen of all stripes. For the post-Gutenberg person, why bother to remember anything at all? The physician, the lawyer, and the merchant all have the books of their trades on their shelves. Today, it is doubtful that these books have even been opened.

The printing press also had several unintended consequences. As the production of books became cheaper and less laborious, book merchants were able to increase their profits. However, the initial market for books was necessarily small, limited to the educated elite who could read Greek or Latin or Hebrew. To expand the field of potential patrons, books had to be translated into vernacular languages. The commercial side of book-printing thus led to the growth of a market for translators. The accessibility of these translations vitiated the need that all scholars once had to seriously pursue philological studies. There was no longer a need to engage deeply with the language and culture of ancient Athens in order to begin to confront Plato. Plato now comes to us speaking our own idiom. With this decline in philology, so too did historical memory deteriorate. Today, we find ourselves entirely at the mercy of the translators and editors.

The Protestant Reformation

Another of the unintended consequences of the Gutenberg press was the doubt thrown upon the teachings of the Catholic Church. Printing allowed universal access to Scripture, which had once been nearly monopolized by the clergy. Of course, most of Europe was at the time unable to make sense of the Latin of the Vulgate Bible printed by Gutenberg, but the intellectual elite of the continent could now read it for themselves. What they found was not always consistent with what they heard from the mouths of the spiritual fathers. It is well known that the clarion call of the reformers was to accept the authority of Scripture alone.

It was Martin Luther who best exemplified this position. In 1521, Luther appeared before the Diet of Worms to answer for certain heretical views, the Emperor Charles V presiding. Amongst other views that had aroused the Church, Luther had seriously questioned the legitimacy of the pope and the legitimacy of most of the Holy Sacraments of the Church.[10] At the imperial diet, Luther affirmed authorship of his books and reaffirmed his views. He said that he could recant nothing without a

---

10   See Diarmaid MacCulloch, *The Reformation: A History* (New York: Penguin, 2005), 124–27.

conviction from "scripture or plain reason (for I believe neither in Pope nor councils alone)."[11]

This view was developed in many of Luther's writings, particularly his 1525 diatribe against Erasmus, *De servo arbitrio*. Here, Luther proclaims against the authority of the Church, "The Word of God and the traditions of men fight each other in implacable opposition. God and Satan are personally involved in this same conflict."[12] Later, "Men's ordinances cannot be observed together with the Word of God, because the former bind consciences and the latter looses them. The two things are as much opposed to each other as fire and water."[13] Not only is Scripture the primary source of spiritual truth, it is the *only* legitimate source. The traditional teachings of the Church and the popes are placed on a level with the will of Satan. In Luther's teaching, the two are utterly opposed and do not coincide whatsoever. Not only is Scripture the only source of truth, but Luther says "of the whole of Scripture that I do not allow any part of it to be called obscure. ... The word of God is to us a lamp shining in a dark place."[14] Scripture is always clear and never subject to subjective interpretation. The three intellectual lights that Luther allows are "the light of nature, the light of grace, and the light of glory."[15] This is a reaffirmation of his declaration at Worms that Scripture and plain reason are alone the proper guides of religion.

Luther substituted these two items, Scripture and plain reason, for the authority and tradition of the Church. This view was not unique to Luther; it was the central article of faith of most of his fellow early reformers, however they may have disagreed on doctrine. Because of the force of their characters and the simple reason behind their position, Protestantism spread rapidly throughout Europe and shaped the political climate of the west for more than a century.

What is relevant for our inquiry is the impact that this had on the memory tradition. It is evident that the dogmas of Protestantism did not encourage the cultivation of philosophical memory. If the whole of Christian faith is contained in Scripture, and Scripture is accessible to everyone, then all one must do is read one's Good Book. The book is always there, and natural reason is sufficient to engage it. One need re-

---

11 Quoted at ibid., 127.
12 Martin Luther, *The Bondage of the Will*, trans. J. I. Packer and O. R. Johnston (Grand Rapids, MI: Baker Academic, 1957), 93.
13 Ibid., 97.
14 Ibid., 129.
15 Ibid., 317.

member nothing more. The Catholic Church demanded obedience to tradition, and tradition is memory. Proper performance of rituals and services require internalized recollection. The Catholic must remember the edicts of the Councils and the lives and doings of the saints. The intricacies of the varieties of sin and punishment require the graphic imagery of Dante's *Inferno* to emblazon them on our mind. The myriad duties and responsibilities of the pious Christian demand a vast storehouse of *memoria*. This is why St. Thomas and St. Albert encouraged the cultivation of trained memories.

Nor does Protestantism tend to embrace the Augustinian conception of memory as the means by which the individual searches for God. Seeking God is no longer a desperate matter, as it is for Augustine. Every schoolchild knows the truth about God, which is impressed upon the soul. In his *Institutio Christianae religionis*, John Calvin writes, "All men of sound judgment will therefore hold, that a sense of Deity is indelibly engraven on the human heart. ... This is not a doctrine which is first learned at school, but one as to which every man is, from the womb, his own master; one which nature herself allows no individual to forget, though many, with all their might, strive to do so."[16] For Calvin, the knowledge of God is suppressed by ignorance, superstition, and human weakness. This language is far from the longing "How then am I to seek for you, Lord?" of Augustine.

I do not mean to defend the abuses and excesses of the Catholic Church or to undermine Protestantism. I only mean to point out that the central doctrines of Protestantism do not require one to care much about memory. Scripture and reason are sufficient for piety. Catholicism demands much more of one's recollection, for better or worse. The Catholic does not live in the moment, nor can the Catholic exercise his or her own judgment in spiritual matters. The whole weight of the collective past bears down upon the faith, and encourages a robust memory of that past. Judgments are received from tradition, and the cohesiveness of the group is at least somewhat a function of recollection.[17]

---

16 John Calvin, *Institutes of the Christian Religion*, trans. Henry Beveridge (Grand Rapids, MI: Eerdmans, 1989), 44–45.
17 We might wonder what Émile Durkheim would have said about this view of the cohesion of Catholicism having to do with the common memory of tradition. For Durkheim, this cohesion of the Catholic community and the consequent feeling of belonging to something larger than oneself are responsible for the lower suicide rates among Catholics than Protestants. See Durkheim, *Suicide*, trans. John A. Spaulding and George Simpson (New York: The Free Press, 1979), bk. 2, chap. 2.

The scientific revolution

The influence of the developments in the physical sciences on the philosophical thought of the seventeenth and eighteenth centuries is well-documented. The discoveries of Copernicus, Kepler, Galileo, Huysmans, Newton, and others, shook and finally destroyed the ancient hold of Aristotle over the western conception of the natural world. I refer both to the experimental discoveries of previously unknown laws and facts of nature, as well as the discovery of new instruments and methods of observation. It is without hyperbole that Whitehead refers to the seventeenth century as "the century of genius."[18]

One of the effects of the Copernican Revolution was the rise of a mathematical conception of the universe. This had a profound impact on philosophical conceptions. Whitehead writes, "The great characteristic of the mathematical mind is its capacity for dealing with abstractions; and for eliciting from them clear-cut demonstrative trains of reasoning, entirely satisfactory so long as it is those abstractions which you want to think about. The enormous success of the scientific abstractions, yielding on the one hand matter with its simple location in space and time, on the other hand mind, perceiving, suffering, reasoning, but not interfering, has foisted onto philosophy the task of accepting them as the most concrete rendering of fact."[19] For Whitehead, this mathematical conceptualization has "ruined" modern philosophy, this "misplaced concreteness" resulting in three extreme lines of thought: the dualists (exemplified by Descartes) and two species of monists, idealists and materialists.[20]

Complementing the metaphysical assumptions drawn from the mathematical view of reality, the new sciences also suggested a mechanistic view of the universe. Physics and astronomy had discovered that the natural world could be understood in terms of the laws of mechanics. Human beings are certainly a part of the natural world. The developing science of motion was bound to eventually infiltrate the realm of voluntary motion. For Descartes, animal movement could be understood by the laws of simple mechanics. However, it soon became usual practice for philosophers to reduce even the behavior of the human individual to mechanistic laws. We see this view informing the work of Pierre Gassendi, the deterministic psychology of Hobbes, and the 1751 treatise

---

18 Alfred North Whitehead, *Science and the Modern World* (New York: Free Press, 1953), ch. 3.
19 Ibid., 55.
20 Ibid.

L'homme machine of Julien de La Mettrie. For La Mettrie, man is simply a complex machine following the laws of mechanics: "Thus the soul is merely a vain term of which we have no idea. ... Given the slightest principle of movement, animate bodies will have everything they need to move, feel, think, repent and, in a word, behave in the physical sphere and in the moral sphere which depends on it."[21]

From the standpoint of the mechanistic philosopher, memory could only have been of interest as a function of physico-organic movements in the brain. Aristotle had privileged the functions of the mind in *De anima*, but now they were reduced to matter in motion. If memory is nothing more than the output of a complex machine, following certain formulae and principles, then there is nothing very significant about it. We will explore how far Descartes held this view to be accurate in the following chapter. More interesting to the modern intellectual would be the anatomy of the *organ* of memory. Galileo, in a 1615 letter to the Grand Duchess Christina, writes, "The eyes of an idiot perceive little by beholding the external appearance of a human body, as compared with the wonderful contrivances which a careful and practiced anatomist or philosopher discovers in that same body when he ... seeks the seat of the vital faculties, notes and observes the admirable structure of the sense organs, and (without ever ceasing in his amazement and delight) contemplates the receptacles of the imagination, the memory, and the understanding."[22] That is to say, the mechanistic philosopher hopes by the eventual growth of neuroscience to reduce memory, imagination, and understanding to mechanistic principles.

It is also pertinent to consider the scientific method of the seventeenth century. This method was best stated by Galileo in his 1623 treatise, *Il saggiatore*. This treatise was part of a long controversy occasioned by the comets of 1618. Galileo used the opportunity to attack the Jesuit Orazio Grassi's scholastic dogmatizing from authority, which was the common scientific practice of the day. Galileo writes, "I discern in Sarsi [Grassi] a firm belief that in philosophizing it is essential to support oneself upon the opinion of some celebrated author, as if when our minds are not wedded to the reasoning of some other person they ought to re-

---

21 Julien Offray de La Mettrie, *Machine Man and Other Writings*, trans. Ann Thomson (New York: Cambridge University Press, 1996), 26
22 Galileo Galilei, *Discoveries and Opinions of Galileo*, trans. Stillman Drake (New York: Doubleday, 1957), 196–97.

main completely barren and sterile."[23] This tendency was characteristic of scientists in the middle ages who hesitated to contradict the authority of Aristotle. The principle of *ipse dixit* stood in place of investigation. The new scientists radically believed that the only adequate source of knowledge about nature was first-hand observation of nature itself.

With regard to his own method, Galileo writes, "Philosophy is written in this grand book—I mean the universe—which stands continually open to our gaze, but it cannot be understood unless one first learns to comprehend the language and interpret the characters in which it is written. It is written in the language of mathematics, and its characters are triangles, circles, and other geometrical figures, without which it is humanly impossible to understand a single word of it; without these, one is wandering about in a dark labyrinth."[24] Only through experimentation and observation can one discover truth in natural science. This truth is inherently mathematical. The method of physics is therefore to observe phenomena and comprehend them in terms of *mathesis universalis*, the language of mathematics.

The significance of this change in the spirit of the times is similar to that brought about by the Protestant Reformation. For the latter, the only authority is Scripture, which each may investigate for himself or herself. Church tradition is of no authority and should not inform spirituality. In the scientific revolution, tradition and authority are likewise disavowed. Nature is an open book that stands before the investigator. The only sources of scientific insight are experimentation and observation, which are matters of the present time. The scholastic master of physics had to have a memory full of the teachings of Aristotle and all those sanctioned sages of natural history that had come before. The new scientists shattered that paradigm. The Galilean physicist had need only for a telescope and human wit.

Modern and contemporary science have little interest in the ideas and paradigms that have preceded the present moment. Science operates along the lines of technique, which we investigated in Chapter 5. If a scientific idea or worldview is superseded by one more useful for whatever the ends of the inquiry may be, then the old model is fully dead. Only the philosopher of science or the antiquarian cares to preserve the older models of the universe. Of course, Thomas Kuhn's insight that historical

---

23 Galilei, *The Assayer*, in *The Controversy of the Comets of 1618*, trans. Stillman Drake and C.D. O'Malley (Philadelphia: University of Pennsylvania Press, 1960), 183.
24 Ibid., 183–84.

studies of science are necessary to inform the present image of science is true, but it is of little significance to practicing scientists.[25] This disconnect from history and tradition leaves the scientist in a position of indifference toward memory.

The burgeoning sciences of the Renaissance and seventeenth century were not altogether hostile to memory. They allowed it a role, though not one of great significance. For Leonardo da Vinci, the faculty of memory was important for enabling us to perceive the "passage of time,"[26] though not for transmitting authority. Francis Bacon (despite his criticisms of *ars memoriae*) encouraged classification systems as "an invaluable mnemonic aid."[27] The purely technical art of memory was widely embraced as a useful tool.[28] As the quantity of scientific information increased, one can easily imagine the expanded need for systematic classification, and the connection such practices might have with the Ciceronian art of memory. Producing a work like the taxonomy of Linnaeus' *Systema naturae* would certainly require a well-trained, deliberately ordered memory. However, for the real work of science—the observation of natural phenomena—memory was not at all necessary.

The rise of democracy

The seventeenth and eighteenth centuries also saw in Europe the rise of a political spirit best characterized by the French motto *liberté, égalité, fraternité*. The tendency toward democracy was informed by those currents of modern thought we have already discussed, namely the printing press, the Protestant Reformation, and the scientific revolution. The first severed the average citizen's dependence on the state as the dispensary of knowledge and truth. The second encouraged individualism and self-reliance, both of which are inimical to monarchy. The third, by overthrowing the classical hierarchical conception of the universe, also brought into question the classical model of the state, which was often presented as the image of the celestial hierarchy.

---

25 See Thomas S. Kuhn, *The Structure of Scientific Revolutions* (Chicago: University of Chicago Press, 1962), ch. 1.
26 Quoted by Eugenio Garin in *Science and Civic Life in the Italian Renaissance*, trans. Peter Munz (Garden City, NY: Anchor Books, 1969), 64.
27 Paolo Rossi, *The Birth of Modern Science*, trans. Cynthia De Nardi Ipsen (Malden, MA: Blackwell, 2000), 180–81.
28 See Gopal P. Sarma, "The Art of Memory and the Growth of the Scientific Method," *Interdisciplinary Description of Complex Systems* 13 (2015): 373–96, and chapter 5 of Rossi, *Logic and Memory* ("Artificial Memory and the New Scientific Method: Ramus, Bacon, Descartes.").

Of course, the seventeenth and eighteenth centuries were in a strictly factual sense the age of the divine right of kings. This was the age of the majesty of the Sun King. Intellectually, one can find the supreme rights of the sovereign defended by Hobbes, Robert Filmer, Jacques-Bénigne Bossuet, and others. Nonetheless, from at least the time of the foundation of the Dutch Republic under William of Orange in 1581, there ran a serious counter-current of political thought, one that would reach its crescendo in the bloody revolutions at the end of the eighteenth century.

In his *Second Treatise of Civil Government*, John Locke declared that the purpose of government was to protect and serve the needs and hopes of the people, and that as soon as government failed to do so it was no longer legitimate. Earlier thinkers had argued that sovereignty could do as it pleased, since there was no higher authority to which the people could appeal. For Locke, to the question, "Who shall be Judge?" the answer is the people themselves. He writes, "If a Controversie arise betwixt a Prince and some of the People, in a matter where the Law is silent, or doubtful, and the thing be of great Consequence, I should think the proper *Umpire*, in such a case, should be the Body of the *People*."[29] The people are always the foundation and object of government, and therefore retain the final word on how they are governed. If they find the actions of their leaders to be unacceptable, it remains the inalienable prerogative of the people to dissolve the government.

Locke's thinking hinges on his notion of the state of nature. The accepted wisdom was that life in the state of nature was "solitary, poor, nasty, brutish, and short."[30] To renounce civil government, however oppressive, was to return oneself to this savage state of nature, something that should be avoided at all costs. For Locke, the state of nature is much more benign. Far from being a state of license, it is governed by natural law. "The *State of Nature* has a Law of Nature to govern it, which obliges everyone: And Reason, which is that Law, teaches all Mankind, who will but consult it, that being all equal and independent, no one ought to harm another in his Life, Health, Liberty, or Possessions."[31] It is fraught with danger, no doubt, and human beings join together politically for the sake of the mutual protection of our natural rights (life, liberty, property).

---

29   John Locke, *Two Treatises of Government*, ed. Peter Laslett (Cambridge: Cambridge University Press, 2009), 427.
30   Thomas Hobbes, *Leviathan*, ed. J.C.A. Gaskin (New York: Oxford University Press, 1996), I.xiii, 84.
31   Locke, *Two Treatises*, 271.

When those rights fail to be protected, or are actively transgressed by the government itself, there is no longer any reason to retain the government. Locke was not the first modern philosopher to encourage the political primacy of the people. However, it was Locke who best exemplified and gave voice to the burgeoning spirit of his times. Renaissance humanists were acutely aware of the successful democratic *poleis* of ancient Greece and admired classical republicanism. Amongst those humanists, Machiavelli's writing certainly advocated the foundation of an Italian republic. The Old Testament Hebrews also served as a model of republicanism for those unhappy with the hegemony of the Church who sought a theological precedent. The egalitarian tendencies of Protestantism pointed in this direction as well. Initially, none of these models suggested pure democracies; the idea was to limit the powers of the monarch and increase popular participation in government.[32] However, this tendency toward liberty, equality, and fraternity was part of a general spiritual transformation in Europe. William Bouwsma has called it the "general shift ... from hierarchy to balance as the basic principle of order."[33] All of the revolutions we have so far considered evince this trend. With the new influx of knowledge into Europe (which is what is meant by Enlightenment), the old monolithic models of power and authority lost their grasp on the individual, and were gradually replaced by more egalitarian, democratic institutions. Later thinkers like Rousseau and Burke would cast serious doubts on whether this trend was for the best, but their scepticism was unable to halt the march of progress.[34]

Alexis de Tocqueville demonstrates just how strong this tendency to shift from hierarchy to balance had become at the time of the French Revolution. What Tocqueville found so surprising about the French Revolution was that it occurred during a period of history in which France had made enormous strides in terms of national prosperity. The standard of living had been steadily increasing, not decreasing, for the average French citizen.[35] Along with the general material prosperity, Louis XVI also attempted to alleviate some of the excessive burdens placed on the French citizens by the machine of the state. This egalitarian undertaking

---

32 See William J. Bouwsma, *The Waning of the Renaissance: 1550–1640* (New Haven, CT: Yale University Press, 2002), 95.
33 Ibid., 96.
34 See Leo Strauss, *Natural Right and History* (Chicago: University of Chicago Press, 1968), ch. 6.
35 Alexis de Tocqueville, *The Old Régime and the Revolution in France*, trans. Stuart Gilbert (Garden City, NY: Doubleday Anchor, 1955), 174–75.

was the great mistake made by the king. Tocqueville writes, "The most perilous moment for a bad government is when it seeks to mend its ways. Only consummate statecraft can enable a King to save his throne when after a long spell of oppressive rule he sets to improving the lot of his subjects. Patiently endured so long as it seemed beyond redress, a grievance comes to appear intolerable once the possibility of removing it crosses men's minds."[36] The upper classes and functionaries of the government, "by thus championing the cause of the underprivileged ... made them acutely conscious of their wrongs."[37]

Tocqueville, with his usual perspicacity, here suggests that by the time of the French Revolution, the average European person loved the *idea* of republicanism enough to fight and die for it even when the abuses and burdens of monarchy were removed. Once the French people were given the slightest suggestion that amelioration was possible, they at once rose up and demanded not just a balance of power, but the whole of civil power. One sees that by this time, the rhetoric of republicanism was very different from what it had been only a century before. Robespierre is not a moderate rhetorician. Even the tone of Thomas Paine's *Common Sense* is quite different than that of Locke's *Second Treatise*.

To outline the complete causes and effects of this shift in the political landscape and the conception of the political amongst the people is beyond the scope of the present study. What is relevant here is the impact this transformation had on memory. Once again, we see that the trend is to break with tradition and authority in favor of the authority of simple reason. The older political model, hierarchical in nature, suggested that government was the province of a certain kind of wisdom, not shared by all. The democratic spirit assumes that all citizens have the same right to participate in politics because all have the same capacity to judge of what is good or bad for themselves. Individualism is the rule of the day.[38] The inner light of reason is enough to inform one of what should be done. This inner light is, of course, influenced by private emotions, passions, and desires, but nonetheless we assume that the general consensus will for the most part adequately reflect the rational will of the people. The old ways of the past are irrelevant for each new generation, which must make its own decisions about the shape of its government. The average

---

36 Ibid., 177.
37 Ibid., 180.
38 On individualism (particularly American individualism) and its shortcomings, see Alexis de Tocqueville, *Democracy in America*, trans. Harvey C. Mansfield and Delba Winthrop (Chicago: University of Chicago Press, 2000), 482–84.

participant in government, which now refers to each and every citizen, is no longer required to cultivate a political memory.

Vico says that the three forms of government each have their own principles of rule. In pure monarchies, "kings, at their own pleasure, rule both public and private affairs by means of custom." In a pure aristocracy, "whose basic structure is the conservation of the laws, everything proceeds according to unwritten precedent." In a pure democracy (or free commonwealth, as Vico says), "power resides in a multitude of people, and these people understand only natural equity. Natural equity is judged according to the merits of each individual case, and the cases differ according to circumstances, and circumstances are infinite in number. A free people would enshrine its wishes in laws. Thus a free society lives according to laws—countless laws." Most societies are of a mixed type, comporting themselves partly to customs, partly to precedents, and partly to laws.[39]

This is an over-simplification, but it is not inapposite. Monarchies and aristocracies are always concerned to preserve the ways that things are done, the *nomoi* or *mœurs* of the nation. The sovereign will has the force carried by law in a democracy, so it is incumbent upon all to remember every decree of the sovereign, every precedent. The subject, to fulfill his or her duty, must remember the past, and fall in with traditional custom. This is akin to what the good Catholic must do with regard to the decrees of ecclesiastical authority. The subject, qua subject, lives in a world governed by memory. The citizen of a democracy lives in a world governed by laws, all of which are published. The laws of the past do not concern the present. The proclamations of politicians do not carry any force. All authority is invested in promulgated law. The law code is enormous, and one would do well to commit much of it to memory, but this is merely the psychological memory and does not concern the past whatsoever. All law is contemporary, and no individual's opinion carries the authority of law. The good democratic citizen need not bear the full weight of the past in order to understand the present. Like all of the previously discussed social currents of modernity, democracy annuls memory.

---

39   Vico, *Universal Law*, 1: 214–15.

The new philosophy

The final intellectual shift to occur during the age now under discussion is much more limited in scope and social importance than the others, but worth considering for our purposes. I am referring to the change in the object of philosophical investigation. The seventeenth and eighteenth centuries saw the decline of metaphysical speculation. Metaphysics had been the primary interest of those calling themselves philosophers from antiquity through the age of Scholasticism. It was considered first philosophy because all other philosophical questions depended upon the solutions to metaphysical problems. Metaphysics is the science of the real, and its object is truth. In place of metaphysics, epistemology or theory of knowledge came to dominate western philosophical thought. Epistemology is the investigation of what we as human beings can possibly know. It is the science of certainty, not truth. Far from embracing the Hermetic image of man as a micro-cosmos, the epistemologists of early modernity conceived human cognition as extremely limited. They theorized about the limits of this cognition. The apex of this tradition was certainly Kant's *Critique of Pure Reason*, which arrived at the obvious conclusion of this philosophical trend: the real world cannot be known to us at all.

This epistemological turn correlated to the greater social fluctuations of the time. With the decay of authority and tradition in all of their most humane forms (religious, political, scientific), thought was forced to turn inward for answers. Faith in institutions was replaced by faith in the individual subject, who arose as the source of authority for what was true and false, right and wrong. This applies to the individual Protestant as arbiter of religious matters, the individual scientist as investigator of natural phenomena, and the individual citizen as locus of the legitimacy of the state. The fragile human ego, it was thought, was sufficient for any and all intellectual endeavors.

However, when responsibility for all meaningful truth lost its social aspect and fell upon the shoulders of the individual, recognition of the limits of the investigator had to arise simultaneously. As long as the search for truth and meaning was a joint venture undertaken by the human species throughout the ages—that is, when intellectual difficulties could be solved by turning to tradition—the whole of the human species was implicated, and the insufficiency of its instruments were not so apparent. This is the reason ancient and medieval philosophers were so little concerned with epistemology. When each human is left alone on his *poêle* to meditate upon the most important things without the support of any authority, then the weakness of the human mind becomes readily apparent, and this becomes the new central concern for philosophy. The epistemological turn has a social basis.

Descartes and Locke stand at the forefront of this movement. We will explore Descartes' epistemology in the following chapter. Here, let us consider Locke's *Essay Concerning Human Understanding*, which begins with the following claim: "Since it is the *understanding* that sets man above the rest of sensible beings, and gives him all the advantage and dominion which he has over them; it is certainly a subject, even for its nobleness, worth our labor to inquire into. The understanding, like the eye, whilst it makes us see and perceive all other things, takes no notice of itself; and it requires art and pains to set it at a distance and make it its own object."[40] A few paragraphs later, Locke writes, "If we can find out how far the understanding can extend its view; how far it has faculties to attain certainty; and in what cases it can only judge and guess, we may learn to content ourselves with what is attainable by us in this state."[41]

We can see at once what is at stake in Locke's *Essay*. The human understanding, taxed with so much, finds itself inadequate to the task. It strives to embrace all things, but it is unable to do so. There is an urgent need for philosophers to investigate the very limits of knowledge so that the understanding can be taught to find satisfaction in those things it can achieve, and to stay within its bounds. Was the understanding not always unruly and presumptuous? Of course it was. However, when social institutions like the Church and the state stood over and against it as authorities, it was held in check and intuited its own insufficiency. Modernity promised the sanctity and autonomy of the individual. This created the problem of knowledge. It is meaningful that Bertrand Russell says that lack of dogmatism is characteristic of Locke, and that this temper is "connected with religious toleration, with the success of parliamentary democracy, with *laissez-faire*, and with the whole system of liberal maxims."[42] Locke was very much the voice of the spirit of his times as an epistemologist, just as we saw he is also was as a political philosopher.[43]

---

40 Locke, *Essay*, 1: 25.
41 Ibid., 1: 29.
42 Bertrand Russell, *A History of Western Philosophy* (New York: Simon and Schuster, 1945), 606–7.
43 Paul Hazard's *The Crisis of the European Mind: 1680–1715* touches on similar points, especially Parts 2 and 3 ("The War on Tradition" and "The Task of Reconstruction"). Hazard sees Locke as the perfect philosopher for the task of finding a new philosophy.

The effects of this inward turn in philosophical orientation on the significance of memory mirror the effects of all of the other paradigm shifts of the age. If the central object of philosophy is the limits of knowledge, this is not an inquiry that requires any deep notion of philosophical recollection. The quest for *self-knowledge*, which may seem the same as epistemology, is wildly different. Self-knowledge, we saw in the first part of this book, goes back to Socrates and the Delphic maxim, *gnōthi seauton*, "know thyself." Knowing oneself is a task that entails a cultivated philosophical memory, imagination, and *ingenium*. It demands a lifetime of meditative contemplation. Theory of knowledge merely seeks to demarcate the efficacy of human thought. One can perform the latter task and come no closer to achieving self-knowledge.

Theory of knowledge in not reliant on memory, and it is born out of the decline of tradition. To the epistemologists, memory is an object of study, not a tool for investigation. As a part of human thought (we no longer speak of "faculties" as the ancients once did), memory is considered only in its purely mechanical sense. This is the sense Hegel speaks of when he refers to *Gedächtnis*, psychological memory. We will soon see that for Descartes, memory is entirely mechanical, not at all spiritual. It can be understood along the same lines as a *canard digérateur*.

This overview of the dominant social forces and tendencies of the seventeenth and eighteenth centuries over-simplifies much and is not meant to be exhaustive. Nor is this meant as a polemic. It would be strange to say that the revolutions in thought that occurred during this age were not generally for the better. My intention was merely to outline some currents of human history that erupted at around the same time and led to the devaluation of memory. The psychological form of memory simply becomes less useful in modernity, its cultivation less a matter of life and death. There is no denying this. The history of science is no longer relevant to science, nor is the history of faith any longer relevant to faith. We can relegate these things to a bookshelf. However, the psychological form of memory is not the only form of memory.

The ingenious, *making* memory, the philosophical memory, is of a different sort altogether. The doctrine of memory as philosophy has little interest in tradition and authority. Its most ingenious intellectual products always arise over and against the established wisdom of the day. Plato, Vico, Hegel—these men explode upon the scene as daring iconoclasts. However, modern intellectual currents tend to fail to make this distinction between psychological and philosophical memory. We have come to believe that psychological memory is the whole of memory.

The project of this book is to revisit this assumption. The fact that memory was largely pushed aside from philosophical thought depended on particular social conditions and was therefore contingent. It could have been otherwise. In the following chapter, we will look in particular at the role played by Descartes in the undermining of memory. In the final chapters, we will see that Hegel does not accept the relegation of memory to mere mechanism.

XII: Descartes and His Children

Mathesis universalis

We have briefly considered some of the effects of the scientific revolution of the seventeenth century in the previous chapter, and discovered a double tendency: the rise of a mathematical view of the cosmos, and the reduction of all physical phenomena to simple mechanics. These two tendencies are inseparable. Mathematics is the language and logic of mechanics. If all matter follows the same laws of motion, then the universe can be interpreted by means of a few simple formulae, taking into consideration mass, trajectory, acceleration, and so on. The fewer the formulae, the better. If we were to discover one single formula to explain the whole of material motion in the cosmos, this would be the secular equivalent of the name of God. *Mathesis universalis*, universal mathematics, is Descartes' term for the mathematical-mechanistic view of nature. He writes, "I came to see that the exclusive concern of mathematics is with questions of order or measure and that it is irrelevant whether the measure in question involves numbers, shapes, stars, sounds, or any other object whatever. This made me realize that there must be a general science which explains all the points that can be raised concerning order and measure irrespective of the subject-matter, and that this science should be termed *mathesis universalis*—a venerable term with a well-established meaning."[1]

If we assume that animals lack autonomous minds or souls, as Descartes and most Cartesians do, then animal behavior and movement is likewise reducible to mechanical principles. The life of the animal is not an expression of any sort of meaningful endeavor. Instead, animals follow the same principles as stones rolling down a hill, with only slightly more complexity. Descartes refers to the animal as *bête machine*. In the *Discours*, he writes, "[Animals] have no intelligence at all, and ... it is nature which acts in them according to the disposition of their organs. In the same way a clock, consisting only of wheels and springs, can count the hours and measure time more accurately than we can with all our

---

[1] Descartes, *Rules*, rule 4 (1: 19); see also rules 12 and 14. For a good account of the meaning of *mathesis universalis* for Descartes and how it fits into his philosophical project, see L. J. Beck, *The Method of Descartes: A Study of the* Regulae (Oxford: Clarendon Press, 1952), 194–202.

wisdom."[2] Descartes believes that it is not beyond human wit to design machines able to perfectly replicate all of the functions and organic processes of beasts. The non-human animal is simply a highly complex machine without soul, like a clockwork. The unfortunate consequences of this view—particularly the belief that animals cannot feel pain—are well known.[3]

La Mettrie would take this view to its logical conclusion in the following century. *L'homme machine* is merely the development of the logic of *bête machine*. For Descartes, however, man is not quite a machine. Human behavior is the one thing he is not quite willing to explain away by the formulae of physics.[4] The rational soul is what separates humans from animals. Descartes' dualism of body and soul only applies to the human animal. Of all things under the sun, man alone is autonomous. Descartes' evidence is that man alone is capable of meaningful speech and able to act from understanding, neither of which machines or animals can simulate. "It is for all practical purposes impossible for a machine to have enough different organs to make it act in all the contingencies of life in the way in which our reason makes us act."[5] Descartes' conception of the rational soul cannot be derived from matter. It is the first logical article of certainty, prior to the existence of bodies.[6]

The human body is, however, a different matter. The body considered by itself is simply corporeal matter. It is therefore just as subject to the laws of mechanics as any other corporeal object. The human body is a machine. What privileges this particular machine is that it can be set in motion by the rational soul, whereas all other matter is condemned to be moved from without. In his reply to Antoine Arnauld's objections to the *Meditations*, Descartes writes, "Both in our bodies and those of the

---

2   Descartes, *Discourse* 5 (1: 141).
3   Among the many contemporaries or near-contemporaries who objected to Descartes' doctrine of animals were Henry More and Ralph Cudworth in England, and Antoine Arnauld in France. For Arnauld's criticism, see *Objections and Replies* to Descartes' *Meditations*, obj. 4 (2: 144). For the historical context of the debate about sensation in animals, see Desmond M. Clarke, *Descartes's Theory of Mind* (Oxford: Clarendon, 2003), 71–77.
4   Nevertheless, Descartes suggest that the practical science of morals is among the fruits of physics. "The whole of philosophy is like a tree. The roots are metaphysics, the trunk is physics, and the branches emerging from the trunk are all the other sciences, which may be reduced to the three principal ones, namely, medicine, mechanics and morals." Descartes, *Principles*, 1: 186. *Mathesis universalis* promises to perfect ethics as it does mechanics. It is noteworthy that Descartes never wrote a substantive ethical treatise.
5   Ibid., 5 (1: 139–40).
6   See Descartes, *Second Meditation*.

brutes, no movements can occur without the presence of all the organs or instruments which would enable the same movements to be produced in a machine. So even in our own case the mind does not directly move the external limbs, but simply controls the animal spirits which flow from the heart via the brain into the muscles, and sets up certain motions in them. ... Now a very large number of the motions occurring inside us do not depend on the mind."[7]

The human body is an organic automaton, a machine in motion with an intricate internal mechanism. The mind is not able to facilitate this body violating the laws of mechanics. All it can do is indirectly set up certain motions in the body, that is, give a new impetus to motion or operate as a secondary cause of motion. This is what the meteor hurdling through space and the small game animal charmed by the snake cannot do. For the most part, the operations of the body are not subject to the rational mind, and function according to the corporeal mechanism. Descartes includes heartbeat, digestion, nutrition, and respiration among these automatic movements of the human machine, as well as unconscious walking and singing, which may occur without the attention or direction of the mind. Instinct is also included amongst mechanical processes.[8] The falling person who sticks out his or her arms is not subject to a rational process. Instead, certain visual stimuli agitate the brain in such a way that it responds by agitating the nerves of the arms to produce a movement. The entire process is explicable by mechanistic laws.

In Descartes' philosophy, the brain is not the mind. The mind is ethereal, non-corporeal. Mind is the one thing that is by nature not body; the two are separable by their very essences. The brain itself, on the other hand, is entirely material. It is a particularly complex organ, and the organ that informs the mind, but it is nevertheless matter and therefore subject to the laws of mechanics. The rational intellect exists outside of the brain (though "outside" still suggests that it exists in space; the mind is utterly non-spatial). The brain regulates the autonomic processes of the rest of the human machine, but its most significant function with regard to the mind is to provide the data of sensation.

Desmond Clarke writes of Descartes' general theory of the brain, "Once a shape or pattern is impressed on an external sensory organ, it is subsequently transmitted to the so-called common sense (*sensus communis*), the internal organ in the brain in which all incoming sensory

---

7   Descartes, *Objections and Replies*, set 4 (2: 161).
8   Ibid.

stimuli are synthesized. The common sense, in turn, must act like a seal when it forms on the passive, waxlike material of the phantasy or imagination all the shapes or ideas that result from external stimuli."[9] The brain then stimulates the body's nerves in response to these patterns. The body moves according to general rules of stimulus-response, with the brain as medium. This process would occur, as Descartes believes it does in animals, without any intervention on the part of mind.[10]

However, the brain is also connected to the mind in some obscure way. Spiritual or mental activity is not a process of the brain, but the brain informs the mind, which alone is outside of the physical nexus of causality. "All our sensations undoubtedly come to us from something that is distinct from our mind."[11] The sensations that are impressed on the matter of the brain as patterns are accessible to the mind, which uses them as the occasion for autonomous activity and indirect influence on the human machine. More precisely, the arrangement of the parts of the brain from which the nerve fibers issue is the means by which the mind is able to know the situation of the body.[12] This is to say that there are two sorts of processes: (1) Organic processes that occur through the brain, and are purely mechanical, governed by the laws of movement and of causality. (2) Rational processes that occur in the mind. Only the latter are spiritual activities. Of which sort is memory?

For Descartes, "to philosophize" means to set about acquiring perfect knowledge "deduced from first causes."[13] This is a spiritual activity, not a corporeal activity. If it turns out that memory is an organic, bodily process, then it can be an object of philosophical inquiry, but it cannot be the instrument of philosophical investigation.

The Treatise on Man

In Descartes' earliest philosophical work, *Rules for the Direction of the Mind*, he writes, "The phantasy is a genuine part of the body [i.e. of the brain], and is large enough to allow different parts of it to take on many different figures and generally, to retain them for some time; in which

---

9   Clarke, *Descartes's Theory*, 48. It is notable that this understanding of sensation resonates with that of Aristotle.
10 See Descartes, *Rules*, rule 12 (1: 39–51).
11 Descartes, *Principles*, pt. 2, prin. 1 (1: 223).
12 Descartes, *The Treatise on Man*, in *The World and Other Writings*, ed. and trans. Stephen Gaukroger (New York: Cambridge University Press, 1998), 131.
13 Ibid., preface (1: 179).

case it is to be identified with what we call 'memory'."[14] Memory, then, is corporeal, and located at a particular place within the brain. It is the seat of images, and the ancient image of wax, upon which images are impressed, is apt. It is also worth noting that Descartes believes "memory is no different than imagination,"[15] which is the same position Vico takes. However, the implications of this belief are quite different for Descartes and Vico. For Descartes, memory is a function of the brain, not the mind. Memory-images have a real efficacy with regard to stimulating reactions in the nerves of the body, and these images are also accessible to rational thought. However, memory is not properly a part of rational thought.[16]

Descartes goes most deeply into the nature of memory as a brain process in another early work, his *Treatise on Man* [*L'homme*]. In this treatise, Descartes promises to discuss first the human body, then the mind, and finally the manner in which these two natures are joined together. This project was never completed, and the treatise in fact only discusses the first of these items, the human body. Since the body is under review in itself, abstracted from the mind, Descartes proposes to treat it entirely as a "machine made of earth," a machine more complex than a clock or a mill, but still inherently of the same order.[17] Throughout the work, comparisons to other man-made mechanisms abound: "The nerves of the machine I am describing can indeed be compared to the pipes in the mechanical parts of these fountains [of the royal gardens], its muscles and tendons to various other engines and springs which serve to work these mechanical parts," and so on.[18]

The body as such, without the oversight of the mind, is still capable of forming ideas in the brain, and these ideas are able to become memories. Descartes writes, "I ask you to consider what is most noteworthy

---

14   Descartes, *Rules*, rule 12 (1: 41–42).
15   Ibid., 1:43.
16   Bergson disagrees that memory is inherently material. He writes, "When we pass from pure perception to memory, we definitely abandon matter for spirit." Bergson, *Matter and Memory*, 235. Because Bergson believes memories are not "located" spatially in the brain, they can never properly speaking be destroyed. Failures in recollection, e.g. because of cerebral lesions, are failures of the body to adopt the right attitude for recollection, *not* indications that the memory itself has been destroyed. See ibid., 107–8.
17   Descartes, *Treatise*, 99.
18   Ibid., 107. Stephen Gaukroger suggests that the mechanical images Descartes employs are derived from the devices in the grottoes at the Saint-Germain gardens. See Gaukroger, "The Resources of a Mechanist Physiology and the Problem of Goal-Directed Processes," in *Descartes' Natural Philosophy*, ed. S. Gaukroger, Stephen Schuster, and John Sutton (New York: Routledge, 2000), 386.

about the brain during the time of waking: namely, how ideas of objects are formed in the place assigned to the imagination and to the common sense, how these ideas are retained in the memory, and how they cause the movement of all the bodily parts."[19] Only figures "traced in the spirits on the surface of gland H" (that is, the pineal gland) become ideas.[20] Impressions on the organs of sense or the inner surface of the brain are the occasion for this cerebral response, but they are not yet ideas. Only impressions on the pineal gland, the place of *sensus communis*, are able to properly become ideas.

The mechanistic construction of memory proceeds from here. Upon issuing from the pineal gland, the "spirits" that formed idea-impressions on the gland pass into the pores between the fibers of the brain. Here, they enlarge these openings slightly, and alter the position of the fibers in various ways. This procedure traces figures in the cerebral gaps, which correspond to those of the object of sensation. Descartes writes, "At first they do this less easily and perfectly here than on gland H, but they gradually improve as their action becomes stronger and lasts longer, or is repeated more often. Which is why in such cases these patterns are no longer easily erased, but are preserved in such a way that the ideas that were previously on this gland can be formed again long afterwards without requiring the presence of the objects to which they correspond. And this is what memory consists in."[21] Physical spirits forcefully rearrange brain fibers, and open new neural passageways, and the path of their violence leaves an impression on the surface of the brain. These image-spirits have the corporeal effect of a signet-ring. If this neural model is correct, then a good neurologist might be able to reconstruct a human's memories by observing these corporeal traces, just as a good tracker can tell what animals have run through a clearing by examining the twigs broken upon the ground.

To better illustrate the process of memory-formation, Descartes uses the analogy of needles being passed through a cloth. The tiny holes formed would either stay open or, if they closed, they would be quite easy to open again with the proper stimulation. Descartes suggests that if these holes had been made several times, and had always been opened

---

19 Descartes, *Treatise*, 146.
20 Ibid., 149.
21 Ibid., 150. Descartes says this procedure specifically occurs "on the internal part of the brain, marked B" (ibid.), but he fails to give any indication to which of his many diagrams he is referring, so it is unclear what area of the brain he believes to be the seat of memory. Nonetheless, he does have in mind one specific physical location.

simultaneously, then just opening some of the holes would cause the others to open. This is his corporeal explanation of the association of ideas that occurs in memory. He writes, "This shows how the recollection of one thing can be excited by that of another which has been imprinted in the memory at the same time. For example, if I see two eyes with a nose, I immediately imagine a forehead with a mouth and all the other parts of a face, because I am unaccustomed to seeing the former without the latter."[22] The old impressions inscribed in the fibers of the brain are reawakened through the agitation of correlated areas of the brain. Associative memory is therefore a sort of mechanical habit of the surface of the brain.

All of this takes place in Descartes' theoretical body without a soul, through purely mechanical processes that are reasonably simple. Descartes' final word on the nature of memory reaffirms its material basis: "But the effect of memory that seems to me to be most worthy of consideration here is that, without there being any soul present in this machine, it can naturally be disposed to imitate all the movements that real men— or many other similar machines—will make when it is present."[23] The ideas synthesized by the pineal gland, which proceed to form neural memory pathways, inform the soul about the state of the body and its relation to the outside world, assuming the machine already has a soul. However, even if there is *no soul at all*, the mechanism of memory functions just the same and the manner in which it alters brain fibers informs the unintelligent movements of the body. Spirit may allow itself to be informed by the memories of the body, but it need not. Memory is not at all a spiritual process. Its role is secondary, that of a handmaid. Therefore, it cannot be an instrument of philosophical investigation, nor of humane wisdom.

This purely mechanical understanding of memory is not unique to the early stage of Descartes' career. He reaffirms it several times in his later writings and never moves away from it. In his reply to Pierre Gassendi's objections to the *Meditations* (1641), he writes, "So long as the mind is joined to the body, then in order for it to remember thoughts which it had in the past, it is necessary for some traces of them to be imprinted on the brain; it is by turning to these, or applying itself to them, that the mind remembers."[24] In a 1640 letter to Lazare Meyssonnier, he

---

22 Ibid., 151–52.
23 Ibid., 157.
24 Descartes, *Objections and Replies*, set 5 (2: 247).

writes, "As for the impressions preserved in memory, I imagine they are not unlike the folds which remain in this paper after it has once been folded; and so I think that they are received for the most part in the whole substance of the brain."[25] This image of the folded paper is not quite as apt as his image of the needles, since the holes of tiny needles do close up, while the folds of a piece of paper can never be removed.

In several places, Descartes acknowledges what he refers to as "intellectual memory."[26] Frans Burman reports that Descartes said in conversation, "I do not refuse to admit intellectual memory: it does exist. When, for example, on hearing that the word 'R-E-X' signifies supreme power, I commit this to my memory and then subsequently recall the meaning by means of my memory, it must be the intellectual memory that makes this possible. For there is certainly no relationship between the three letters and their meaning, which would enable me to derive the meaning from the letters."[27] However, the nature of this intellectual memory and how it differs from bodily memory are never quite clear. L. J. Beck suggests that it is a memory of clear and distinct ideas, and therefore exempt from confusion.[28] Descartes' example here involves the memory of a connection discovered by an intellectual process, which the brute body would be incapable of uncovering by itself. It is most likely that by the "intellectual memory" Descartes understood a mechanical process of the same type as that applying to bodily memories, but one that dealt with the data of reasoning and thought rather than the data of sensation.

What significance does this view of memory have for Descartes' philosophical project, and why does he insist on relegating memory to a bodily process? The reason is the same as the reason memory was undermined by the dominant intellectual trends of the seventeenth and eighteenth centuries discussed in the previous chapter.

Descartes' new method for philosophy entails a refusal to submit to tradition. His view of history is apparent in the first chapter of the *Discours*. After discussing the value of the various fields of education, he turns to the limits of traditional learning. He writes, "But I thought I had already given enough time to languages and likewise to reading the

---

25 Descartes, *Letters*, 3: 143. For further, similar claims about memory made by Descartes, see Clarke, *Descartes's Theory*, 94–96.
26 For more substantial studies of the "intellectual memory" in Descartes, see Beck, *Method*, 121–26, and Clarke, *Descartes's Theory*, 99–105.
27 Descartes, *Letters*, 3: 336–37 (translation altered).
28 Beck, *Method*, 122–23.

works of the ancients, both their histories and their fables. For conversing with those of past centuries is much the same as travelling. It is good to know something of the customs of various peoples, so that we may judge our own more soundly. ... But one who spends too much time travelling eventually becomes a stranger in his own country; and one who is too curious about the practices of past ages usually remains quite ignorant about those of the present."[29] Once he was old enough to do so, Descartes tells us, he "entirely abandoned the study of letters. Resolving to seek no knowledge other than that which could be found in myself or else in the great book of the world. ... For it seemed to me that much more truth could be found in the reasonings which a man makes concerning matters that concern him than in those which some scholar makes in his study about speculative matters."[30]

Timothy Reiss points out, "Reason, mind, that was to say, had no history."[31] The image we most associate with Descartes is that of the solitary philosopher, alone with his thoughts upon the *poêle*. The philosopher must cast off all dogmas and all received opinions in order to meditate upon truth. This is why Descartes allows radical skepticism into his system at the very beginning. Reason has no history, and in each philosopher it must begin at the beginning, without the help of anyone or anything else. That is the prerequisite for the discovery of meaningful truths. Tradition and authority count for nothing and the individual ego is everything.

This is Protestantism and democracy applied to philosophy. A good memory is of some use in this project, and we would be wise to make use of the aid it provides.[32] After all, the philosopher must be able to run through the series of truths he discovers through reflection. However, it is not properly a part of the meditation of the philosopher, not an organon for the discovery of truth. Memory has absolutely no role in the work of philosophy, and, as the young Descartes says, it has absolutely no role in any of the sciences. Descartes discovered many fine things. However, he has no notion of any philosophical sense of memory. Unfortunately for the doctrine that I am advocating, most philosophers since the time of Descartes have been his intellectual children.

---

29   Descartes, *Discourse* 1 (1: 113–14).
30   Ibid., 1: 115.
31   Timothy J. Reiss, "Denying the Body? Memory and the Dilemmas of History in Descartes," *Journal of the History of Ideas* 57 (1996): 591.
32   Descartes, *Rules*, rule 12 (1: 39).

The legacy of Descartes

When I refer to most of the philosophers to follow Descartes as his children, I do not necessarily mean that they were Cartesians. I mean that Descartes' writing set the agenda and delineated the topics and problems appropriate for philosophical discourse over the ensuing centuries. Whether the particular philosopher tended to embrace Cartesian positions or argue fiercely against them, the specter of Descartes loomed over the landscape of philosophy. He was, and still is, inescapable. The philosophical world given shape by Descartes tended to view memory as a bodily process, at best an aid to the proper faculties of investigation and discovery. This is in stark contrast to the view of the ancients and Renaissance humanists.

For Hobbes, memory is "decaying sense." In *Leviathan* (1651), he writes, "This *decaying sense*, when we would express the thing itself, we call *imagination*, as I said before: but when we would express the decay, and signify that the sense is fading, old, and past, it is called *memory*. So that imagination and memory are but one thing."[33] A great deal of memory is experience, which conditions and determines much of human behavior. However, the decaying images of memory are always the products of simple sensory impressions. Remembrance is a sort of "sixth sense," an internal sense that receives its data from the five external senses.[34] The contents of memory are entirely dependent on the body's organs, and memory lacks any autonomous creative power. This materialistic position was shared in the following century by the Abbé de Condillac.[35]

Spinoza is no more generous in his treatment of memory. In the *Ethics* (written 1664–65, pub. 1677), he embraces Descartes' notion of the association of ideas as the central element of memory. Spinoza writes, "We clearly understand what memory is. It is a simple linking of

---

33 Hobbes, *Leviathan*, I.ii, 12. By identifying imagination with memory, Hobbes may be the source for Vico's similar doctrine. David Hume, notably, denies the identity of the two faculties. For Hume, the difference is that memory is restrained "to the same order and form [of] the original impressions." *A Treatise of Human Nature*, ed. L. A. Selby-Bigge (New York: Clarendon Pres, 1978), 9. Hume therefore lacks the notion of memory as *ingegno*, the third sense given to it by Vico.

34 Hobbes, *Human Nature*, in *The Elements of Law Natural and Politic*, ed. J. C. A. Gaskin (New York: Oxford University Press, 1994), III, 29.

35 See Étienne Bonnot, Abbé de Condillac, *A Treatise on the Sensations*, in *Philosophical Writings*, trans. Franklin Philip and Harlan Lane (Hillsdale, NJ: Lawrence Erlbaum Associates, 1982): "Sensations ... give rise to the whole system of man" (158). For Condillac, memory is entirely subject to organic sensations (167–68).

ideas involving the nature of things outside the human body, a linking which occurs in the mind parallel to the order and linking of the affections of the human body." He also emphasizes that memory only concerns "the linking of those ideas that involve the nature of things outside the human body, not of those ideas that explicate the nature of the said things."[36] As with Hobbes, Spinoza (a fellow determinist) believes that memory is effectively a mechanical process, one that extends only to sensations and has nothing to do with rational understanding. The machine of the body, without the presence of soul, can generate the associative memory through the movements of the sensory organs and the brain. The mechanistic principle is the same as Descartes': the stimulation of certain cerebral fibers entails the concurrent indirect stimulation of other fibers.

Father Malebranche also shares this conception. In the *Search after Truth* (1674–75), he writes, "For the explanation of *memory*, it is sufficient to understand this truth well: That all our different perceptions are attached to the changes occurring in the fibers of the principal part of the brain, where the soul resides more particularly; because assuming this single principle, the nature of memory is explained. ... Our brain fibers, having once received certain impressions through the flow of the animal spirits and by the action of objects, retain some facility for receiving these same dispositions for some time."[37] Since this passage is almost a facsimile of the language and meaning of Descartes' own words, no commentary is needed. It is significant, however, that Malebranche also discusses the objection to this theory the idea that the brain is far too small to admit so many physical traces of impressions. He calls this a "prejudice" from which we must be delivered.[38] If we recall that for Descartes the location of these memory traces is not the entirety of the brain's surface, but only one particular segment of the brain, not clearly identified, and if we also consider that upon this segment must be physically inscribed the whole of the past (perhaps seventy years of unremitting sensation), this criticism does not seem so unfair a "prejudice."

Other philosophers were able to think beyond this view of memory as a purely material process of the body. Locke, for one, does not tie himself to the corporeal model of Descartes; in his *Essay on Human Understanding* (1689), he repeatedly calls memory an act of mind, and says

---

36   Baruch Spinoza, *The Ethics*, trans. Samuel Shirley (Indianapolis: Hackett, 1992), II.xviii, schol., 79.
37   Malebranche, *Search after Truth*, 106.
38   Ibid., 107.

that it is the process by which mind is able to revive ideas that, once imprinted, have disappeared. Locke describes memory as a "storehouse of our ideas." He says that "the mind has a power in many cases to revive perceptions which it has once had, with this additional perception annexed to them, that *it has had them before*."[39] However, memory requires repetition. The storehouse must be visited from time to time, for if ideas are not repeated, they fall into oblivion, without a trace.[40] The cultivation of memory is of the utmost importance for Locke. He says that "where it is wanting, all the rest of our faculties are in great measure useless."[41]

Of particular interest to contemporary philosophers is the role of memory in Locke's doctrine of personal identity. How far are we justified in saying that this person before us is the identical person that we met yesterday or ten years ago? What determines the identity of the individual? For Locke, the answer is memory. One is the same person insofar as one participates in the same continued life. However, we cannot say that the same continued life means the same body abides through time. The parts of the body are subject to annihilation and regeneration; cells decay and new cells take their place. The body is no more stable than the classical ship of Theseus. The part of the ego that participates continuously in the same life must, then, be mental. An uninterrupted consciousness is what makes one the same self, the same "I" through time. Should that consciousness be transplanted into some other body, the new body would be the seat of the "I" that previously abided elsewhere. How are we to know that this current "I" is the same as some other of a past time? Because one remembers the past. My present consciousness has the memories of the consciousness of the "I" of yesterday and the day before and so on. It is memory that makes personal identity.[42] Locke elevates memory to the status of a mental process, and grants it this central role in personal identity. However, Locke does not allow memory any greater

---

39 Locke, *Essay*, 1: 193–94.
40 Bergson agrees that memories are intellectual things, but he argues that *because* of this they cannot ever be destroyed. Locke would have done well to distinguish the oblivion of the memory from what really occurs, that is a cognitive failure in the human subject to access the memory. See n. 16 of this chapter, above.
41 Locke, *Essay*, 1: 198. In his editorial note (n. 3), Alexander Campbell Fraser takes issue with Locke's insertion of the phrase "in great measure." It would be more apt to say that without memory, one's other faculties would be entirely useless. The neurologist Oliver Sacks has asked: "What sort of life (if any), what sort of a world, what sort of self, can be preserved in a man who has lost the greater part of his memory and, with this, his past, and his moorings in time?" See Sacks, "The Lost Mariner," in *The Man Who Mistook His Wife for a Hat* (New York: Touchstone, 1998), 23.
42 Ibid., 1: 448–68.

efficacy. Like Descartes, Locke recognizes reflection as the primary instrument of philosophical inquiry.

Leibniz is another philosopher who was able to think about memory without stumbling into Descartes' position. The influence of the classical tradition of *ars memoriae* on Leibniz's early interest in the idea of a "Universal Character" has been demonstrated at length by Paolo Rossi.[43] This was at a time (c. 1678–79) when this tradition had been condemned to irrelevance by most of his contemporaries. However, Leibniz never developed his own doctrine of memory.

There was always a counter–current of resistance to Cartesian philosophy, which Isaiah Berlin called a "counter-Enlightenment." Giambattista Vico, whom Karl-Otto Apel accurately called the "owl of Minerva of Italian Renaissance culture,"[44] was among the most significant voices of this resistance, though he was largely unknown at the time he was writing. Vico was deeply suspicious of the intellectual transition from Renaissance rhetorico-memorial philosophy to the Cartesian critical philosophy. In his *Autobiography*, Vico relates how, after nine years' absence from Naples, he returned home to find himself "a stranger in his own land"—a turn of phrase borrowed directly from Descartes' thoughts on education in the *Discours*. He found "the physics of Descartes at the height of its renown among the established men of letters. That of Aristotle … had now become a laughingstock. As for metaphysics … it was now thought worthy only of being shut up in the cloisters."[45] Unlike many of his contemporaries, trained in Cartesian philosophy, "Vico blessed his good fortune in having no teacher whose words he had sworn by."[46]

Against the project of Cartesianism, Vico objects, "Speculative criticism, the main purpose of which is to cleanse its fundamental truths not only of all falsity, but also of the mere suspicion of error, places upon the same plane of falsity not only false thinking, but also those secondary verities and ideas which are based on probability alone, and commands us to clear our minds of them. Such an approach is distinctly harmful. … Probabilities stand, so to speak, midway between truth and falsity, since

---

43   See Rossi, *Logic and Memory*, chapter 8 ("The Sources of Leibniz's Universal Character").
44   Karl-Otto Apel, *Die Idee der Sprache in der Tradition des Humanismus von Dante bis Vico* (Bonn: Bouvier Herbert Grundmann, 1975), 320–21.
45   Giambattista Vico, *The Autobiography of Giambattista Vico*, trans. Max Harold Fisch and Thomas Goddard Bergin (Ithaca, NY: Cornell University Press, 1975), 132.
46   Ibid., 133.

things which most of the time are true, are only very seldom false."[47] The idolization of certainty is detrimental to prudence, which is based on probabilities. Vico, as a teacher of rhetoric, also objects to the rejection of the art of topics: "Again I say, this is harmful, since the invention of arguments is by nature prior to the judgment of their validity, so that, in teaching, that invention should always be given priority over philosophical criticism."[48]

We have considered Vico's view of the structure and significance of memory in the third chapter of this book. We saw that in his *New Science*, Vico says that memory is threefold, *memoria*, *fantasia*, and *ingegno*, and he develops a doctrine of *ingegno* (informed by *memoria* and *fantasia*) as the central organon of philosophy. For Vico, the history of philosophy must move around Descartes, not through him. Vico confronts the critical philosophy with the humanistic Renaissance philosophy that it supplanted. He appropriates all of the strongest elements of the classical doctrine of memory as philosophy, while avoiding the hyperbolic claims of a Camillo. Memory will not make us gods, and we will learn nothing about divine things.[49] However, we will be able to better understand human things. The *New Science* portrays the city of the human race, not the city of God.[50] Vico says that the *New Science* is the contemplation of "providence in respect of that part of [nature] which is most proper to men, whose nature has this principal property: that of being social."[51] Vico's new science of memory promises wisdom concerning human things and human institutions, which is the most important thing for us human beings to know. However, Vico's call to arms failed to resonate in Cartesian Europe.

The greatest of Descartes' children was Immanuel Kant. Descartes had separated the body and the mind, and for nearly two centuries, phi-

---

47 Giambattista Vico, *On the Study Methods of our Time*, trans. Elio Gianturco (Ithaca, NY: Cornell University Press, 1990), 13.
48 Ibid., 14.
49 Nor is it to the technical *ars memoria* that Vico wishes to return. Even in his pedagogy Vico rejected the utility of mnemotechnics as a tool for students of rhetoric. In his *Institutiones Oratoriae*, from which he taught his courses on "Latin eloquence," he devotes a single paragraph to the topic: "There is nothing we can say here on memory. It is indeed an innate virtue which is maintained and kept by usage, and if there is an art to this, which I do not think there is, the proper one is that which is called mnemonics (*ars mnemoneutica*)." Vico, *The Art of Rhetoric*, trans. Giorgio A. Pinton and Arthur W. Shippee (Atlanta: Rodopi, 1996), 207.
50 See Dustin Peone, "Vico and His Patron Saint: The City of Man and the City of God," *Clio* 45 (2015): 9.
51 Vico, *New Science*, §2.

losophers argued over how the two substances interacted. Kant's great insight into metaphysics was that there is no interaction at all. Kant's *Critique of Pure Reason* is the logical culmination of the Cartesian project. He grants no communication whatsoever between being-in-itself and the subject's experience of the world. Kant's doctrine of the *noumenon* has been discussed above, in the third chapter.

In another sense, Kant is the methodological heir to Descartes. In Descartes' writing, the hero figure of philosophy is the solitary scholar alone atop the *poêle*. This character is no less the philosophical hero for Kant. In his preface to the first *Critique*, Kant writes, "The chief question is always simply this:—what and how much can the understanding and reason know apart from all experience?"[52] In the preface to the second edition, he writes, "Metaphysics is a completely isolated speculative science of reason, which soars far above the teachings of experience, and in which reason is indeed meant to be its own pupil. Metaphysics rests on concepts alone—not, like mathematics, on their application to intuition."[53] It is a godlike task that the philosopher undertakes. The metaphysician must slough off the world and ascend to the pure concept. Experience counts for nothing in the critical project. The true Kantian would do well to find a nice warm stove and bolt the doors of his house for a few days.

Kant's critical philosophy is a philosophy of reflection through and through, as has already been discussed; Hegel's application of the term *Reflexionsphilosophie* to him is quite apt. It is no surprise that memory plays no role at all in Kant's work. It is not a faculty the metaphysician needs to do his work. Memory can never extricate itself from its connection to intuition. Therefore, it is positively harmful if assumed to be a source of knowledge by the critical philosopher. Transcendental logic, for instance, must abstract not just from the data of sensation, but from the "laws of memory" as well, from everything corporeal.[54] The ego must learn to become indifferent to the Muses when they sing of what was, is, and shall be.

This was the general trend in philosophy following Descartes: memory was first removed from the mind and identified with the processes of the body. Its role in philosophy was solely to aid the intellect by

---

52 Kant, *Critique of Pure Reason*, A xvii.
53 Ibid., B xiv. Similarly, Kant views moral philosophy as entirely a matter of concepts abstracted from lived experience in the *Critique of Practical Reason* and *Groundwork of the Metaphysics of Morals*.
54 Ibid., A 53, B 77.

supplying images. It was then stripped of this privilege as philosophy became transcendental. Vico, the child not of Descartes but of the Renaissance, understood this trend but his influence was unable to extend beyond Naples until he was rediscovered by Jules Michelet a century later. The great defense and resuscitation of "memory as philosophy" required the genius of Hegel.

Hegel was almost certainly unaware of Vico, though their affinities have been emphasized by Benedetto Croce.[55] In particular, the two philosophers share a negative outlook on the critical project. The final two chapters of this book will analyze Hegel's philosophical thought, considering him as the greatest post-Cartesian proponent of "memory as philosophy."

Like Vico, Hegel was born into a philosophical landscape dominated by criticism and method. His earliest published essays were written in the same decade as Kant's third *Critique*, and Kant died only three years before the publication of the *Phenomenology of Spirit* (1807). To the extent that Descartes had to confront the specter of Montaigne in order to carve out his own philosophical *topos*, Hegel had to confront the specter of Kant, not to mention Jacobi, Fichte, Schelling, and other popular philosophers more or less indebted to Kant. For this confrontation, Hegel had to find some way around the critical philosophy and its reflective method, some way around the century and a half of modern philosophy entangled in the web of Descartes. The faculty that Hegel rediscovered as the master key to his speculative philosophy was recollection, *Erinnerung*.[56] Let us now examine the role of memory in Hegel's reaction to the project of modernity.

---

55 See Benedetto Croce, "An Unknown Page from the Last Months of Hegel's Life," trans. James W. Hillesheim and Ernesto Caserta, *The Personalist* 45 (1964), 329–353. In this fictitious essay, a visitor shows Hegel some of Vico's works, and Hegel admits that they agree with his own.

56 There have been several books written on the role of recollection (*Erinnerung*) and memory (*Gedächtnis*) in Hegel's philosophy, notably Donald Phillip Verene, *Hegel's Recollection*; Thamar Rossi Leidi, *Hegels Begriff der Erinnerung*; Angelica Nuzzo, *Memory, History, Justice in Hegel*; and Rebecca Comay and John McCumber, eds., *Endings: Questions of Memory in Hegel and Heidegger*, as well as numerous articles on this topic, including Ernst Bloch, "Hegel und die Anamnesis"; Valerio Verra, "Storia e memoria in Hegel"; and a series of articles by Nuzzo. Few of these authors, however, place Hegel in the context of the memory tradition or interpret *Erinnerung* as the key to the Hegelian dialectic.

XIII: Hegel's Philosophy of *Erinnerung*

Describing his philosophical system in the *Encyclopedia Logic*, Hegel writes, "Each part of philosophy is a philosophical whole, a circle rounded and complete in itself. In each of these parts, however, the philosophical idea is found in a particular specificity or medium. ... The whole of philosophy in this way resembles a circle of circles. The Idea appears in each single circle, but, at the same time, the whole Idea is constituted by the system of these peculiar phases, and each is a necessary member of the organization" (*EL*, §15). In this and the following chapter, I will consider the role of recollection in the major works published in Hegel's lifetime, in order to illuminate how this faculty fits into the several circles of his system, which is a circle of circles. Because the *Phenomenology of Spirit* gives the model for the role of recollection in the later works, and links Hegel's project with the memory tradition, I will devote most of the present chapter to a discussion of this work. I will then consider the role that memory plays in Hegel's later works: the *Science of Logic*, the *Encyclopedia of the Philosophical Sciences*, and the *Philosophy of Right*. Throughout the entire system, the absolute [*das Absolute*] is always identical with *Erinnerung*. As a preliminary, we must consider Hegel's relationship to *ars memoriae*.

Hegel and *ars memoria*

While Hegel developed his own philosophical doctrine of memory independent of any influence from Vico or Montaigne, he was certainly aware of the classical and Renaissance memory tradition with which they were both in dialogue. He was educated from his youth in classical rhetoric. Hegel's education at the Gymnasium Illustre in Stuttgart was largely based on memory and application. John H. Smith writes, "The principles that guided Hegel's instruction in every discipline ... can be summarized as the memorization and exercise of *praecepta* in order to attain a mastery of stylistic decorum modeled on past masters so that the student can enter the public sphere. In the eighteenth century, then, Hegel's school resembled its earlier condition under humanism and baroque rhetorical theory rather than a modern Enlightenment institution."[1]

---

1 Smith, *Spirit and Its Letter*, 70–71. This book gives the most extensive account of Hegel's rhetorical *Bildung* and its influence on his mature philosophy.

As part of his rhetorical training, Hegel, like the young Montaigne, was educated in eloquence by exercises in translating and emulating the style of Cicero.[2] There were also well-known contemporaries of Hegel's who continued to peddle the classical memory techniques, most notably the German mnemonist Gregor von Feinaigle, who wrote *The New Art of Memory* (1812), a recapitulation of the technique of memory found in Cicero and Quintilian.[3]

In his *Lectures on the History of Philosophy*, Hegel discusses at length the memorial arts of Ramon Lull and Giordano Bruno, showing admiration for these efforts. He writes, "There is then in Bruno a great beginning at thinking the concrete, absolute unity. The other great thing is his attempt to grasp and exhibit the universe in its development, in the system of its [progressive] determination, to show how the outward realm is a sign of the ideas" (*LHP*, 72). He also claims, in the *Encyclopedia*, that Plato's doctrine of *anamnesis* accords with his own doctrine of the *Begriff* (*EL*, §161, Z).

Despite this admiration for Bruno and Lull, Hegel always adopts a dismissive tone when he explicitly mentions the classical mnemotechnic. He sees the art of memory as a moment in the history of philosophy, but a moment that it was necessary to overcome. In the *Encyclopedia*, he writes: "The recent attempts—already, as they deserved, forgotten—to rehabilitate the mnemonic of the ancients, consist in transforming names into images, and thus again deposing memory to the level of imagination. The place of the power of memory is taken by a permanent tableau of a series of images, fixed in the imagination." For Hegel, this reduces ideas to the level of the shallowest picture-thinking. He continues, "The attachment cannot be made otherwise than by shallow, silly, and utterly accidental links. Not merely is the mind put to the torture of being worried by idiotic stuff, but what is learnt by rote is just as quickly forgotten, seeing that the same tableau is used for getting by rote other series of ideas." The objects of the mnemonic are not *erinnert*, not truly internalized. They do not affect the character of the individual: "What is

---

2   See ibid., 94–95. See also H. S. Harris, *Hegel's Development* (New York: Oxford University Press, 1972), 1: 47–56, on the lost collection of excerpts from Hegel's student days, several of which treat of Cicero.
3   It is this Feinaigle who is the subjects of Byron's lines,
    For her Feinagle's was a useless art,
    And he himself obliged to shut up shop—he
    Could never make a memory so fine as
    That which adorned the brain of Donna Inez.
    Lord Byron, *Don Juan* (Boston: Houghton Mifflin, 1958), I: xi.

mnemonically impressed is not like what is retained in memory really got by heart, i.e. strictly produced from within outwards, from the deep pit of the ego, and thus recited, but is, so to speak, read off the tableau of fancy.—Mnemonic is connected with the common prepossession about memory, in comparison with fancy and imagination; as if the latter were a higher and more intellectual activity than memory" (*PM*, §462).

In the *Lectures on the History of Philosophy*, Hegel makes a connection between Bruno and Lull on the one hand, and the mnemotechnic of the *Ad Herennium* on the other. Regarding the art of memory, he writes, "It is just a matter of definite images in the imagination. One fixes these images firmly and transfers to them all the individual representations of all particular contents and objects one seeks to know by heart. ... The difficulty lies only in forming a conjunction between the content and the images. This too is an inferior art. Anyone practiced in it can learn something by heart with a greater ease" (*LHP*, 68–9). This reflects Quintilian's suspicions and doubts about the efficacy of the technical art of memory. Hegel believes that Bruno ultimately goes much further than this mere tableau of pictures and gives "a system of ideas, thought-determinations or universal representations. Bruno passes over to this art from his universal ideas" (ibid., 69).

Hegel suggests that the weaknesses of the mnemonic system advocated by the author of the *Ad Herennium* are apparent. It places things in an entirely artificial order. It grants only a turbid, mechanical, and accidental grasp of things, and in no way fosters the true internalization of the essence of things. For Hegel, true recollection is an answer to the question, "What is the real?" The mnemotechnic cannot begin to answer this question; it rests, uncritically, at the level of immediate sense-perception. However, this is not to say that Hegel is not interested in arts of memory as such. The error of the mnemotechnic is not that it emphasizes recollection; it errs by neglecting what is truly philosophical about recollection. Bruno's art comes closer to Hegel's idea of memory. Bruno deals with universal ideas rather than the matter-at-hand. Thought precedes the art of memory, and the purpose of the art is to internalize these ideas and thereby to grasp the really real. Memory is the meeting place of the inner and the outer. Hegel praises Bruno's Hermetic attempt to grasp the *cosmos* through recollection: "Thinking is activity, and in [Bruno's] view it portrays inwardly, by means of an inner script, what nature portrays outwardly, by means of an outer script. The understanding takes the outer script of nature up within itself, and the inner script is also imaged in the outer; there is one form that develops [in both]. It is one and the same principle—what the understanding organizes outside itself, and what thinks within the human mind" (*LHP*, 71).

Hegel's thinking, as I have already mentioned, was profoundly influenced by Hermeticism, though this intellectual debt has only recently been explored. Glenn Alexander Magee has discussed the "lasting influence of [Bruno's] memory system on German Hermeticism" that resulted from Bruno's time in Wittenberg.[4] The mnemotechnic is an insufficient tool for reaching the position of absolute knowing, but the art of Bruno, which both cancels and preserves the classical mnemonics, comes much closer. Hegel wishes to resuscitate the Renaissance idea of memory, not its technical line. The notion of *theatrum mundi*, with its cosmic presumptions, was an object of scorn for modern rationalism. There is no place for Bruno's esoteric dark arts in the method of Descartes or the system of Kant. Kant is the furthest thing from a *magus*. However, Hegel was interested in overcoming the limitations of these analytic philosophies of reflection and bringing subject and object into some kind of unity. For him, the discarded memory tradition appeared as a perfect instrument, a perfect starting point for his own philosophical project. His appropriation of the memorial arts is evident in the final chapter of the *Phenomenology*, which will be discussed in the next chapter. Hegel's effort to carry philosophy forward begins with taking up again that strand of thought that modern philosophy had worked to forget.

In an early manuscript, entitled "Über Mythologie, Volksgeist und Kunst," Hegel articulates certain early opinions on memory and history that persist throughout his body of work. He writes, "Mnemosyne, or the absolute Muse, art, assumes the aspect of presenting the externally perceivable, seeable, and hearable forms of spirit. This Muse is the generally expressed consciousness of a people. The work of art of mythology propagates itself in living tradition. As peoples grow in the liberation of their consciousness, so the mythological work of art continuously grows and clarifies and matures. This work of art is a general possession, the work of everyone. Each generation hands it down embellished to the one that follows; each works further toward the liberation of absolute consciousness." Later in the manuscript, he writes, "There is always one who brings it to its final completion by being the last to work on it and he is the darling of Mnemosyne."[5]

---

4 Magee, *Hegel and the Hermetic Tradition*, 34.
5 Translated by Verene, in *Hegel's Recollection*, 36–37.

Mnemosyne, memory, is the "absolute Muse." She must therefore be the Muse of philosophy, which is concerned not with particulars and accidents, but with absolute knowing. Mnemosyne and her memory of what was, is, and shall be, is the source of philosophical knowledge. Philosophy is the practice of discovering the necessary, inner form of things. Hegel has in mind a "perennial philosophy,"[6] knowledge not just of how things have always been, but also of how they are and how they will always be. In this fragment, Hegel suggests that spirit develops through history, as a shared consciousness of a people, toward its final goal of absolute consciousness. The work of art is this cultural development. Absolute consciousness is brought to fruition under the auspices of Mnemosyne, through a memory of the whole. Donald Phillip Verene writes, "Seen from the perspective of these fragments, Hegel is attempting in the *Phenomenology* to connect philosophy with the absolute Muse, Mnemosyne, and to create in the living world of modern culture a philosophy that does not have the character of dreaming."[7]

This announces a much more ambitious project than that of Montaigne. Montaigne never claims that his memorial dialectic is a tool for attaining a position of absolute knowing or knowledge of the truth of the cosmos. In the *Essays*, memory is always ethical; it teaches us how to live well with others. It is prudence for the moment. For Hegel, a more permanent species of truth can be known, and is attained through the grace of the genius of Memory. In the *Encyclopedia*, he writes, "When people assert that man cannot know the truth, they are uttering the worst form of blasphemy. They are not aware of what they are saying. Were they aware of it they would deserve that the truth should be taken away from them" (*PM*, §440, Z). Truth can be known because it has already happened, and it continues along the same lines as it has always followed. As Francis Bacon writes, "Solomon saith, *There is no new thing upon the earth*; so that as Plato had an imagination that all knowledge was but remembrance, so Solomon giveth his sentence, *That all novelty is but oblivion.*"[8] How Mnemosyne connects with Hegel's philosophy of absolute knowing becomes clear in the final pages of his first major book, the *Phänomenologie des Geistes*.

---

6 See Magee, *Hegel and the Hermetic Tradition*, 86–87.
7 Verene, *Hegel's Recollection*, 37.
8 Francis Bacon, "Of Vicissitude of Things," in *Essays*, 235. This is also the epigraph of Jorge Luis Borges' story, "The Immortal."

Erinnerung in the *Phenomenology*

Hegel can only give a concise description of the process and content of the *Phenomenology* at the end of the work because, as he establishes in its Preface, it is not possible to give in advance of a work of philosophy a clear statement of what it hopes to achieve, except on the most superficial levels. The content of the work only becomes clear in the work itself, its "inner meaning" showing itself in "the result together with the process through which it came about" (*PS*, §§1–3; *W*, III: 11–13). What is the process by which the "result" of the *Phenomenology*—that is, the posture of "absolute knowing"—comes about? In the final paragraph of the work, Hegel uses the word *Erinnerung* four times to describe the project he has just undertaken. This paragraph is worth quoting in full:

> But the other side of its [spirit's] becoming, *history*, is that *knowing*, self-*mediating* becoming—spirit externalized [*entäußerte*] into time; but this externalizing is just as much the externalizing of itself; the negative is the negative of itself. This becoming exhibits a slow movement and succession of spirits, a gallery of images [*Galerie von Bildern*], each of which, endowed with the full richness of spirit, is so slow moving because the self has to penetrate and digest all of this richness of its substance. Since its completion consists of perfectly *knowing* what *it is*, its own substance, so this knowing is its *going-into-itself*, in which it relinquishes its concrete existence [*Dasein*] and gives its shape over to recollection [*Erinnerung*]. In its going-into-itself, it is absorbed into the night of its self-consciousness, but its vanished existence is preserved in it, and this absorbed yet preserved [*aufgehobne*] existence—the preceding one, but born anew from knowing—is the new existence, a new world and new shape of spirit. It has to begin anew unconstrainedly from its immediacy and to raise itself up again to maturity, as if all that had preceded it was lost and it had learned nothing from the experience of the earlier forms of spirit. But the re-collection [*Er-Innerung*][9] has preserved it and is the inner being and, in fact, the higher form of substance. So when this form of spirit starts its education [*Bildung*] anew, seeming to begin only from itself, it at the same time starts on a higher level. The realm of spirits that have in this way formed themselves within existence make a succession in which one replaces the other and each has taken over the realm of the world from its predecessor. Its goal is the revelation of what is innermost, and this is *the absolute concept* [*der absolute Begriff*]; this revelation is herewith the cancelling but preserving [*Aufheben*] of its innermost being or its *expansion*, the negativity of this "I" as being-in-itself, which is its alienation

---

9   I have translated *Er-Innerung* as "re-collection", but there is no adequate way to neatly capture its sense in English. By hyphenating the word, Hegel emphasizes the German root *Innerung*. The word is here being used to indicate the inwardizing or internalizing function of recollection. I have considered translating *Er-Innerung* as either "inwardizing recollection" or "inner recollection", but neither turn of phrase does full justice to the German. Hegel also hyphenates the word in the Religion section of the *Phenomenology* (*PS*, §753; *W*, III: 548).

[*Entäußerung*]¹⁰ or substance—and its *time*, in that this alienation is as such an alienation of itself and thus in its expansion, as well as in its depth, is the self. *The goal*, absolute knowing, or spirit knowing itself as spirit, has for its path the recollection [*Erinnerung*] of the forms of spirit as they are in themselves and as they execute the organization of their realm. Their retention, from the side of free existence appearing in the form of contingency, is history, but from the side of their conceptually grasped [*begriffnen*] organization is the *science* of *phenomenal knowing*; both together—"conceptually grasped history"—form the recollection [*Erinnerung*] and the Calvary [*Schädelstätte*] of absolute spirit, the reality, truth and certainty of its throne, without which it would be lifeless solitude; only—

> out of the chalice of this realm of spirits
> foams to Him His infinity (*PS*, §808; *W*, III: 590–91, my translation).

The surprising revelation of this final paragraph is that "absolute knowing," the joyous mountain that spirit has sought throughout the text, *is*, as I have suggested several times, nothing more than the "path of recollection." Absolute knowing is spirit recollecting its own progress. How are we to understand this claim, and what is its relevance in Hegel's system? This requires examining first what Hegel says in the Preface of the *Phenomenology*.

The Preface to the *Phenomenology*

In the Preface, which was written only after the rest of the text was completed, Hegel foreshadows what is eventually made explicit. He writes, "The task of leading the individual from his uneducated standpoint to knowledge had to be seen in its universal sense. ... The single individual is incomplete spirit, a concrete shape in whose whole existence *one* determinateness predominates, the others being present only in blurred outline. In a spirit that is more advanced than another, the lower concrete existence has been reduced to an inconspicuous moment; what used to be the important thing is now but a trace; its pattern is shrouded to become a mere shadowy outline" (*PS*, §28; *W*, III: 31–32). As one ascends the ladder of knowledge, the moments of one's education are *aufgehoben*, both cancelled and preserved.

Hegel continues, "The individual whose substance is the more advanced Spirit runs through this past just as one who takes up a higher sci-

---

10 The German *Entäußerung* could also be translated as "externalization," as I have translated *entäußerte* as "externalized," above. On one level, Hegel is contrasting *Entäußerung* and *Erinnerung* in this paragraph. C.f. Jean-Louis Vieillard Baron, "Hegel, philosophe de la reminiscence," *International Studies in Philosophy* 8 (1976): 158. Vieillard Baron calls *Erinnerung* and *Entäußerung* a "reciprocal set of concepts" (my translation).

ence goes through the preparatory studies he has long since absorbed, in order to bring their content to mind: he *recalls* them to the inward eye, but has no lasting interest in them. The single individual must also pass through the formative stages of universal Spirit so far as their content is concerned, but as shapes which Spirit has already left behind, as stages on a way that has been made level with toil" (ibid., emphasis mine). After advancing to a higher position, spirit is able to look back and recall, as dead matter, all of its previous, lower positions. Philosophical *Bildung* requires that the individual pass through these earlier stages, but preserve them all in recollection.

In the following paragraph, Hegel writes, "The *length* of this path has to be endured, because, for one thing, each moment is necessary; and further, each moment has to be *lingered* over, because each is itself a complete individual shape, and one is only viewed in absolute perspective when its determinateness is regarded as a concrete whole." Because these stages, on which one lingers, are in the past, "It is no longer existence in the form of *being-in-itself* ... but is now the *recollected in-itself*, ready for conversion into the form of *being-for-self*" (*PS*, §29; *W*, III: 33–34). The conversion from being-in-itself to being-for-itself depends upon recollection, *Erinnerung*, as its middle term.[11] The "absolute perspective" requires that one simultaneously hold in mind all of the stages that precede this perspective; this alone constitutes the "concrete whole." As H. S. Harris says, "Phenomenological Science must not only display the 'shaping' of what has sunk into being the 'property' of the mature culture as a distinct moment in its development; it must also display the movement of culture through which this transformation happened; and it must display it 'in its full detail and necessity.' ... The philosophical phenomenologist must experience the *Bildung* of the *Weltgeist* in the way that an artist copies a painting."[12]

A few paragraphs later, Hegel connects this act of *Erinnerung* with the "labor of the negative." He writes, "That an accident as such, detached from what circumscribes it, what is bound and is actual only in its context with others, should attain an existence of its own and a separate freedom—that is the tremendous power of the negative; it is the energy

---

11 Verene refers to this as the "double Ansich." He reads the *Phenomenology* as a two-step movement in which the distinction "between the *Ansich* and the *Ansich* known" is developed but never synthesized by consciousness. See Verene, *Hegel's Recollection*, 15–16. Hegel's clearest statements about the connection between in-itself and for-itself are at *PS*, §§85–86; *W*, III: 77–79.
12 H. S. Harris, *Hegel's Ladder* (Indianapolis: Hackett, 1997), 1: 71.

of thought, of the pure 'I'. Death, if that is what we want to call this non-actuality, is of all things the most dreadful, and to hold fast what is dead requires the greatest strength" (*PS*, §32; *W*, III: 36). Lived experience is dead matter when it is past. As lived, it possesses the immediate status of being-in-itself, but after it has been lived through, this privileged status is effaced. What once *was* is now dust, a corpse or *caput mortuum*. This is the death captured by Shelley in his poem "Ozymandias":

> 'My name is Ozymandias, king of kings:
> Look on my works, ye Mighty, and despair!'
> Nothing beside remains. Round the decay
> Of that colossal wreck, boundless and bare
> The lone and level sands stretch far away.[13]

It is also, as Angelica Nuzzo has pointed out, "memory that first declares the dead as dead and sanctions the past as past in order to make it live on."[14] Memory is what kills, as well as what preserves.

Hegel continues, "But the life of spirit is not the life that shrinks from death and keeps itself untouched by devastation, but rather the life that endures it and maintains itself in it. It wins its truth only when, in utter dismemberment, it finds itself. ... Spirit is this power only by looking the negative in the face, and tarrying with it. This tarrying with the negative is the magical power that converts it into being" (*PS*, §32; *W*, III: 36). This gaze that spirit casts upon the dead matter of its own history is the gaze of *Erinnerung*. Recollection dwells amongst the dead. It takes up what no longer has being and transforms it into the "recollected in-itself." It *internalizes* what was once simple being, what once stood opposite the subject as an other. This element of internalization is etymologically present in the German *Erinnerung*, the root of which is *inner*, from *das Innere*.[15]

To undertake the philosophical act of *Erinnerung* demands the fortitude of Aeneas, the courage to venture amongst the shades. Such a journey is not for most. Like Aeneas, we must withstand the wailing

---

13 Percy Bysshe Shelley, "Ozymandias," in *The Complete Poetical Works of Percy Bysshe Shelley*, ed. Thomas Hutchinson (New York: Oxford University Press, 1965), 550, lines 10–14.
14 Angelica Nuzzo, *Memory, History, Justice in Hegel* (New York: Palgrave Macmillan, 2012), 29. This passage first appears in Nuzzo's "History and Memory in Hegel's Phenomenology," *Graduate Faculty Philosophy Journal* 29 (2008): 195.
15 On the four structural parts of the word *Erinnerung*, see David Farrell Krell, "Of Pits and Pyramids: Hegel on Memory, Remembrance, and Writing," in *Of Memory, Reminiscence, and Writing: On the Verge* (Bloomington, IN: Indiana University Press, 1990), 235–36.

voices of the dead. We must confront, with tears and regret, our own ghosts in the fields of mourning. The purpose of this journey is the pursuit of self-knowledge. Only through this descent can we grasp the significance of the long path of our own history, as Virgil tells us (*Aen.*, VI). Aeneas' expedition from Troy to Latium is the journey of every individual spirit, a journey that only acquires its full significance when it looks backward by way of a totalizing recollection. Hegel is the ferryman who ushers us into the land of the dead, so that we may pursue self-knowledge. The *Phenomenology* as a whole is the autobiography of spirit, for those with the courage to undertake the project of recollection. Courage is always a necessary virtue for the philosopher.

Harris writes that this paragraph "validates my comprehensive interpretation of *Erinnerung* as a death and resurrection of experience in memory."[16] Memory is not, however, a true resurrection. What is recollected does not come to life again. Life takes place in a temporal stream, but memory holds its objects outside of time. The content of memory is eternal because it is atemporal. The negativity of the dead past is always preserved in one sense, though it is cancelled in another. It is cancelled through internalization, in the conversion from being-in-itself to the recollected in-itself. It is preserved insofar as it remains as a moment in the whole. Each moment is taken up as a part of absolute knowledge, but none is sufficient by itself to be the absolute position.

It is noteworthy that Hegel begins this paragraph by emphasizing the insufficiency of the analytical approach. He writes, "This analysis, to be sure, only arrives at *thoughts* which are themselves familiar, fixed, and inert determinations. But what is thus separated and non-actual is an essential moment; for it is only because the concrete does not divide itself, and make itself into something non-actual, that it is self-moving. The activity of dissolution is the power and work of the *understanding* [*Verstand*], the most astonishing and mightiest of powers, or rather the absolute power [*absolute Macht*]" (ibid.). The "analytic" approach Hegel mentions is the philosophical method of Descartes.[17] Hegel is careful to distinguish his own philosophical system from that of the Cartesians. The latter is problematic because it defines and forever fixes its ideas. Analysts fail to account for the perpetual movement of all things, to which Montaigne and Hegel were both so particularly attuned. These fixed de-

---

16 Harris, *Hegel's Ladder*, 1: 77.
17 Harris suggests that Hegel has in mind the traditions of both Descartes and Locke, and their unification in Kant. See Harris, *Hegel's Ladder*, 1: 78.

terminations are inert. True philosophical thought, on the other hand, gives vitality to what is dead; it captures the self-moving nature of things, rather than fixing things down once and for all. This is the "absolute power" of thought. Hegelian *Erinnerung* is introduced as an alternative to the analytic-reflective tradition, as a means of avoiding its hazards.

Hegelian *Vergessen*

The dramatic progression of the *Phenomenology* is the journey of spirit as it attempts to reconcile *das Ansich* [the in-itself] and *das Fürsich* [the for-itself], and to thereby reach a position of absolute knowing. This position, we have seen, cannot be reached by the philosophies of reflection practiced by Descartes and Kant, which always hold the object at a distance. The chapters of the *Phenomenology* are all moments in this journey, all stopping points at which spirit believes itself finally at home. Each fails in its turn. Spirit moves from the position of sense-certainty and immediate consciousness, to self-consciousness, to reason, and so on. It is not my intention to offer an analysis of the various stages of the *Phenomenology*, or the dialectical leaps that carry us from one to the next. There are countless commentaries on the structure and content of the book, and some are even worth reading.[18] I will only mention a few places in the body of the text that bear directly on the question at hand, the role of memory in Hegel's philosophy. In particular, we must focus on several moments in the dialectic of the *Phenomenology* at which Hegel speaks of the forgetfulness of spirit, its *Vergesslichkeit*.

What does Hegel mean by the forgetfulness of spirit? In the first chapter of the *Phenomenology*, "Sense-Certainty," he writes, "It is clear that the dialectic of sense-certainty is nothing else but the simple history of its movement or its experience, and sense-certainty itself is nothing else but just this history." This history is simple because it has not been internalized. It is the immediately given, which has not yet died. Hegel continues, "That is why the natural consciousness, too, is always reaching this result, learning from experience what is true in it; but equally it is always forgetting it and starting the movement all over again" (*PS*, §109; *W*, III: 90).

Hegel connects this passage with "the ancient Eleusinian mysteries of Ceres and Bacchus," saying that those stuck on the level of sense-

---

18 Among the best and most well-known are John N. Findlay's *Hegel: A Re-Examination*, H. S. Harris' *Hegel's Ladder*, and Jean Hyppolite's *Genesis and Structure in Hegel's* Phenomenology of Spirit.

certainty "have still to learn the secret meaning of the eating of bread and the drinking of wine. For he who is initiated into these mysteries not only comes to doubt the being of sensuous things, but to despair of it; in part he brings about the nothingness of such things himself in his dealings with them, and in part he sees them reduce themselves to nothingness" (ibid.; *W*, III: 91). If spirit is unable to learn the inherent nothingness of the object—and this is a difficult mystery to learn, because to comprehend it is to *despair*—we are, as Verene writes, "doomed to be forever returning to the barren plain of sense-certainty as the ground of knowing being."[19] If spirit continuously forgets the process of experience, it is unable to advance beyond this initial stage and repeats the same thing over and over again.

In a later passage, *Vergesslichkeit* is the device by which Hegel explains the transition from "Self-Consciousness" to "Reason." At the beginning of this stage, idealism stakes a claim for itself: "Reason is the certainty of consciousness that it is all reality." Concerning this new standpoint, which is likely a caricature of the idealism of Fichte, Hegel writes, "The consciousness which is this truth has this path behind it and has forgotten it, and comes on the scene *immediately* as reason; in other words, this reason which comes immediately on the scene appears only as the certainty of that truth. Thus it merely asserts that it is all reality, but does not itself comprehend this; for it is along that forgotten path that this immediately expressed assertion is comprehended. And equally, anyone who has not trodden this path finds this assurance incomprehensible when he hears it in its pure form" (*PS*, §233; *W*, III: 180).

In this passage, it is evident that the dialectical leap from one stage of the *Phenomenology* to the next, so baffling to literal-minded thinkers in search of an *argument* to justify these leaps, is at least some of the time a matter of forgetting. No stage is an entire break from that which precedes it, but we forget that this is the case. Because consciousness forgets the path it has trod to reach the stage of "Reason", it believes itself to have alit suddenly in an entirely new reality. It asserts its new doctrine of ideality as a simple truth, but it cannot justify this assertion because it has forgotten the progress that has gone toward reaching this standpoint. For those who have not travelled this far along the path, the claims it makes must be incomprehensible nonsense. Recollection is always the engine by which we move forward in the dialectic, whereas forgetting leaves us stranded at one stage or other. Recollection is the se-

---

19   Verene, *Hegel's Recollection*, 35.

cret of the dialectical leaps. We are left unable to progress from a given stage if we do not know from whence we have come. We become like the goldfish, who forgets that he was not always trapped in the tank. In order to advance beyond its present negative state and adopt a new form, spirit has to recollect something from the states through which it has already passed.

In the two penultimate paragraphs of the *Phenomenology*, Hegel discusses spirit as nature. He writes, "Science contains within itself this necessity of externalizing the form of the pure concept [*reinen Begriffs*], and it contains the passage of the concept into *consciousness*" (*PS*, §806; *W*, III: 589, translation altered). However, "This externalization is still incomplete; it expresses the connection of its self-certainty with the object which, just because it is thus connected, has not yet won its complete freedom. The self-knowing spirit knows not only itself but also the negative of itself. ... This last becoming of spirit, *nature*, is its living immediate becoming; nature, the externalized spirit, is in its existence nothing but this eternal externalization of its *continuing existence* and the movement which reinstates the *subject*" (*PS*, §807; *W*, III: 590).

Spirit is natural, but to view spirit as *only* natural is incomplete and dangerously one-sided. Hegel says in the following paragraph that on the other side of its becoming, spirit is also *historical*. The historical side of spirit is a product of its *Erinnerung*. The natural side of spirit is a product of its *Vergesslichkeit*. Taken as nature, spirit is simply "living immediate becoming," which the Stoics called *species transitivae* and Whitehead called "vacuous actuality." It forgets its own history, its own autobiography. While *Erinnerung* is internalization, spirit taken as nature is externalization. Verene writes, "Spirit as the form of nature is a form of forgetting, of wandering with strange companions, not itself. It saves itself from these strange companions, the objects of nature, by remembering it has another life—the life of self images."[20] Spirit taken solely as nature can never advance beyond immediacy. Absolute knowing depends on the richer, historical sense of spirit; it depends on recollection. This discussion of nature sets the stage for the final paragraph of the *Phenomenology*, in which Hegel finally gives the key to the entire work.

---

20   Ibid., 5.

Erinnerung as absolute knowing

We are now in a position to evaluate this final paragraph and its four different uses of the word *Erinnerung*. Hegel introduces in this paragraph a surprising metaphor to describe the *Phenomenology* as a whole. He says that the "becoming" of the book "exhibits a slow movement and succession of spirits, a gallery of images [*Galerie von Bildern*], each of which, endowed with the full richness of spirit, is so slow moving because the self has to penetrate and digest all of this richness of its substance." The *Phenomenology* is a "gallery of images."[21] This claim aligns the *Phenomenology* with the Renaissance idea of *theatrum mundi*.[22]

The "gallery of images" is the collection of all of those failed attempts of spirit to attain direct knowing. As Angelica Nuzzo writes, "[Memory's] living flux is preserved in a gallery of still (dead and past) images whose flow is cancelled in the instantaneous present; history is *aufgehoben* ... in the atemporal and aspacial dimension of the pure 'concept.'"[23] These still images are all on stage at once for spirit to behold, as a totality. The cast comes out together to take its bows. This "gallery" mirrors the Renaissance idea of *theatrum mundi*. At a single glance, the spectator can observe all the failed stages of his or her own progress. The gallery is the secret to absolute knowing. It offers the complete view of the whole. It is not memory in the service of the image (which is Hegel's criticism of Cicero), but the image in the service of memory. We will recall that ordering the contents of memory in a single theater was the project of the divine Camillo. By doing so, one was supposed to be able to attain the wisdom and powers of the cosmos.

Following Vico, I have argued that the philosophical act of *ingenium* depends upon a memory fertile with images. The theatrical presentation of these memory images gives thinking a stage from which it can reorder its knowledge or impart a new twist to things. The *Galerie von Bildern* is the vehicle for *ingenium*.[24] The dialectic of the *Phenomenology*

---

21 Harris reads the "gallery of images" as a reference to the religious images of Chapter VII of the *Phenomenology*. See Harris, *Hegel's Ladder*, 2: 749. I believe that this gallery refers instead to the complete progress of spirit throughout the text.
22 Verene's book, *Hegel's Recollection*, focuses on the images of the *Phenomenology* as the key to understanding the role of *Erinnerung* in the work. I mention the "gallery of images" not to cover the same ground, but to tie Hegel's thinking to *ars memoriae*. On the significance of the *Galerie von Bildern*, see *Hegel's Recollection*, 4; and Verene, "Two Sources," 45.
23 Nuzzo, *Memory, History, Justice*, 48.
24 Verene makes the same claim: "In my view the dialectic in Hegel's *Phenomenology* becomes a kind of ingenuity (*ingenium*) to move the recollection in the direction of

proceeds from the standpoint of Hegel's absolute knowing, though the reader must begin from immediate sense-certainty and slowly ascend to Hegel's position. The dialectical movements, connections, and leaps from one stage to the next are one and all the work of *ingenium*. The images in the gallery are moved about by Hegel's genius, until they find an order that adequately expresses their inner form, their inner connections. This is why I have suggested that Hegel may not be as systematic a thinker as he claims. The perambulations and transitions of his dialectic all depend on *ingenium*, which is always more playful than systematic, and cannot be taught. The subsequent history of philosophy is littered with the stillborn progeny of Hegelians who lacked *ingenium*.

Having reached this interpretation of the overall role of *Erinnerung* in the *Phenomenology*, it will be worthwhile to consider Hegel's four uses of *Erinnerung* in the book's final paragraph, taking them one at a time.

(1) "Since [spirit's] completion consists of perfectly *knowing* what *it is*, its own substance, so this knowing is its *going-into-itself*, in which it relinquishes its concrete existence [*Dasein*] and gives its shape over to recollection [*Erinnerung*]. In its going-into-itself, it is absorbed into the night of its self-consciousness, but its vanished existence is preserved in it, and this absorbed yet preserved existence—the preceding one, but born anew from knowing—is the new existence, a new world and new shape of spirit. It has to begin anew unconstrainedly from its immediacy and to raise itself up again to maturity, as if all that had preceded it was lost and it had learned nothing from the experience of the earlier forms of spirit." This claim relates to the two paragraphs immediately preceding, in which spirit was considered as nature. Natural spirit is unfulfilled because it is externalized. Herbert Marcuse has pointed out, "The fundamental nature of the history of Spirit is formed through the interdependence of externalization and recollection, objectification and its overcoming. ... The fulfillment of Spirit implies the *abandonment* of its 'existence' to the *perishing* of every objective form of being, to the '*disappearance*' of each actual 'realm of the world,' for every such realm is intrinsically one of externalization and objectification."[25]

This first moment of recollection also relates to Hegel's "gallery of images." These images pass slowly before the spirit, which makes them

---

the speculative apprehension. ... The dialectic is not a method but a name for ingenuity, ingenious activity itself, which takes a continually varying shape depending on the content before it." Verene, *Hegel's Recollection*, 11.

25 Herbert Marcuse, *Hegel's Ontology and the Theory of Historicity*, trans. Seyla Benhabib (Cambridge, MA: MIT Press, 1987), 315.

its own. Spirit's perfect self-knowledge, its withdrawal into itself, is a terrifying procedure. The withdrawal from the external world is a descent into the realm of dead images. The "realms of the world" that disappear from immediacy are preserved as ghosts haunting the recollection, ghosts that demand to be recognized. The "night of its self-consciousness" is at first a haunting existential carnival in which, without appeal to the external world, the wraith-like images of the gallery are empowered. This is the nightmare of Aeneas' descent to the underworld. In this first moment, the images are not yet made one's own. Hegel writes, "[Spirit] has to begin anew unconstrainedly from its immediacy and to raise itself up again to maturity, as if all that had preceded it was lost and it had learned nothing from the experience of the earlier forms of spirit."

(2) "But the re-collection [*Er-Innerung*] has preserved it and is the inner being and, in fact, the higher form of substance. So when this form of spirit starts its education anew, seeming to begin only from itself, it at the same time starts on a higher level." This sinking into the "night of its self-consciousness" is not a return to the beginning of the dialectic. We find ourselves repeating the same things over and over again only when we *forget* our progress. This is the second moment of *Erinnerung*, at which recollection realizes its positive power to internalize the ghostly images. The hyphenation of the word emphasizes its role in internalizing what is external.[26] In this moment, by inwardizing the images that pass before it in recollection, spirit is able to begin anew at a higher level than when it merely took the gallery of images as a spectacle. It starts afresh, from a content now made its own, rather than from something external. Hegel's critique of the mnemotechnic is that it is *Erinnerung* without *Innerung*, and thus inadequate for a proper *Bildung*. The inwardizing moment of *Erinnerung* is the basis of true education.

Hegel continues, "The realm of spirits that have in this way formed themselves within existence make a succession in which one replaces the other and each has taken over the realm of the world from its predecessor. Its goal is the revelation of what is innermost, and this is *the absolute concept*."[27] The *absolute*, as Hegel uses the term here, is reached by way

---

26   Marcuse observes, "As the (negative) dimension of mere inwardness, this right is at the same time the (positive) dimension of inwardizing, the realm of true 'recollection'." Marcuse, *Hegel's Ontology*, 316.
27   Harris, who understands the history of self-consciousness as the "biography of God," interprets this succession of spirits as a progression of "community-spirits," or "shapes of God." See *Hegel's Ladder*, 2: 747. I understand the history of self-consciousness in the *Phenomenology* as the potential or ideal autobiography of all individual spirits, a *storia ideale eterna*. I do not read *Erinnerung* as a particularly religious concept.

of the series of images displayed in the gallery, through which spirit slowly makes its way. He continues, "This revelation is herewith the cancelling but preserving of its innermost being or its *expansion*, the negativity of this 'I' as being-in-itself, which is its alienation or substance—and its *time*, in that this alienation is as such an alienation of itself and thus in its expansion, as well as in its depth, is the self." Recollection adds the element of temporality and history to the concept; it raises it above vacuous actuality. At the same time, it negates the status of the "I", the individual spirit, as a mere being-in-itself. Recollection externalizes the "I", just as it internalizes the gallery of images.

(3) "*The goal*, absolute knowing, or spirit knowing itself as spirit, has for its path the recollection [*Erinnerung*] of the forms of spirit as they are in themselves and as they execute the organization of their realm." This sentence gives the key to the text as a whole. For Hegel, the path of *Erinnerung* is the path of absolute knowing, because absolute knowing is self-knowledge, spirit that knows itself as such, Aristotle's *noēsis noēseōs*. To know itself, spirit must recollect itself, and pass through all those forms and errors in which it previously persisted. This path brings together the two independent moments of *Erinnerung*: the negative inwardizing, and the positive internalizing. Spirit must have the courage to stand naked before itself, and then to make what it sees its own. In the first moment of *Erinnerung* we *behold*; in the second moment we *know*. The higher level of recollection is the truth and unity of the two moments, and as such it is a pathway, the progress of consciousness. Absolute knowing is not something apart from the engagement of recollection with its gallery of images. We attain the stage of the absolute by recalling all of the stages through which spirit has passed to reach its destination. This is spirit's liberation from simple existence in the world of external things. If spirit continues to exist merely in the immediate world, its existence is externalized, and self-knowledge is accordingly limited to externalization. If we would know ourselves in our truth and essence, this external form of existence must pass away.

(4) "Their retention, from the side of free existence appearing in the form of contingency, is history, but from the side of their conceptually grasped organization is the *science* of *phenomenal knowing*; both together—'conceptually grasped history'—form the recollection [*Erinnerung*] and the Calvary of absolute spirit, the reality, truth and certainty of its throne, without which it would be lifeless solitude; only—

out of the chalice of this realm of spirits
foams to Him His infinity."

Here, Hegel uses *Erinnerung* to refer again to the unification of the first two moments of recollection. Recollection, as the production of images *and* the internalization of these images, is comprehended history.

Significantly, the recollection of absolute spirit is joined with the "Calvary [*Schädelstätte*] of absolute spirit." Calvary, or Golgotha, was the mount outside of Jerusalem on which Jesus was crucified. The Gospel of Mark says, "Then they brought Jesus to the place called Golgotha (which means the place of the skull), and they offered him wine mixed with myrrh; but he did not take it. And they crucified him, and divided his clothes among them, casting lots to decide what each should take" (Mark 15: 22–24).[28] *Schädelstätte* literally means "place of the skull." What, then, are we to make of this reference, at the end of the text, to the "Calvary of absolute spirit"? Harris interprets this in its religious sense, arguing that the *Phenomenology* ends in despair for those who abandon faith in a "beyond."[29] Stephen Crites suggests that Hegel has in mind the Stations of the Cross.[30] Verene emphasizes the significance of the visual aspect of the image, the *calvaria* (the skull without the lower jaw and face), and relates this image to the *Phenomenology*'s critique of *Schädellehre*.[31] Hegel was surely well aware of the depth of his image's ambiguity, and all of these interpretations are partial truths.

Most relevant to the discussion of *Erinnerung* is the connection of the image of Calvary to death and the possibility of resurrection. Comprehended history is the combination of the two moments of *Erinnerung*, in which spirit both beholds its dead images and then makes these images its own. Calvary represents the crucifixion of the immediately given, the first death of the body that recollection must first impose upon its objects, as foreshadowed in the Preface. The images then appear to spirit as haunting, ghostly apparitions, arisen from the dead. When Jesus returns from the dead, he is at first taken to be an apparition (John 20: 26–8). The second moment, recollection proper, is the positive internalization of these images. This is the day of Pentecost, the moment at which the tongues of fire descend upon the apostles and they internalize the Holy Spirit (Acts 2: 1–4). *Erinnerung* is this bodily death and spiritual resur-

---

28 Biblical quotations are from *The New Oxford Annotated Bible*, third edition, ed. Michael D. Coogan (New York: Oxford University Press, 2001).
29 Harris, *Hegel's Ladder*, 2: 750–53, 774–75.
30 Stephen Crites, "The Golgotha of Absolute Spirit," in *Method and Speculation in Hegel's* Phenomenology, ed. Merold Westphal (Atlantic Highlands, NJ: Humanities Press, 1982), 47–56. This article is the most extensive treatment of the Calvary image.
31 Verene, *Hegel's Recollection*, 5–6 and 88–89.

rection of every stage that has come before, and it is necessary to take up all of these stages once more. Forgetfulness of our progress always throws us back upon some earlier stage. Absolute knowing—spirit knowing itself—requires that the whole, along with all of its stages taken separately, be maintained in its resurrected internalization.

John N. Smith is entirely correct when he observes, "The irony of the last figure of the Spirit ... is that it tells us that we will not find 'absolute knowledge' beyond the dialogic exchange of positions, for absolute knowledge consists in that very dialogue. The highest formation of consciousness consists in the memory of its own development."[32] Absolute knowledge is not a "beyond." It is the sum total of what is here before us, in the spacious storehouses of memory. Augustine asked, "How then am I to seek for you, Lord?" and found the answer within. Hegel asks, "How then am I to seek for me?" and arrives at the same solution.

It is not accidental that Hegel concludes the chapter on absolute knowing with an image. This indicates that this stage is not a sharp break from the path of consciousness that has brought us to this point. Absolute knowing is another stage in the series. Like all of the others, the stage of absolute knowing is itself an image that must be taken up into the gallery of images and internalized. The recollection of the whole includes the absolute standpoint as a part of the whole. Absolute knowing is not an outsider's perspective on a closed set of scenes and images. The contents of this perspective include the absolute itself, spirit's self-knowledge. The two lines with which Hegel ends the book are an intentional misquotation of Schiller's poem, "Die Freundschaft." They suggest that the divinity, like the individual spirit at the end of the *Phenomenology*, is left contemplating His own infinity. God's form of knowing is the infinite recollection of His own creation. Likewise, we readers of Hegel are left contemplating the recollection of our own infinite spirits.

The revelation promised by absolute knowing, the great reconciliation that we sought at new every stage of spirit, is revealed to have already taken place. *Absolutes Wissen* is the recollection of what has already happened, and needed only to come forward in its true light.[33] The work of phenomenology, for Hegel, is a work of recollection. It is recol-

---

32 Smith, *Spirit and Its Letter*, 237.
33 Nuzzo says that *absolutes Wissen* is "nothing but the final recollection of what has already happened—the recollection of something that 'in itself' has already taken place and needs only be brought forth in its true and most 'proper form'. Such form is the 'simple unity of the concept' to which all figurative phenomenological determination must conclusively yield." "History and Memory," 189–90.

lection, with its two distinct moments taken together, which transforms substance into subject. Self turns out to be identical to being.[34] Recollection shows spirit to itself, and thus reveals to spirit what the real is and has always been.[35]

---

[34] See Jean Hyppolite, *Structure and Genesis of Hegel's* Phenomenology of Spirit, trans. Samuel Cherniak and John Heckman (Evanston, IL: Northwestern University Press, 1974), 591.

[35] In my interpretation of Hegel, recollection is always an ontological matter. This reading accords with Marcuse, who writes that *Erinnerung* is a "universal *ontological* category." See *Hegel's Ontology*, 68. It differs from the interpretation of Nuzzo, who reads *Erinnerung* in an ethical sense in Hegel's early work—"*Erinnerung* becomes *sittlich*"—and as related to justice in his later work. See Nuzzo, "History and Memory," and Nuzzo, "Memory, History, and Justice in Hegel's System," *Graduate Faculty Philosophy Journal* 31 (2010): 349–89. It also differs from Ernst Bloch, who interprets Hegel's "*Anamnesis*" as bound entirely to the past and therefore inadequate to ontology. See Bloch, "Hegel und die Anamnesis," *Hegel-Studien* (1964): 167–80.

XIV: Hegel's Later Works

Hegel published four major works in his lifetime: The *Phenomenology of Spirit* (*Phänomenologie des Geistes*, 1807), the *Science of Logic* (*Wissenschaft der Logik*, 1812, 1813, and 1816), the *Encyclopedia of the Philosophical Sciences* (*Enzyklopädie der philosophischen Wissenschaft*, in three parts, 1817, 1827, and 1830), and the *Elements of the Philosophy of Right* (*Grundlinien der Philosophie des Rechts*, 1821). I have said above that Hegel viewed his system as a series of circles, which together make up a "circle of circles." It is not my intention to attempt to work out how the various pieces of the system fit together.[1] I do, however, wish to consider the role that recollection plays in each of these works.[2] I will begin by discussing the *Logic*, treating as a pair the *Science of Logic* and the first volume of the *Encyclopedia*, which I will refer to as the *Lesser Logic*. I will then discuss the three volumes of the *Encyclopedia* as a whole, reading the *Lesser Logic* alongside Hegel's Philosophy of Nature and Philosophy of Mind. Finally, I will discuss the *Philosophy of Right* along with Hegel's related lectures on the *Philosophy of History*.

Hegel's *Logic*

In the final chapter of the *Phenomenology*, Hegel writes, "In [absolute] knowing, then, spirit has concluded the movement in which it has shaped itself, in so far as this shaping was burdened with the difference of consciousness [of subject and object], a difference now overcome. ... Whereas in the phenomenology of spirit each moment is the difference of knowledge and truth ... science on the other hand does not contain this difference and the cancelling of it. On the contrary, since the moment has

---

1 The most accessible articulation of Hegel's project as a whole is John N. Findlay's *Hegel: A Re-Examination*.
2 While there is a great deal of secondary literature on the significance of *Erinnerung* in the *Phenomenology*, there is significantly less that considers its role in Hegel's later writings. Most of the literature that discusses these later works focuses on the psychological treatment of recollection and memory found at the end of the *Philosophy of Mind*. W. T. Stace, for instance, never discusses Hegel's notion of recollection expressed in reference to this section. See *The Philosophy of Hegel* (New York: Dover, 1955), 365–67. In Glenn Alexander Magee's *Hegel Dictionary*, the entry for "recollection" is grouped with "imagination" and "memory", and refers only to this section. See *The Hegel Dictionary* (New York: Continuum, 2010), 196–97. This part of the *Philosophy of Mind* is psychologically interesting, but it is not particularly philosophical. I have discussed this above, in the fourth chapter.

the form of the [concept], it unites the objective form of truth and of the knowing self in an immediate unity" (*PS*, §805; *W*, III: 588–89). This "science" is the *Science of Logic*, the second part of Hegel's system.[3] Absolute knowledge is a goal shared by both projects, because they are ultimately two parts of the same philosophical science. Several attempts have been made to read the *Phenomenology* through the lens of the *Logic*.[4] While this approach may be suspect, it is clear that Hegel had in mind a general outline of his entire project while writing the *Phenomenology*.

We saw in the third chapter that, in the *Science of Logic*, recollection is the faculty by which the subject apprehends *essence*. Hegel writes, "The truth of *being* is *essence*. Being is the immediate. Since knowing has for its goal knowledge of the true, knowledge of what being is *in and for itself*, it does not stop at the immediate and its determinations, but penetrates it on the supposition that at the back of this being there is something else, something other than being itself, that this background constitutes the truth of being" (*SL*, 389; *W*, VI: 13, partially quoted above). It is not sufficient for spirit to rest at the apprehension of immediate being because immediate being is merely vacuous stuff, without history and without inner meaning. Before me stands some rubble: that is its being. However, this rubble was once a deeply ingrained element within a vibrant civilization: now we are coming closer to its essence. The mineral material of this rubble has a long, long history that sees it rise as it is out of a series of geological cataclysms: now we are closer still to its essence. To speak in Hegelian terms, immediate being is not yet in and for itself; it is only in-itself. It is therefore not yet "truth," because truth requires the identity of the thing and its concept.

Hegel continues, "Not until knowing *inwardizes*, *recollects* [*erinnert*] itself out of immediate being, does it through this mediation find essence. ... This path is the movement of being itself. It was seen that being inwardizes itself through its own nature, and through this movement into itself becomes essence" (ibid.). The inwardizing of being is the procedure explained at the end of the *Phenomenology*. It is the two-moment

---

3   As Merold Westphal observes, "Hegel's ontologically grounded Logic will presuppose the unity of thought and being developed in the *Phenomenology*." *History and Truth in Hegel's* Phenomenology (Bloomington, IN: Indiana University Press, 1998), 224.

4   This is the approach that Stanley Rosen takes to the *Phenomenology*. See Rosen, *G. W. F. Hegel: An Introduction to the Science of Wisdom* (New Haven, CT: Yale University Press, 1974), especially Rosen's discussion of the absolute, 229–60. Hyppolite also emphasizes the connection between the two works and the transition from the one to the other, in *Structure and Genesis*, 573–606.

process of death and resurrection, of seeing and knowing. Recollection inwardizes the thing, makes it spirit's own. Hegel writes, "Cognition certainly cannot stop short at manifold *determinate being*, nor yet at *being*, *pure being*; the reflection that immediately forces itself on one is that this *pure being*, the *negation* of everything finite, presupposes an *internalization*, a *recollection* [*Erinnerung*] and movement which has purified immediate, determinate being to pure being" (ibid.; *W*, VI: 13–14).

How does this purification occur? Recollection, we have seen, annuls the character of immediate being. The recollected form of the thing is atemporal and aspacial; it is eternal. It is no longer determinate or bound to particular locations in space or time. Essence, therefore, "is past—but timelessly past—being" (*SL*, 389; *W*, VI: 13). In the *Lesser Logic*, Hegel clarifies what he means by this claim: "There is a permanence in things, and that permanent is in the first instance their Essence. ... In the German auxiliary verb, *sein*, the past tense is expressed by the term for Essence [*Wesen*]: we designate past being as *gewesen*. This anomaly of language implies to some extent a correct perception of the relation between being and essence. Essence we may certainly regard as past being, remembering however meanwhile that the past is not utterly dead, but only laid aside and thus at the same time preserved" (*EL*, §112, Z). Essence is past being. While being simply *is*, essence *was*. We have already worked through the sense in which philosophical recollection is able to get behind being to uncover what it has always been, and thereby to reveal its essence and truth. This is a process in which ingenious, philosophical thought must cooperate with memory.

After introducing "essence" as a possible object of cognition dependent on the process of recollection, Hegel writes, "The negativity of essence is *reflection*; and the determinations are *reflected*, posited by essence itself and remaining in essence as sublated [*aufgehoben*]. ... At first, essence *shines* or *shows* [*scheint*] *within itself*, or is reflection; secondly, it *appears* [*erscheint*]; thirdly, it *manifests* [*offenbart*] itself" (*SL*, 391; *W*, VI: 15–16). In the corresponding section of the *Lesser Logic*, he writes, "The point of view given by the essence is in general the standpoint of 'reflection'. This word 'reflection' is originally applied, when a ray of light in a straight line impinging upon the surface of a mirror is thrown back from it" (*EL*, §112, Z). Hegel's commentary here on the concept of reflection shows a sensitivity to its origins as an optical term. Descartes—and probably Locke also—borrowed the term from the science of optics. I have argued above that recollection and reflection are alternative approaches to philosophical thought. What are we to make of Hegel here suggesting that the standpoint of essence, which depends upon recollection, is in fact reflection?

John Findlay, suggesting Fichte as the immediate source of Hegel's idea of reflection, writes, "[Hegel] tells us, also, that he has chosen a word from a strange language ['reflection'] to express the position of an appearance that has become *estranged* from its own immediacy. ... The connection of 'Reflection' with 'Essence' lies in the fact that the Essence of anything is the antithesis of what it presents to the immediate view: it is something which lies behind or within the immediate surface of appearance, and which is only reached by penetrating beneath it. Such penetration is reflective. ... The word 'Reflection' is further connected by Hegel with relativity and relationships."[5] This idea of antithesis is of the utmost importance for understanding Hegel's thought. Cognition of essence is *not* the level at which one attains absolute knowing. It is a positive step beyond the apprehension of being, but this new stage presents its own dilemmas. Essence is itself deeply problematic.

When it first appears, essence is nothing more than the opposite of immediate being; it is that which stands over and against being. In this relationship, being is considered "unessential" (*SL*, 394; *W*, VI: 17). In this sense, being is "illusory." Hegel writes, "It is *reflected* immediacy, that is, immediacy which *is* only by means of its negation [of its essence]" (ibid., 396; *W*, VI: 20). This illusory being "is the same thing as *reflection*; but it is reflection as *immediate*. For illusory being that has withdrawn into itself and so is estranged from its immediacy, we have the foreign word *reflection* [*Reflexion*]" (ibid., 399; *W*, VI: 24). The relationship between essence and being is a matter of relativity. The perception of either as true entails the perception of the other as illusory. Spirit is able, if it so chooses, to oscillate between one point of view and the other.

The sphere of essence is a sphere in which thinking cannot get beyond the properties of this relativity. Reflection always holds its objects at a distance, and reflective thinking always entails a distinction between subject and object. Reflective thinking is always relational. *Erinnerung* is necessary in the *Logic* in order to progress from the stage of being to the stage of essence, just as it is a requirement for each dialectical advance in the *Phenomenology*. Recollection is the vessel that carries thought from one stage to the next. Every transition in the texts is the result of *Erin-*

---

5   Findlay, *Hegel*, 185–86.

nerung. However, recollection is never the faculty through which we encounter the world while we abide at any particular stage. At any particular moment of the journey, it is some other cognitive faculty that assumes dominance, and hopes in vain to finally reconcile subject and object, or in-itself and for-itself. *Erinnerung* is absolute knowing not because it is the characteristic faculty of any one of these stages of logical thought, but because it alone grasps the whole of the journey of thought, including recollection itself.

At the level of essence, thinking becomes reflective because immediately perceived being is opposed to an other for the first time. *Erinnerung* reveals this otherness, but reflection forgets the source of this revelation. In order to move past this stage, in which reflection is dominant, we must be careful that spirit not forget its journey thus far. Reflection externalizes, and progress requires that what is externalized become internalized. Reflective thinking is not altogether harmful, but by itself it is not sufficient for philosophical thinking. Because it apprehends individual moments, it is a necessary preliminary for internalization.[6] However, it cannot move past these moments as long as they are kept asunder. Hegel writes, "This relation of the determining is thus the mediation of each with itself through its own non-being; but these two mediations are one movement and the restoration of their original identity—the recollection of their outwardness [*die Erinnerung ihrer Entäußerung*]" (*SL*, 452; *W*, VI: 90, translation altered). Externalization is overcome by recollection. This passage mirrors the two moments of *Erinnerung* at the end of the *Phenomenology*. In the first, we behold the gallery of images, and in the second the gallery is inwardized and becomes *known*. Only after we have discovered what Findlay calls the "necessary relation" between concepts can we pass beyond reflection to the sphere of the *Begriff*.[7]

It is noteworthy that in the *Lesser Logic*, the language of recollection is absent when Hegel introduces his doctrine of essence. Essence is spoken of in terms of reflection, which is the dominant faculty in the logical stage of essence, but not the faculty whereby essence arrives on the scene. Hegel begins this later articulation of the doctrine by writing, "The terms in essence are always mere pairs of correlatives, and not yet abso-

---

6   C.f. Stanley Rosen, *The Idea of Hegel's* Science of Logic (Chicago: University of Chicago Press, 2014): "This passage shows us once more that Hegel does not reject reflection, which is a necessary stage in the development of logical structure. ... It is reflection that provides us with individual moments like identity and difference. Externalization is thus the necessary preparation for internalization or recollection" (316).

7   See Findlay, *Hegel*, 186.

lutely reflected in themselves; hence in essence the actual unity of the notion is not realized, but only postulated by reflection. Essence—which is being coming into mediation with itself through the negativity of itself—is self-relatedness, only in so far as it is in relation to an other—this other however coming to view at first not as something which *is*, but as postulated and hypothesized" (*EL*, §112). Hegel does not speak of essence as the truth of being, as he does in the *Science of Logic*. Instead, he quickly addresses the shortcomings of the stage of essence, its ultimate failures as a reflective stage. Essence is what *was*, but it is not yet the absolute because this past being is only grasped in relation to immediate being.

Because essence and being are the limits of one another, either pole on its own falls short of the true infinite (*wahrhaft Unendliche*). In the *Lesser Logic*, Hegel calls the true infinite "the fundamental concept [*Grundbegriff*] of philosophy" (*EL*, §95). In the *Science of Logic*, he describes the concept in this way: "Finitude *is* only a transcending of itself; it therefore contains infinity, the other of itself." The infinite, though, is not merely the negation of the finite. "Similarly, infinity *is* only as a transcending of the finite; it therefore essentially contains its other and is, consequently, in its own self the other of itself. The finite is not sublated [*aufgehoben*] by the infinite as by a power existing outside it; on the contrary, its infinity consists in sublating its own self" (*SL*, 145–46; *W*, V: 160). For Hegel, a "bad infinite" (*Schlecht-Unendliche*) is any conception that takes the infinite as merely the beyond of the finite. This is bad because such an infinite is not truly infinite, insofar as it still has a limit, namely finitude. A conception of the true infinite must negate this opposition and contain both the infinite and the finite.[8] The stage of essence is a bad infinite, because, though it embraces the whole of what lies behind mere being, it is still limited by being. The true infinite, which is what absolute knowing seeks, must annul the opposition and contain both being and essence. In order to do so, spirit must recollect that the stage of essence follows from the stage of being, and preserve both moments while negating their independence.

When Hegel does appeal to *Erinnerung* in the *Lesser Logic*, it is much later in the text than the doctrine of essence, toward the end of the doctrine of the *Begriff*, the concept. On the level of the *Begriff*, a contradiction arises between the impulse for good and the idea of truth. Hegel writes, "In point of form however this contradiction vanishes when the

---

8   On Hegel's notion of the "true infinite," see Peone, "Ethical Negativity: Hegel on the True Infinite."

action supersedes the subjectivity of the purpose, and along with it the objectivity, with the contrast which makes both finite; abolishing subjectivity as a whole and not merely the one-sidedness of this form of it. ... This return into itself is at the same time the content's own 'recollection' [*Erinnerung*] that it is the good and the implicit identity of the two sides—it is a 'recollection' of the presupposition of the theoretical attitude of mind that the objective world is its own truth and substantiality" (*EL*, §234).

For the contradiction between the subjectively good and the objectively true to be annulled, thinking must take up an earlier presupposition. This entails the faith of reason in "the virtual identity between itself and the absolute world," and its faith that the objective world is its own truth (*EL*, §224). The contradiction is overcome only when the two sides recollect their own inherent identity: internalized substance becomes subject. This is spirit's return into itself. In a passage parallel to the end of the *Phenomenology*, Hegel writes, "This life which has returned to itself from the bias and finitude of cognition, and which by the activity of the notion has become identical with it, is the speculative or absolute idea" (*EL*, §235). This recollection is a partial return to the beginning of the *Logic*, in which spirit has naïve faith in the truth of immediate being, except that what was then merely an assumption is now properly an article of *cognition*. This return at the end of the *Logic* to its beginning exemplifies the circular nature of the parts of the Hegelian system.

Though Hegel employs the term *Erinnerung* at different stages in the two *Logics*, I do not see any contradiction in the way it is used. *Erinnerung*, as I have suggested, is behind every dialectical advance. It powers the transition from being to essence. Forgetfulness of this advance leaves one stranded at the level of essence. However, *Erinnerung* is not itself the characteristic faculty of any one level.

Recollection is the only power whereby we can attain the absolute idea, which is the unity of the subjective and objective ideas, the idea thinking itself, *noēsis noēseōs*.[9] Subjective and objective only come together in memory, as Bergson also understood. In the *Logic*, as in the *Phenomenology*, absolute knowing is recollection itself. The difference is that, while the *Phenomenology* is a history of the individual spirit and therefore relies on a gallery of personal images, the *Logic* is the universal history of pure logical thought, and its form of recollection can manage

---

9 Hegel borrows this term from Aristotle when commenting on the absolute idea. See *EL*, §236, Z.

without imagistic thinking (although Hegel does still rely on striking images in certain important passages of both versions of the *Logic*). Logical thought must recollect itself from its own determinations.

The *Encyclopedia of Philosophical Sciences*

Hegel wrote the three-volume *Encyclopedia of the Philosophical Sciences* while a professor of philosophy in Heidelberg. The first edition was published in 1817, with two revised editions following, in 1827 and 1830.[10] Logic, nature, and mind—the general topics of the three parts of the *Encyclopedia*—characterize the path the philosopher must take to attain a fully reconciled position of thought thinking thought, in the world.[11] In broad terms, the first volume is the development of philosophical thought as such, the second is the development of the external world, the negation of abstract thought, and the third is the development of spirit in the world. The *Encyclopedia* ends where it begins: "Its result is the logical system but as a spiritual principle" (*PM*, §574).

Erinnerung is not always used in a philosophical sense in the *Encyclopedia*. In the "Psychology" section of the Philosophy *of Mind*, recollection and memory [*Erinnerung* and *Gedächtnis*] are analyzed, along with the imagination [*Einbildungskraft*], as psychological faculties of representation (*PM*, §§451–64). Hegel here places these faculties alongside the other faculties of the soul and describes them mechanistically. In their psychological senses, he considers recollection to be an act of inwardly assuming the contents of intuition in the form of an image (*PM*, §452), and memory to be the production of a permanent synthesis between name and meaning that completes the transformation of intuition into representation (*PM*, §461).[12] Hegel's analysis here is close to Aristo-

---

10 For a brief account of the publication history of this text, see William Wallace's bibliographical notice at the beginning of *EL*, xxxi–xliii.

11 Glenn Alexander Magee suggests that the trinity of Logic-Nature-Spirit owes much to Lull's *ars combinatoria*. Lull replaces the sensuous images of the classical *ars memoriae* with "a quasi-algebraic notation and a 'method.'" See Magee, *Hegel and the Hermetic Tradition*, 181. While I agree that Hegel's idea of memory was influenced by Lull, Hegel does not abandon the use of sensuous imagery after the *Phenomenology*.

12 David Farrell Krell considers the psychological treatment of memory and recollection to still be philosophical, and considers the structure of this section as "matters of firsts and thirds for Hegel, beginnings and ends, precisely because their function is to rescue seconds, midpoints, mediations, and differences." See Krell, "Of Pits and Pyramids," 206. If memory is a matter of rescuing midpoints, then it is connected to *ars topica*. I do not think this post-modern interpretation is sustainable, given the content of this section of the *Encyclopedia*.

tle's treatment of these faculties in *De memoria*.¹³ Taken one-dimensionally as a psychological faculty, recollection is not the fountainhead of all philosophy, but a middle term between intuition and thinking. This is how memory is understood in the Aristotelian schema.¹⁴

In the *Encyclopedia* as a whole, however, *Erinnerung* retains its philosophical sense. Hegel tells us that, though memory has a mechanistic side, this side is subordinate (*EL*, §195, Z). The *Encyclopedia* is ultimately concerned with spirit in the world, and with the possibility of making the whole of the cosmos one's own. With this end in view, *Erinnerung* assumes a much more Hermetic role in the encyclopedic project than in Hegel's earlier works, in which its application was limited to the autobiography of the individual spirit or the abstract forms of logical thinking.

Hegel introduces the *Encyclopedia* by writing, "The objects of philosophy, it is true, are upon the whole the same as those of religion. In both the object is truth, in that supreme sense in which God and God only is the truth. Both in like manner go on to treat of the finite worlds of nature and the human mind with their relation to each other and to their truth in God. ... But with the rise of this thinking study of things, it soon becomes evident that thought will be satisfied with nothing short of showing the *necessity* of its facts" (*EL*, §1). Philosophy discovers not just the true, but the necessity of the true: the necessary, inner form of what was, is, and shall be. This suggests that Hegel fundamentally understands his own project of philosophical thinking, which he identifies with religious thinking, as an effort to obtain the wisdom of the Muses. In particular, it is the wisdom of Mnemosyne, the "absolute Muse," that the philosopher seeks.

In the introduction to the *Philosophy of Nature*, Hegel employs an evocative image that suggests this is the case. He writes, "This universal aspect of things is not something subjective, something belonging to us: rather it is ... like the Platonic Ideas, which are not somewhere afar off in the beyond, but exist in individual things as their substantial genera. Not until one does violence to Proteus—that is not until one turns one's back

---

13 This has been noted by Daniel Brauer, in "La 'memoria productiva': Acerce de la concepción de Hegel del recuerdo y la memoria," *Revista latinoamericana de filosofía* 28 (2002): 334.

14 For a detailed commentary on the "Representation" section of the *Encyclopedia*, see Jennifer Ann Bates, *Hegel's Theory of Imagination* (Albany: State University of New York Press, 2004), 84–96. Bates unfortunately does not discuss the philosophical sense that *Erinnerung* has elsewhere in Hegel's work.

on the sensuous appearance of nature—is he compelled to speak the truth. The inscription on the veil of Isis, 'I am that which was, is, and will be, and my veil no mortal hath lifted', melts away before thought" (*PN*, §246, Z).

Proteus is an oracular figure of classical literature, with the power to change his form. He speaks the truth only when compelled to do so. It is said by Virgil that he "has knowledge of all things—what is, what hath been, what is in train ere long to happen" (*Georg.*, IV, 392–93). In the *Odyssey*, Homer says that Proteus does not lie, but will only give answers if he can be held down. Menelaus relates that he had to seize Proteus while the latter slept and hold fast while his adversary transformed into a lion, a serpent, and a torrent of water, amongst other forms. Menelaus has the courage to retain his hold despite these apparent transformations, and this finally compels Proteus to speak (*Odys.*, IV, 428–528). In the fourth *Georgic*, Virgil relates the story of Aristaeus, who seeks to learn from Proteus why all of his bees have died. To compel him to speak, Aristaeus too must seize Proteus and hold him tight, disregarding the shapes into which he transforms himself (*Georg.*, IV, 387–414). One must violently restrain Proteus without heeding the sensuous appearances he manifests. Sensuous appearance is immediate intuition; it is the one-sided form in which vacuous being presents itself. Truth is not found in immediately given, externalized being. The philosopher must turn away from vacuous actuality when seeking out the deeper oracular truth. We must have the courage to confront the dreadful immediate being of Proteus with violence. We must turn away from what appears and demand the really real.

Plutarch associates Isis with the Muses of Hermopolis because of her wisdom. The content of her wisdom is, as Hegel says, that which was, is, and will be. This is the wisdom of Mnemosyne, the wisdom that apprehends the inner form of necessity. What will always be is revealed through the knowledge of what has always been. This wisdom does not stop at the external appearance of nature. Apparent actuality is subject to fluctuation and impermanence. The wisdom of the Muses entails, instead, turning away from the apparent and discovering the inner form of things. This is the work of recollection; both the Muses and Isis have the wisdom of perfect recollection. Hegel has figured out the simple key to penetrating the veil of Isis: it "melts away before thought," and the faculty of thought before which it melts away is recollection. Recollective thought simply cuts the Gordian knot. Beneath this veil is revealed the perennial truth of the cosmos, not its accidental manifestations.

Jean Hyppolite recognizes this element of Hegel's thinking. He writes, "If we are to understand Hegel's argument here we must assume that the whole is always immanent in the development of consciousness. ... Were it not for the immanence of the whole in consciousness, we should be unable to understand how negation can truly engender a content."[15] The Hegelian dialectic only moves forward because the whole, which is the true, is already implicitly known by the subject, in the Platonic sense of *anamnesis*. The work of philosophy is making this knowledge explicit to consciousness.[16]

Glenn Alexander Magee, sensitive to the Hermetic elements in Hegel's work, has also recognized the cosmic element of Hegel's notion of recollection. He writes, "All philosophy is implicitly or explicitly dialectical in nature, and the activity of dialectic presupposes that one always already possesses wisdom, but in inchoate form. Dialectic is a recollection and explication of that wisdom. This is true of both Hegelian and Platonic dialectic. ... Hegel's muse is Mnemosyne because his dialectic is a recollection of what our finite individual spirit has somehow already glimpsed of Absolute Spirit."[17] Elsewhere, Magee says that the philosopher "'recollects' this unconscious wisdom [of religion] and expresses it in a fully adequate form."[18]

Hegel asserts that the purpose of philosophy is to make explicit what consciousness already knows—that the work of philosophy is essentially *anamnesis*—from the very beginning of the *Encyclopedia*. He claims that the history of philosophy is a unified process, a development of the various forms of expression of a single perennial philosophy (*EL*, §13). The idea of a perennial philosophy comes from Hermes Trismegistus and was disseminated through Pico della Mirandola's *Oration on the Dignity of Man*. At what do the various imperfect forms of this perennial philosophy aim? Hegel writes, "The business of philosophy is only to bring to explicit consciousness what the world in all ages has believed about thought. Philosophy therefore advances nothing new; and our present discussion has led us to a conclusion that agrees with the natural belief of mankind" (*EL*, §22, Z). Solomon says there is nothing new under

---

15 Hyppolite, *Genesis and Structure*, 15.
16 C.f. Vieillard Baron, "Hegel, philosophe": "Plato's pedagogical theory in the *Meno* is thus explained by Hegel: the goal is thinking in and for itself; the means to achieve this is a formation that does not consist in openness to new knowledge, but rather the fundamental basis of this thinking in and for itself is immanent in spirit, in the soul of man" (153, my translation).
17 Magee, *Hegel and the Hermetic Tradition*, 89–90.
18 Ibid., 224.

the sun (Ecc. 1: 9), and Hegel affirms this. Philosophy recollects what is already known, but forgotten.

Two paragraphs later, Hegel writes, "Philosophy is knowledge, and it is through knowledge that man first realizes his original vocation, to be the image of God. ... On his natural side certainly man is finite and mortal, but in knowledge infinite" (*EL*, §24, *Z*). Man is a microcosm, the image of God, the *imago Dei*.[19] As we have seen with earlier thinkers in the Hermetic tradition like Bruno and Camillo, if man is a microcosm with an infinite capacity for divine wisdom, then recollection opens one to the possibility not just of self-knowledge, but to divine, cosmic knowledge. What is needed to access cosmic recollection? Hegel writes, "Education or development is required to bring out into consciousness what is therein contained. It was so even with Platonic reminiscence" (*EL*, §67). Here Hegel overtly underscores the connection between his own philosophy and the *anamnesis* of Plato. Knowledge of the whole is accessible to all, and can be attained through an inward look, but it requires the promptings of a philosophical guide. Presumably, Hegel is the *magus* required, and his system, his highway of despair, is our initiation into the mysteries, should we dare to walk with him.

Isis is "that which was, is, and shall be," and recollective thinking is the secret to lifting her veil. In the *Philosophy of Nature*, Hegel writes, "In the positive meaning of time, it can be said that only the present *is*, that before and after are not. But the concrete present is the result of the past and is pregnant with the future. The true present, therefore, is eternity" (*PN*, §259, *Z*). The true, which is the whole, is not the protean flux of the apparent world. Past is different than present, and both are distinct from future, insofar as the accidental appearances of the world change. However, the inner form of things is necessity, which is bound to neither time nor space. Necessity is that of which the Muses sing, and that which *ingenium* alone can discover. This discovery entails a grapple with Proteus, wherein the thinker must be able to ignore the surfaces of things. The mirror of reflection cannot penetrate these surfaces.

The final volume of the *Encyclopedia*, the *Philosophy of Mind*, contains Hegel's most explicit articulation of this cosmic form of knowing. In the Introduction, he writes, "This triumph over externality which belongs to the notion of mind, is what we have called the ideality of

---

19 Louis Dupré associates memory in the *Encyclopedia* with the *memoria Dei* of Augustine and the early Latin church fathers. See Dupré, "Hegel Reflects on Remembering," *Owl of Minerva* 25 (1994): 142.

mind. Every activity of mind is nothing but a distinct mode of reducing what is external to the inwardness which mind itself is, and it is only by this reduction, by this idealization or assimilation, of what is external that it becomes and is mind" (*PM*, §381, Z). The triumph over externality is the triumph over nature, the triumph over Proteus. The external world becomes one's own through the internalization of recollection. Hegel uses distinctly Hermetic language to explain this internalization: "The soul, when contrasted with the macrocosm of nature as a whole, can be described as the microcosm into which the former is compressed, thereby removing its asunderness" (*PM*, §391, Z). The whole of nature is contained internally, in the human being's implicit consciousness. This is the teaching of Hermes. It explains why recollection is the key to a divine form of knowing.

Insight into the inner necessity of things also allows us to comprehend how things must be in the future. Commenting on the phenomenon of clairvoyance, which he is willing to accept as at least possible, Hegel returns once again to the image of wisdom veiled. He writes, "It would be desperately wearisome to have exact foreknowledge of one's destiny and then to live through it in each and every detail in turn. But a foreknowledge of *this* kind is an impossibility; for what is yet only in the *future* and therefore merely *implicit* or a *possibility*, this simply cannot be an object of perceptive, intellectual consciousness, since only what *exists* … is perceived."

One cannot have a sensual representation of an experience in advance of that experience. Hegel continues, "The human mind is, of course, able to rise above the knowing which is occupied exclusively with sensibly present particulars; but the *absolute* elevation over them only takes place in the philosophical cognition of the eternal, for the eternal, unlike the particular of sense, is not affected by the flux of coming-to-be and passing-away and is, therefore, neither in the past nor in the future; on the contrary, it is the absolutely *present*, raised above time and containing within itself all the differences of time in their ideality." Contrasted with this philosophical knowing, the clairvoyant contemplates his or her "veiled life" in a concentrated state, in which "the determinations of space and time are also *veiled*" (*PM*, §406, Z). Philosophical "clairvoyance" is nothing more than the grasp of eternal truths.

The image of Isis veiled is the key to understanding Hegel's notion of cosmic recollection in the *Encyclopedia*. In the above passage, Hegel's articulation of his idea of philosophical knowledge relates it to the form of omniscience of Isis and Mnemosyne. The human mind rises above nature to grasp the eternal. The eternal is the necessary, that about which the Muses sing. It is attained through a dissolution of sensuous immediacy, which is accomplished through recollection. We are able to think the eternal (or the absolute) because each human individual is a microcosm—not just of *l'humaine condition*, as Montaigne would have it, but of the divine creator. Clairvoyance, which is still bound to sensory, determinate thinking, is not able to lift the veil of Isis. The veil can only be lifted by philosophical thinking, *absolute thinking*, which is always recollection. The Hegelian system is the lifting of the veil.

Objective spirit[20]

The *Philosophy of Right*, the last of Hegel's works to be published in his lifetime, is his analysis of objective spirit; that is, of morals, politics, and history. In terms of both style and content, this is the most accessible of Hegel's major works. It has therefore become the prism through which many readers of Hegel approach the whole of his system, especially those who are more interested in political theory than ontology. On the other side, there are some Hegelians who view this as the weakest part of his system. Findlay, for instance, writes, "In the *Philosophy of Right*, Hegel shows himself to be literally a reactionary. His dialectic, contrary to its principles, simply harks back to the immediacy on which it had its origin. That Hegel could have come to write as he does, certainly points to a deep loss of integrity both in his character and his thinking."[21] I do not care to take a side in this controversy. I take Hegel at his word that his system is a circle of circles; if this is the case, then any one circle is only a partial truth. To read the whole of Hegel's work through any one particular text is to violate this principle.

In an important sense, politics is always memory. Political morality must be tied to *prudentia*, since it always depends upon the recollection of what has been of benefit to the society or the group in the past. *Iurisprudentia*, that is, the system of legality, is the political codification of *prudentia*. History, too, is memory. History is what *was*; it lies behind

---

20 I have tried to limit my commentary to Hegel's finished and published works, but a complete analysis of the role of memory in his thinking could be taken farther. Much has been written, for instance, about its role in his lectures on aesthetics. See Bates, *Hegel's Theory*, 103–33, and Martin Donougho, "Hegel's Art of Memory," in Rebecca Comay and John McCumber, eds., *Endings: Questions of Memory in Hegel and Heidegger* (Evanston, IL: Northwestern University Press, 1999), 139–59.
21 Findlay, *Hegel*, 324.

immediate being and invests the present with meaning. The interest we take in the past primarily concerns its bearing on the present, as Collingwood has argued. The plane of history is only brought to immediate presence through recollection. In the *Phenomenology*, we saw that Hegel considers history to be a conscious process that depends on the slow progression of the forms of spirit in a gallery of images. The *Philosophy of Right* and the related lectures on history are works in which recollection is always center-stage. What I will consider is the particular manner in which memory is understood in these texts.

The image in the *Philosophy of Right* that has drawn the most commentary is the "owl of Minerva" (there is even an important journal of Hegel studies with this name). In the Preface to the text, Hegel writes, "One word more about giving instruction as to what the world ought to be. Philosophy in any case always comes on the scene too late to give it. As the thought of the world, it appears only when actuality is already there cut and dried after its process of formation has been completed. The teaching of the concept, which is also history's inescapable lesson, is that it is only when actuality is mature that the ideal first appears over against the real. ... The owl of Minerva spreads its wings only with the falling of the dusk" (*PR*, 13; *W*, VII: 28).[22] Philosophy always arrives too late. It is condemned to looking backward and showing what has been, rather than looking forward and predicting the future.

On the surface, this claim seems to argue against the way that Hegel has heretofore used the concept of *Erinnerung*. Isis is that which was, is, and will be. If philosophical thinking cannot extend into futurity, then philosophy cannot lift her veil. If Minerva's owl sees only the day that has just come to a close, then Minerva's wisdom is limited and not divine. Rather than this interpretation, we should relate the owl of Minerva to Hegel's critique of clairvoyance in the *Encyclopedia*. The clairvoyant is bound to a sensual and determinate form of thinking, not the philosophical form of thought. We cannot, it is true, attain a *perceptual* knowledge of the future, or a knowledge of the accidental contents of times to come. The particulars of actual history cannot be fully known because they have not finished unfolding. We can, however, still grasp necessity, which is something different than the collection of factual data.

---

22   Hegel does not employ paragraph numbers in the Preface of the *Philosophy of Right*, but does in the remainder of the text. I have cited the English and German page numbers for quotations from the Preface, and paragraph numbers where applicable.

History, for Hegel, progresses along two lines, the actual and the ideal, and only at times do the two synchronize. He is concerned in the *Philosophy of Right* with the ideal development of history. This ideal historical plan can be known, and in fact always has been known. If a particular nation's actual history does not precisely mirror the philosopher's conception of ideal historical development, all the worse for that nation. In the Preface to the *Philosophy of Right*, Hegel writes, "The truth about right, ethics, and the state is as old as its public recognition and formulation in the law of the land, in the morality of everyday life, and in religion. … It requires to be grasped in thought as well; the content which is already rational in principle must win the *form* of rationality and so appear well-founded to untrammeled thinking" (*PR*, 3; *W*, VII: 13–14).

The *truth* of right and history is already implicitly present in common thinking and religion; philosophy only makes this truth explicit. As Magee says, "The philosopher 'recollects' this unconscious wisdom and expresses it in a fully adequate form."[23] The purpose of the *Philosophy of Right* is "to apprehend and portray the state as something inherently rational" (*PR*, 11; *W*, VII: 26), rather than imposing an "ought" on this rationality. What is the state's rationality? Hegel writes, "The state is the divine will, in the sense that it is mind present on earth, unfolding itself to be the actual shape and organization of the world" (*PR*, §270). In the *Encyclopedia*, the human being, in terms of knowledge, is taken to be the living image of God; human knowledge is potentially divine and infinite. Through the inward gaze of recollection, the individual can cognize the divine necessity unfolding in the cosmos. If the political state is an aspect of the unfolding of the divine will, and this unfolding is a rational process, then consciousness can, in fact, apprehend what *will be* along with what has been. The particulars of the future remain veiled, but the abstract idea of the inner development of the state can be known. Reason is built into the world and accessible through recollection: "In contrast with the truth thus veiled behind subjective ideas and feelings, the genuine truth is the prodigious transfer of the inner into the outer, the building of reason into the real world, and this has been the task of the world during the whole course of its history" (ibid.).

The *Philosophy of Right* ends with a short section on world history, which is "the necessary development, out of the concept of mind's freedom alone, of the moments of reason and so of the self-consciousness and freedom of the mind" (*PR*, §342). This section formed the basis for

---

23 Magee, *Hegel and the Hermetic Tradition*, 224.

Hegel's series of popular lectures on the *Philosophy of History*. While the general concern of the *Encyclopedia* was to illuminate spirit's development in space, the *Philosophy of History* lectures are concerned more with its development in time (*PH*, 72; *W*, XII: 96–97). At the start of these lectures, Hegel says that his subject matter is "universal history itself [*die Weltgeschichte selbst*]," not a collection of observations about factual history (*PH*, 1; *W*, XII: 11). "Philosophical" history is "the thoughtful consideration of [history]" (*PH*, 8; *W*, XII: 20). The one assumption of this "thoughtful consideration" is the presence of reason in the development of the world.

Philosophical thought is concerned with the rational process of history, not its particular events. It is only concerned with particulars insofar as they accord with and illuminate the unfurling of universal reason. Philosophy of history is history seen from within, rather than from without.[24] Hegel writes, "God governs the world; the actual working of his government—the carrying out of his plan—is the history of the world. This plan philosophy strives to comprehend; for only that which has been developed as the result of it, possesses *bonâ fide* reality. That which does not accord with it is negative, worthless existence" (*PH*, 36; *W*, XII: 53).

This view of history, like Hegel's view of the state, considers universal reason to be implicitly present in every individual. He continues, "Religion and morality—in the same way as inherently universal essences—have the peculiarity of being present in the individual soul, in the full extent of their idea, and therefore truly and really; although, they may not manifest themselves in it *in extenso*" (*PH*, 37; *W*, XII: 54). Philosophy, which uncovers reason in history, is a slow apprehension of what is already known. History entails a gallery of images. The philosophy of history, then, is philosophical recollection. The central importance of memory for the investigation of spirit remains consistent throughout Hegel's writing career, under whatever aspect he considers spirit.

History does not unfurl in the same way for every nation. The *Phenomenology* was a universal history of spirit, but each stage of its dialectic was a graveyard from which many individual spirits, through forgetfulness, were unable to advance. The same phenomenon occurs amongst the nations. States that dominate the world-stage at one level of reason's

---

24 R. G. Collingwood writes, "The philosophy of history is for [Hegel] not a philosophical reflection on history but history itself raised to a higher power and become philosophical as distinct from merely empirical, that is, history not merely *ascertained* as so much fact but *understood* by apprehending the reasons why the facts happened as they did." *The Idea of History* (New York: Oxford University Press, 1994), 111–12.

development in history find themselves unable to advance, and become irrelevant in future stages. The Oriental world is overtaken by Greece, Greece by Rome, and Rome by Germany. Findlay correctly notes, "Each State only has the degree of development it has by remembering its origins. It follows that, for Hegel, where there are no historical records, there can also be no real political development. Historians do not merely record political development: they also render it possible."[25]

The development of every state depends on its self-recollection, its memory of the stages along which it has progressed. In the absence of historical memory, a nation mistakes the position it has reached for the absolute. Hegel's three stages of every world-historical nation are growth; independence and prosperity through conquest of the previous world-historical power; and finally decline and fall, brought about by encounters with the succeeding world-historical power. The decline and fall are preceded by internal dissensions, which spring up in the absence of "external excitement" (*PH*, 224; *W*, XII: 276). Prosperity breeds forgetfulness, just as great suffering sharpens the memory. The state loses its internal unity once it has forgotten the need for this unity, and this is the moment at which progress halts.[26]

The most explicit connection between the cosmic recollection of the *Encyclopedia* and the *Philosophy of History* lectures occurs in the paragraph in which Hegel introduces Christianity. He writes, "The absolute object, *truth*, is spirit; and as man himself is spirit, he is present to himself in that object, and thus in his own absolute object has found *his own* essential being" (*PH*, 319; *W*, XII: 386). For Hegel, as for Montaigne and their shared ancestor, Socrates, truth is self-knowledge. Truth, be it historical, scientific, or absolute, is already within spirit. Memory is simply true because it knows what has already happened. It is never an *explanation*; it is just there to be discovered.

In the final paragraph of these lectures, Hegel writes, "Only *this* insight can reconcile spirit with the history of the world—viz., that what has happened, and is happening every day, is not only not 'without God,'

---

25 Findlay, *Hegel*, 333.
26 Hegel says that *every* world-historical nation follows this process (*PH*, 224; *W*, XII: 276–77). This claim refutes the "end of history" thesis often attributed to Hegel, popularized by Francis Fukuyama's article, "The End of History?" *The National Interest* 16 (1989): 3–19. On the myth of Hegel's "end of history" thesis, see Philip T. Grier, "The End of History and the Return of History"; H. S. Harris, "The End of History in Hegel"; and Reinhart Klemens Maurer, "Hegel and the End of History," all of which are in Jon Stewart, ed., *The Hegel Myths and Legends* (Evanston, IL: Northwestern University Press, 1994).

but is essentially his work" (*PH*, 457; *W*, XII: 540). The history of the world is divine reason in the process of revelation. The God of whom Hegel writes is not that of the dogmatists. God is identical to the unfurling of spirit. Philosophy is the thoughtful contemplation of this unfurling. The owl of Minerva bears witness to this process of reason revealed in history. But because man is rational and divine, his hindsight is also foresight. Absolute memory apprehends the universal movement of history, not its accidents.[27] The external world is annulled as external and rises to spirituality in the form of recollection. Absolute knowing is outside of time. It walks amongst the intellectual objects of Plotinus. It grasps the eternal, the unchanging. *Absolute Wissen*, absolute knowing, is the wisdom of the Muses and Isis translated into nineteenth century German.

---

27   C.f. Nuzzo, "Memory, History, and Justice," 381–82.

Postface

I have nothing substantial to add at this point that has not already been said above, but it may be proper here to make a brief backward survey of the path we have taken, our highway of despair.

Hegel's art of memory is not a restatement of the classical art. Hegel combines elements from all of the classical sources, but makes these his own. Recollection is a process led by thought. It is self-knowledge, after the model of Socrates, but at the same time it is cosmic knowledge, after the model of Hermes. Absolute knowing is nothing more nor less than the grasp of the total procession of images and forms through which spirit has passed. The whole is a *theatrum mundi*. The progress of spirit always depends on this total memory. The grasp of the inner movement of spirit is the work of *ingenium*. Forgetfulness leaves spirit stranded at some stage short of the absolute.

Montaigne's art of memory is not the same as Hegel's, and I never meant to imply that they were at all similar in approach or *raison d'être*. Montaigne ultimately rejects the idea of a perfect knowledge of the fluctuating world. In his dialectic, memory is always ethical. It always teaches prudence. Memory helps us to orient ourselves to what is good and what is bad in the world as it confronts us. Montaigne's teaching (if it is acceptable to distill it down to a pithy caricature) concerns how to live well. Hegel's art aims at the real and the true. His recollection is ontological, and he begins from the presupposition that this knowledge of the true is unlimited.

In the contemporary world, under the lasting influence of Descartes, Kant, and the general socio-political project of modernity, philosophy has taken up method, criticism, and reflection as its characteristic starting points. We forget that these have not always been the centerpieces of philosophical thought. I thought it expedient to analyze Montaigne and Hegel as models of rebellion against the dominant epistemological trend of modernity. Montaigne and Hegel are both absolutely new philosophical figures in many ways, but in other ways they personify the continuation of an ancient tradition. Classical *ars memoriae* were destined to perish when it became apparent that they could not adequately confront the new philosophical problems raised by the scientific revolution. Nonetheless, the memory tradition is not a carcass best left alone. Montaigne and Hegel both offer solutions to some of the pressing philosophical problems of the modern, scientific world while retaining creative, vital conceptions of memory. Fundamentally, the dialectics of Montaigne and Hegel can be read as new arts of memory.

The philosophical tradition of memory, like everything past, can never die an absolute death. In our contemporary world, our technological age, "memory as philosophy" finds itself in a period of decay. This historical fact does not, however, mean that "memory as philosophy" can never again be taken up. For spirit to progress, it must remember whence it has come and through what it has already passed. Spirit calls out once more for a new art of memory. I have tried to articulate my own doctrine of "memory as philosophy," but there is much more to be said on the matter. The work done here is not exhaustive. I encourage others to add to this doctrine, or replace it altogether with their own.

One final question remains. Why undertake this investigation at all? In a sense, this question presupposes the idea that philosophy ultimately must have some exchange value, or some social utility, which is an idea I reject, and I think that most philosophers throughout time would reject. To rephrase the question, it may be posed as an accusation: Is this all not the sort of whimsical thinking of someone grown disenchanted with contemporary thought? Not exactly. The main currents of professional philosophical discourse appear to be quite sedimentary and static at present, but that is usually true of the main currents of thought at any given time. I find that much interesting thought still bubbles to the surface, both from within the analytic and continental traditions, and from without. What I am opposed to is not at all a contemporary idea, but the inheritance of Cartesian thought, namely the shibboleth of certainty as the cornerstone of all philosophy. This dogma tends to obscure from the philosophical mind what is most clear to all forms of ordinary thinking. The "I" and the world, the individual and the cosmos, the human and divine, slip further and further from our grasp the more scientific and methodical our thinking becomes. Metaphysics and moral philosophy more and more appear to be mechanical ducks, quacking monstrosities with nothing inside.

I begin and end with a simple intuition to oppose this tendency. That is, that wisdom (I nearly said knowledge, but wisdom, *sapientia*, is more accurate; I want no struggle with the epistemologists)—wisdom is not so eternally receding as it may appear. It is only the over-cultivated and over-educated modern mind that believes this. Those old masters to whom I have referred throughout this book were not at all of the same mind. We are within the cosmos, but the cosmos is therefore within us.

There is no infinite divide between knower and known. The knower already carries the known within. Anamnesis is therefore a doctrine worth revisiting. I say that this is a simple intuition, which is to say that it will not admit of "proof" in the sense of the logicians. It is a starting point, a *topos*, for reason. It will therefore be a notion inimical to many of our great scholars. This is fine, since all children of Socrates know they must follow their own daemons.

My proposal is that if we revisit the old idea of memory as philosophy, there may be a positive yield that allows philosophy to move forward into new domains. It may turn out that truth is not so foreign to our thought as it would appear in the age of post-post-modernity, the age of blind technique and increasingly fractured psyches. I assume that we have all had those sudden ineffable moments of clarity, in which it becomes apparent just for a moment that in fact it is all very simple, all very knowable. It is just possible that these moments are not mere illusion. I propose "memory as philosophy" because it seems to me that the dual questions of what reality is, and how we should live within it, are actually questions that we can grapple with, as the ancient heroes grappled with Proteus. I say that wisdom is possible, and the manner of approach is much closer than it seems—it is already within you.

Bibliography

Apel, Karl-Otto. *Die Idee der Sprache in der Tradition des Humanismus von Dante bis Vico*. Bonn: Bouvier Herbert Grundmann, 1975.

Adorno, Theodor W. "The Essay as Form." *New German Critique* 32 (1984): 151–71.

Alighieri, Dante. *The Divine Comedy*. Trans. John Aitken Carlyle, Thomas Okey, and Philip H. Wicksteed. New York: Vintge, 1959.

Aquinas, St. Thomas. *Summa Theologica*. Trans. Fathers of the English Dominican Province. 5 Vols. Westminster, MD: Christian Classics, 1981.

Aristotle. *Complete Works*. Ed. Jonathan Barnes. 2 Vols. Princeton, NJ: Princeton University Press, 1984.

———. *Parva naturalia*. Trans. W.D. Ross. New York: Oxford University Press, 1959.

Auerbach, Erich. "L'Humaine Condition." In *Mimesis: The Representation of Reality in Western Literature*. Trans. Willard R. Trask. Princeton, NJ: Princeton University Press, 1953, 285–311.

St. Augustine. *The City of God against the Pagans*. Trans. R.W. Dyson. New York: Cambridge University Press, 1998.

———. *Confessions*. Trans. Henry Chadwick. New York: Oxford University Press, 2009.

Aurelius, Marcus. *Meditations*. Trans. Robin Hard. New York: Oxford University Press, 2011.

Averröes. *Epitome of Parva Naturalia*. Trans. Harry Blumberg. Cambridge, MA: The Mediaeval Academy of America, 1961.

Bacon, Francis. *Essays and New Atlantis*. New York: Walter J. Black, 1942.

Bakewell, Sarah. *How to Live, or A Life of Montaigne in One Question and Twenty Attempts at an Answer*. New York: Other Press, 2010.

Bates, Jessica Ann. *Hegel's Theory of Imagination*. Albany: State University of New York Press, 2004.

Beck, L. J. *The Method of Descartes: A Study of the Regulae*. Oxford: Clarendon Press, 1952.

Berkeley, George. *Three Dialogues Between Hylas and Philonous*. New York: Bobbs-Merrill, 1954.

Bergson, Henri. *An Introduction to Metaphysics*. Trans. T.E. Hulme. Indianapolis, IN: Hackett, 1999.

———. *Matter and Memory*. Trans. Nancy Margaret Paul and W. Scott Palmer. New York: Zone Books, 1991.

———. "Memory of the Present and False Recognition." In *Mind-Energy*. Trans. H. Wildon Carr. New York: Henry Holt and Company, 1920, 134–85.

Bernheimer, Richard. "Theatrum Mundi." *The Art Bulletin* 38 (1956): 225–47.

Blavatsky, H. P. *Isis Unveiled*. 2 Vols. Wheaton, IL: Theosophical Publishing House, 1972.

Bloch, Ernst. "Hegel und die Anamnesis." *Hegel-Studien* (1964): 167–80.

Bolzoni, Lina. *The Gallery of Memory: Literary and Iconographic Models in the Age of the Printing Press*. Trans. Jeremy Parzen. Toronto: University of Toronto Press, 2001.

Borges, Jorge Luis. *Collected Fictions*. Trans. Andrew Hurley. New York: Viking, 1998.

Bouwsma, William J. *The Waning of the Renaissance, 1550–1640*. New Haven, CT: Yale University Press, 2000.

Brauer, Daniel. "La 'memoria productiva': Acerca de la concepción de Hegel del recuerdo y la memoria." *Revista latinoamericana de filosofía* 28 (2002): 319–37.

Bruno, Giordano. *The Ash Wednesday Supper*. Trans. Edward A. Gosselin and Lawrence S. Lerner. Toronto: University of Toronto Press, 1995.

———. *De umbris idearum*. Trans. Scott Gosnell. Huginn, Muninn & Co, 2013.

Byron, George Gordon, Lord. *Don Juan*. Boston: Houghton Mifflin, 1958.

Calvin, John. *Institutes of the Christian Religion*. Trans. Henry Beveridge. Grand Rapids, MI: Eerdmans, 1989.

Campanella, Tomasso. *The City of the Sun: a poetical dialogue*. Trans. Daniel J. Donno. Berkeley: University of California Press, 1981.

Caplan, Harry. *Of Eloquence: Studies in Ancient and Mediaeval Rhetoric*. Ed. Anne King and Helen North. Ithaca, NY: Cornell University Press, 1970.

Carruthers, Mary. *The Book of Memory: A Study of Memory in Medieval Culture*. New York: Cambridge University Press, 2008.

Carruthers, Mary, and Jan M. Ziolkowski, eds. *The Medieval* Craft *of Memory: An Anthology of Texts and Pictures*. Philadelphia: University of Pennsylvania Press, 2003.

Cassirer, Ernst. *An Essay on Man*. New Haven, CT: Yale University Press, 1972.

———. "Form and Technology." Trans. Wilson McClelland Dunlavey and John Michael Krois. In *Ernst Cassirer on Form and Technology: Contemporary Readings*. Ed. Aud Sissel Hoel and Ingvilo Folkvoro. New York: Macmillan, 2012, 15–53.

———. *The Individual and the Cosmos in Renaissance Philosophy*. Trans. Mario Domandi. Mineola, NY: Dover, 2000.

———. *The Philosophy of Symbolic Forms, Vol. 2: Mythical Thought*. Trans. Ralph Manheim. New Haven, CT: Yale University Press, 1955.

———. *The Philosophy of Symbolic Forms, Vol. 3: The Phenomenology of Knowledge*. Trans. Ralph Manheim. New Haven, CT: Yale University Press, 1957.

Castor, Grahame. *Pleiade Poetics: A Study in Sixteenth-Century Thought and Terminology*. Cambridge: Cambridge University Press, 1964.

Cicero. *De inventione*. Trans. H.M. Hubbell. Loeb Classical Library. Cambridge, MA: Harvard University Press, 1949.

———. *De oratore*. Trans. E.W. Sutton and H. Rackham. Loeb Classical Library. 2 Vols. Cambridge, MA: Harvard University Press, 1942.

———. *Tusculan Disputations*. Trans. J.E. King. Loeb Classical Library. Cambridge, MA: Harvard University Press, 1942.

[Cicero.] *Rhetorica ad Herennium*. Trans. Harry Caplan. Loeb Classical Library. Cambridge, MA: Harvard University Press, 1954.

Clarke, Desmond M. *Descartes's Theory of Mind*. Oxford: Clarendon, 2003.

Collingwood, R. G. *An Essay on Philosophical Method*. Wiltshire: Thoemmes Press, 1995.

———. *The Idea of History*. New York: Oxford University Press, 1994.

Comay, Rebecca, and John McCumber, eds. *Endings: Questions of Memory in Hegel and Heidegger*. Evanston, IL: Northwestern University Press, 1999.

Condillac, Étienne Bonnot, Abbé de. *A Treatise on the Sensations*. In *Philosophical Writings*. Trans. Franklin Philip and Harlan Lane. Hillsdale, NJ: Lawrence Erlbaum Associates, 1982.

Crites, Stephen. "The Golgotha of Absolute Spirit." In *Method and Speculation in Hegel's* Phenomenology. Ed. Merold Westphal. Atlantic Highlands, NJ: Humanities Press, 1982, 47–56.

Croce, Benedetto. "An Unknown Page from the Last Months of Hegel's Life." Trans. James W. Hillesheim and Ernesto Caserta. *The Personalist* 45 (1964): 329–53.

Descartes, René. *Œuvres*. 11 Vols. Paris: Vrin, 1996.

———. *The Philosophical Writings of Descartes*. 3 Vols. Trans. John Cottingham, Robert Stoothoff, and Dugald Murdoch. New York: Cambridge University Press, 1985.

———. *The World and Other Writings*. Ed. and trans. Stephen Gaukroger. New York: Cambridge University Press, 1998.

Dupré, Louis. "Hegel Reflects on Remembering." *The Owl of Minerva* 25 (1994): 141–46.

Durkheim, Émile. *Suicide*. Trans. John A. Spaulding and George Simpson. New York: The Free Press, 1979.

Eco, Umberto. *Foucault's Pendulum*. Trans. William Weaver. New York: Harcourt Brace, 1989.

———. *The Name of the Rose*. Trans. William Weaver. Orlando, FL: Harcourt Brace, 1994.

Eliot, T. S. *The Complete Plays and Poems: 1909–1950*. New York: Harcourt, Brace & World, 1962.

———. The Use of Poetry and the Use of Criticism. London: Faber and Faber, 1964.

Ellmann, Richard. *James Joyce*. New York: Oxford University Press, 1982.

Ellul, Jacques. *The Technological Society*. Trans. John Wilkinson. New York: Knopf, 1964.

Emerson, Ralph Waldo. "Montaigne; or, the Skeptic." In *Representative Men*. New York: Marsilio, 1995, 80–101.

———. "Natural History of Intellect." In *The Complete Works of Ralph Waldo Emerson*. New York: Houghton, Mifflin & Co., 1921, 12: 1–110.

Engel, William E. "The Renaissance *Ars Memorativa* and Montaigne's Scene of Writing." In *The Order of Montaigne's Essays*, ed. Daniel Martin. Amherst, MA: Hestia, 1989, 33–49.

Epicurus. *The Epicurus Reader: Selected Writings and Testimonia*. Trans. and ed. Brad Inwood and L.P. Gerson. Indianapolis: Hackett, 1994.

Ficino, Marsilio. *Platonic Theology*. Trans. Michael J.B. Allen. I Tatti Renaissance Library. 6 Vols. Cambridge, MA: Harvard University Press, 2001–06.

Findlay, John N. *Hegel: a Re-Examination*. New York: Collier, 1962.

Frame, Donald M. *Montaigne: A Biography*. New York: Harcourt, Brace & World, 1965.

———. *Montaigne's* Essais*: A Study*. Englewood Cliffs, NJ: Prentice-Hall, 1969.

Freud, Sigmund. *New Introductory Lectures on Psychoanalysis*. Trans. James Strachey. New York: W.W. Norton & Co., 1964.

———. *On the History of the Psycho-Analytic Movement*. Trans. Joan Riviere, revised James Strachey. New York: W.W. Norton & Co., 1990.

———. *The Psychopathology of Everyday Life*. Trans. James Strachey. New York: W.W. Norton & Co., 1960.

Friedrich, Hugo. *Montaigne*. Trans. Dawn Eng. Berkeley: University of California Press, 1991.

Fukuyama, Francis. "The End of History?" *The National Interest* 16 (1989): 3–19.

Galilei, Galileo. *The Assayer*. In *The Controversy of the Comets of 1618*. Trans. Stillman Drake and C.D. O'Malley. Philadelphia: University of Pennsylvania Press, 1960.

———. *Discoveries and Opinions of Galileo*. Trans. Stillman Drake. New York: Doubleday, 1957.

Galton, Francis. *Inquiries into Human Faculty and Its Development*. London: The Eugenics Society, 1951.

Garin, Eugenio. *Science and Civic Life in the Italian Renaissance*. Trans. Peter Munz. Garden City, NY: Anchor Books, 1969.

Gaukroger, Stephen. "The Resources of a Mechanist Physiology and the Problem of Goal-Directed Processes." In *Descartes' Natural Philosophy*, ed. S. Gaukroger, Stephen Schuster, and John Sutton. New York: Routledge, 2000, 383–400.

Gombrich, E. H. Symbolic Images: Studies in the Art of the Renaissance. London: Phaidon, 1972.

Gracián, Baltasar. *The Art of Worldly Wisdom*. Trans. Joseph Jacobs. Boston: Shambhala, 2006.

Grassi, Ernesto. *The Primordial Metaphor*. Trans. Laura Pietropaolo and Manuela Scarci. Binghamton, NY: Medieval & Renaissance Texts & Studies, 1994.

———. *Rhetoric as Philosophy: The Humanist Tradition*. Trans. John Michael Krois and Azizeh Azodi. Carbondale, IL: Southern Illinois University Press, 2001.

Gulley, Norman. *Plato's Theory of Knowledge*. London: Metheun & Co., 1962.

Hajdu, Helga. *Das mnemotechnische Schrifttum des Mittelalters*. Amsterdam: E.J. Bonset, 1967.

Harris, H. S. *Hegel's Development*. 2 Vols. New York: Oxford University Press, 1972.

———. *Hegel's Ladder*. 2 Vols. Indianapolis: Hackett, 1997.

Hartle, Ann. *Michel de Montaigne: Accidental Philosopher*. New York: Cambridge University Press, 2003.

———. *Montaigne and the Origins of Modern Philosophy*. Evanston, IL: Northwestern University Press, 2013.

———. *Self-Knowledge in the Age of Theory*. Lanham, MD: Rowman & Littlefield, 1997.

Hazard, Paul. *The Crisis of the European Mind: 1680–1715*. New York: New York Review of Books, 2013.

Hegel, G. W. F. *Faith and Knowledge*. Trans. Walter Cerf and H.S. Harris. Albany: State University of New York Press, 1988.

———. *Lectures on the History of Philosophy 1825–6*. Trans. R.F. Brown and J.M. Stewart. 3 Vols. New York: Oxford University Press, 2009.

———. *Logic: Being Part One of the Encyclopaedia of the Philosophical Sciences*. Trans. William Wallace. New York: Oxford University Press, 1975.

———. *Phenomenology of Spirit*. Trans. A.V. Miller. Oxford: Oxford University Press, 1976.

———. *Philosophy of History*. Trans. J.M. Sibree. Mineola, NY: Dover, 2004.

———. *Philosophy of Mind: Being Part Three of the Encyclopaedia of the Philosophical Sciences*. Trans. William Wallace and A.V. Miller. New York: Oxford University Press, 1971.

———. *Philosophy of Nature: Being Part Two of the Encyclopaedia of the Philosophical Sciences*. Trans. A.V. Miller. New York: Oxford University Press, 1970.

———. *Philosophy of Right*. Trans. T.M. Knox. New York: Oxford University Press, 1967.

———. *Science of Logic*. Trans. A.V. Miller. Atlantic Highlands, NJ: Prometheus Books, 1991.

———. *Werke*. Ed. Eva Moldenhauer and Karl Markus Michel. 20 Vols. Frankfurt am Main: Suhrkamp, 1969.

Heisenberg, Werner. "The Copenhagen Interpretation of Quantum Theory." In *Physics and Philosophy: The Revolution of Modern Science*. New York: Harper Perennial, 2007, 18–32.

[Hermes Trismegistus.] *Asclepius: The Perfect Dialogue of Hermes Trismegistus*. Trans. Clement Salaman. London: Duckworth, 2007.

———. *Hermetica*. Trans. Brian P. Copenhaver. New York: Cambridge University Press, 1992.

Herodotus. *The Persian Wars*. Trans. A.D. Godley. Loeb Classical Library. 4 Vols. Cambridge, MA: Harvard University Press, 1920.

Hesiod. *Theogony*. Trans. Glenn W. Most. Loeb Classical Library. Cambridge, MA: Harvard University Press, 2006.

Hillgarth, J. N. *Ramon Lull and Lullism in Fourteenth-Century France*. New York: Oxford University Press, 1971.

Hobbes, Thomas. *The Elements of Law Natural and Politic*. Ed. J.C.A. Gaskin. New York: Oxford University Press, 1994.

———. *Leviathan*. Ed. J.C.A. Gaskin. New York: Oxford University Press, 1996.

Homer. *The Iliad*. Trans. A.T. Murray. Loeb Classical Library. 2 Vols. Cambridge, MA: Harvard University Press, 1925.

———. *The Odyssey*. Trans. A.T. Murray. Loeb Classical Library. 2 Vols. Cambridge, MA: Harvard University Press, 1995.

Hunter, I. M. L. *Memory: Facts and Fallacies*. Baltimore: Penguin, 1966.

Huxley, Aldous. *Collected Essays*. New York: Harper, 1955.

Hyde, Lewis. *Trickster Makes this World: Mischief, Myth, and Art*. New York: Farras, Straus & Giroux, 1988.

Hyppolite, Jean. *Genesis and Structure in Hegel's* Phenomenology of Spirit. Trans. Samuel Cherniak and John Heckman. Evanston, IL: Northwestern University Press, 1974.

Iamblichus. *Life of Pythagoras*. Trans. Thomas Taylor. Rochester, VT: Inner Traditions, 1986.

Israel, Cynthia. "Montaigne and Proust: Architects of Memory." *Romance Languages Annual* 6 (1994): 105–9.

James, William. *The Principles of Psychology*. 2 Vols. New York: Dover, 1950.

———. *The Varieties of Religious Experience*. New York: Signet Classics, 2003.

Jaspers, Karl. *Man in the Modern Age*. Trans. Eden Paul and Cedar Paul. Garden City, NY: Doubleday Anchor Books, 1957.

Jorgensen, Larry M. "Leibniz on Memory and Consciousness." *British Journal for the History of Philosophy* 19 (2011): 887–916.

Joyce, James. *Finnegans Wake*. New York: Penguin, 1986.

———. *A Portrait of the Artist as a Young Man*. Ware, Hertfordshire: Wordsworth, 1992.

Kandel, Eric R. *In Search of Memory*. New York: W.W. Norton & Company, 2006.

Kanelos, Peter. "Montaigne and the Grotto of Memory." *Proteus: A Journal of Ideas* 19, no. 2 (2002): 12–18.

Kant, Immanuel. *Critique of Judgment*. Trans. Paul Guyer and Eric Matthews. New York: Cambridge University Press, 2000.

———. *Critique of Pure Reason*. Trans. Norman Kemp Smith. New York: St. Martin's Press, 1965.

———. *Groundwork of the Metaphysics of Morals*. Trans. Mary Gregor and Jens Timmermann. New York: Cambridge University Press, 2012.

Krell, David Farrell. "Of Pits and Pyramids: Hegel on Memory, Remembrance, and Writing." In *Of Memory, Reminiscence, and Writing: On the Verge*. Bloomington, IN: Indiana University Press, 1990, 205–39.

Kristeller, Paul Oskar. *Renaissance Thought: The Classical, Scholastic, and Humanist Strains*. New York: Harper & Row, 1961.

Kritzman, Lawrence D. *The Fabulous Imagination: On Montaigne's Essays*. New York: Columbia University Press, 2009.

Kuhn, Thomas S. *The Structure of Scientific Revolutions*. Chicago: University of Chicago Press, 1962.

La Mettrie, Julien Offray de. *Machine Man and Other Writings*. Trans. Ann Thomson. New York: Cambridge University Press, 1996.

Lang, Helen S. "On Memory: Aristotle's Corrections of Plato." *Journal of the History of Philosophy* 18 (1980): 379–93.

Leidi, Thamar Rossi. *Hegels Begriff der Erinnerung: Subjektivität, Logik, Geschichte*. Frankfurt am Main: Lang, 2009.

Leonhardt, Jürgen. *Latin: Story of a World Language*. Trans. Kenneth Kronenberg. Cambridge, MA: Belknap Press, 2013.

LePort, Aurora K. R., et al. "Behavioral and Neuroanatomical Investigation of Highly Superior Autobiographical Memory (HSAM)." *Neurobiology of Learning and Memory* 98 (2012): 78–92.

Locke, John. *An Essay Concerning Human Understanding*. 2 Vols. New York: Dover, 1959.

———. *Two Treatises of Government*. Ed. Peter Laslett. Cambridge: Cambridge University Press, 2009.

Lowenthal, Marvin, ed. and trans. *The Autobiography of Michel de Montaigne*. New York: Houghton, Mifflin & Co., 1935.

Lowes, John Livingston. *The Road to Xanadu: A Study in the Ways of the Imagination*. New York: Houghton Mifflin, 1927.

Lukács, George. *Soul and Form*. Trans. Anna Bostock. Cambridge: MIT Press, 1974.

Lull, Ramon. *Doctor Illuminatus: A Ramon Llull Reader*. Ed. Anthony Bonner. Princeton, NJ: Princeton University Press, 1985.

———. *Selected Works of Ramon Llull*. Trans. and ed. Anthony Bonner. 2 Vols. Princeton, NJ: Princeton University Press, 1985.

Luria, Aleksandr R. *The Mind of a Mnemonist*. Trans. Jerome S. Bruner. Cambridge, MA: Harvard University Press, 1987.

Luther, Martin. *The Bondage of the Will*. Trans. J.I. Packer and O.R. Johnston. Grand Rapids, MI: Baker Academic, 1957.

MacCulloch, Diarmaid. *The Reformation: A History*. New York: Penguin, 2005.

Magee, Glenn Alexander. *Hegel and the Hermetic Tradition*. Ithaca, NY: Cornell University Press, 2001.

———. *The Hegel Dictionary*. New York: Continuum, 2010.

Malcolm, Norman. "Memory and Representation." *Noûs* 4 (1970): 59–70.

Malebranche, Nicolas. *The Search After Truth*. Trans. Thomas M. Lennon and Paul J. Olscamp. New York: Cambridge University Press, 1997.

Marcuse, Herbert. *Hegel's Ontology and the Theory of Historicity*. Trans. Seyla Benhabib. Cambridge, MA: MIT Press, 1987.

———. *One-Dimensional Man*. Boston: Beacon Press, 1964.

Martin, Daniel. *L'Architecture des Essais de Montaigne: mémoire artificielle et mythologique*. Paris: Librairie A.-G. Nizet, 1992.

McLuhan, Marshall. *The Gutenberg Galaxy*. New York: Signet, 1969.

———. *Understanding Media: The Extensions of Man*. New York: McGraw-Hill, 1964.

Merleau-Ponty, Maurice. "Reading Montaigne." In *Signs*. Trans. Richard McCleary. Evanston, IL: Northwestern University Press, 1964, 198–210.

Montaigne, Michel de. *The Complete Essays*. Trans. Donald M. Frame. Stanford, CA: Stanford University Press, 1958.

———. *The Complete Works*. Trans. Donald M. Frame. New York: Modern Library, 2003.

———. *Les Essais*. Ed. Pierre Villey and V.-L. Saulnier. 3 Vols. Paris: Quadridge/PUF, 1988.

Moore, Kate Gordon. "Theory of Imagination in Plotinus." *The Journal of Psychology* 22 (1946): 41–51.

Nietzsche, Friedrich. *On the Genealogy of Morality*. Trans. Maudemarie Clark and Alan J. Swenson. Indianapolis, IN: Hackett, 1998.

———. "On the Uses and Disadvantages of History for Life." In *Untimely Meditations*. Trans. R.J. Hollingdale. Cambridge: Cambridge University Press, 1992, 57–123.

Nuzzo, Angelica. "Dialectical Memory, Thinking, and Recollecting: Logic and Psychology in Hegel." In *Mémoire et souvenir: Six études sur Platon, Aristote, Hegel et Husserl*. Ed. Aldo Brancacci and Gianni Gigliotti. Napoli: Bibliopolis, 2006, 89–120.

———. "History and Memory in Hegel's 'Phenomenology'." *Graduate Faculty Philosophy Journal* 29 (2008): 161–98.

———. *Memory, History, Justice in Hegel*. New York: Palgrave Macmillan, 2012.

———. "Memory, History, and Justice in Hegel's System." *Graduate Faculty Philosophy Journal* 31 (2010): 349–89.

Ortega y Gasset, José. *Meditaciones del Quijote: Ideas sobre la novela*. Madrid: Espasa-Calpe, 1963.

———. *The Revolt of the Masses*. Trans. Anonymous [J.R. Carey]. New York: W.W. Norton, 1957.

Ovid. *Tristia*. Trans. A.L. Wheeler, rev. G.P. Goold. Loeb Classical Library. Cambridge, MA: Harvard University Press, 1924.

Peone, Dustin. "Ethical Negativity: Hegel on the True Infinite." In *The Meaning and Power of Negativity*. Ed. Ingolf U. Dalferth and Marlene A. Block. Tübingen: Mohr Siebeck, forthcoming.

———. "Forgetting and Philosophy." *Proceedings of the Southeast Philosophy Congress* 8 (2015): 37–49.

———. "Vico and His Patron Saint: The City of Man and the City of God." *Clio* 45 (2015): 1–14.

Pico della Mirandola, Gianfrancesco. *On the Imagination*. Trans. Harry Caplan. New Haven, CT: Cornell University Press, 1930.

Pico della Mirandola, Giovanni. *Oration on the Dignity of Man*. Trans. A. Robert Caponigri. Washington, DC: Regnery, 1956.

Pinch, Geraldine. *Handbook of Egyptian Mythology*. Santa Barbara, CA: ABC-Clio, 2002.

Plato. *Complete Works*. Ed. John M. Cooper. Indianapolis, IN: Hackett, 1997.

Pliny. *Natural History*. Trans. H. Rackham. Loeb Classical Library. 10 Vols. Cambridge, MA: Harvard University Press, 1942.

Plotinus. *The Six Enneads*. Trans. Stephen MacKenna and B.S. Page. Chicago: Encyclopaedia Britannica, 1955.

Plutarch. *Moralia*. Trans. Frank Cole Babbitt. Loeb Classical Library. 16 Vols. Cambridge, MA: Harvard University Press, 1957.

Quintilian. *The Orator's Education*. Trans. Donald Russell. Loeb Classical Library. 5 Vols. Cambridge, MA: Harvard University Press, 2001.

Reiss, Timothy J. "Denying the Body? Memory and the Dilemmas of History in Descartes." *Journal of the History of Ideas* 57 (1996): 587–607.

Ricoeur, Paul. *Freud and Philosophy*. Trans. Denis Savage. New Haven, CT: Yale University Press, 1977.

———. *Memory, History, Forgetting*. Trans. Kathleen Blamey and David Pellauer. Chicago: University of Chicago Press, 2004.

Rorty, Richard. *Philosophy and the Mirror of Nature*. Princeton, NJ: Princeton University Press, 1979.

Rosen, Stanley. *G. W. F. Hegel: An Introduction to the Science of Wisdom*. New Haven, CT: Yale University Press, 1974.

———. *The Idea of Hegel's Science of Logic*. Chicago: University of Chicago Press, 2014.

Rossi, Paolo. *The Birth of Modern Science*. Trans. Cynthia De Nardi Ipsen. Malden, MA: Blackwell, 2000.

———. *Logic and the Art of Memory: The Quest for a Universal Language*. Trans. Stephan Clucas. Chicago: University of Chicago Press, 2000.

Rossington, Michael, and Anne Whitehead, eds. *Theories of Memory*. Baltimore: The Johns Hopkins University Press, 2007.

Rousseau, Jean-Jacques. *The Basic Political Writings*. Trans. Donald A. Cress. Indianapolis: Hackett, 1987.

———. *Emile, or On Education*. Trans. Allan Bloom. New York: Basic Books, 1979.

Russell, Bertrand. *A History of Western Philosophy*. New York: Simon and Schuster, 1945.

Russell, Nicolas. *Transformations of Memory and Forgetting in Sixteenth-Century France*. Lanham, MD: University of Delaware Press, 2011.

Sacks, Oliver. *The Man Who Mistook His Wife for a Hat*. New York: Touchstone, 1998.

Santayana, George. *Scepticism and Animal Faith*. New York: Dover, 1955.

Sarma, Gopal P. "The Art of Memory and the Growth of the Scientific Method." *Interdisciplinary Description of Complex Systems* 13 (2015): 373–96.

Schopenhauer, Arthur. *The World as Will and Representation*. Trans. E.F.J. Payne. 2 Vols. New York: Dover, 1966.

Shaftesbury, Anthony Ashley Cooper, third Earl of. *Characteristics of Men, Manners, Opinions, Times*. New York: Bobbs-Merrill, 1964.

Singer, Dorothea Waley. *Giordano Bruno: His Life and Thought*. New York: Henry Schuman, 1950.

Smith, John H. *The Spirit and Its Letter: Traces of Rhetoric in Hegel's Philosophy of Bildung*. Ithaca, NY: Cornell University Press, 1988.

Snell, Bruno. *The Discovery of the Mind in Greek Philosophy and Literature*. Trans. T.G. Rosenmeyer. New York: Dover, 1982.

Sorabji, Richard. *Aristotle on Memory*. Providence, RI: Brown University Press, 1972.

Spence, Jonathan D. *The Memory Palace of Matteo Ricci*. New York: Penguin, 1985.

Spinoza, Baruch. *The Ethics*. Trans. Samuel Shirley. Indianapolis: Hackett, 1992.

Squire, Larry R., and Eric R. Kandel. *Memory: From Mind to Molecules*. Greenwood Village, CO: Roberts and Company, 2009.

Stace, W. T. *The Philosophy of Hegel*. New York: Dover, 1955.

Starobinski, Jean. *Montaigne in Motion*. Trans. Arthur Goldhammer. Chicago: University of Chicago Press, 1985.

Stewart, Jon, ed. *The Hegel Myths and Legends*. Evanston, IL: Northwestern University Press, 1996.

Strauss, Leo. *Natural Right and History*. Chicago: University of Chicago Press, 1968.

Tell, Dave. "Beyond Mnemotechnics: Confession and Memory in Augustine." *Philosophy and Rhetoric* 39 (2006): 233–53.

Tocqueville, Alexis de. *Democracy in America*. Trans. Harvey C. Mansfield and Delba Winthrop. Chicago: University of Chicago Press, 2000.

———. *The Old Régime and the Revolution in France*. Trans. Stuart Gilbert. Garden City, NY: Doubleday Anchor, 1955.

Todorov, Tzvetan. *Imperfect Garden: The Legacy of Humanism*. Trans. Carol Cosman. Princeton, NJ: Princeton University Press, 2002.

Verene, Donald Phillip. *Hegel's Recollection: A Study of Images in Hegel's Phenomenology of Spirit*. Albany: SUNY Press, 1985.

———. *Philosophy and the Return to Self-Knowledge*. New Haven, CT: Yale University Press, 1997.

———. *Speculative Philosophy*. Lanham, MD: Lexington Books, 2009.

———. "Two Sources of Philosophical Memory: Vico versus Hegel." In *Philosophical Imagination and Cultural Memory: Appropriating Historical Traditions*. Ed. Patricia Cook. Durham, NC: Duke University Press, 1991, 40–61.

Verra, Valerio. "Storia e memoria in Hegel." In *Letture hegeliane: idea, natura e storia*. Bologna: Il Mulino, 1992, 13–40.

Vico, Giambattista. *The Art of Rhetoric*. Trans. Giorgio A. Pinton and Arthur W. Shippee. Atlanta: Rodopi, 1996.

———. *The Autobiography of Giambattista Vico*. Trans. Max Harold Fisch and Thomas Goddard Bergin. Ithaca, NY: Cornell University Press, 1975.

———. *The New Science*. Trans. Thomas Goddard Bergin and Max Harold Fisch. Ithaca, NY: Cornell University Press, 1948.

———. *On the Most Ancient Wisdom of the Italians, Unearthed from the Origins of the Latin Language*. Trans. L.M. Palmer. Ithaca, NY: Cornell University Press, 1988.

———. *On the Study Methods of our Time*. Trans. Elio Gianturco. Ithaca, NY: Cornell University Press, 1990.

———. *Universal Law, Book 1: On the One Principle and One End of Universal Law*. Trans. John D. Schaeffer. New Vico Studies 21 (2003): 23–274.

Vieillard Baron, Jean-Louis. "Hegel, philosophe de la reminiscence." *International Studies in Philosophy* 8 (1976): 145–66.

Villey, Pierre. *L'influence de Montaigne sur les idées pédagogiques de Locke et de Rousseau*. Paris: Hachette, 1911.

———. *Les sources & l'évolution des essays de Montaigne*. 2 Vols. Paris: Hachette, 1933.

Virgil, *Aeneid*. Trans. H. Rushton Fairclough. Loeb Classical Library. 2 Vols. Cambridge, MA: Harvard University Press, 1935.

———. *Georgics*. Trans. H. Rushton Fairclough. Loeb Classical Library. Cambridge, MA: Harvard University Press, 1935.

Vives, Juan Luis. "A Fable about Man." Trans. Nancy Lenkeith. In *The Renaissance Philosophy of Man*. Ed. Ernst Cassirer, Paul Oskar Kristeller and John Herman Randall, Jr. Chicago: University of Chicago Press, 1948, 387–93.

Vlastos, Gregory. "Anamnesis in the *Meno*." *Dialogue: Canadian Philosophical Review* 4 (1965): 143–67.

Wenneker, Lu Beery. "An Examination of *L'Idea del Theatro* of Giulio Camillo, Including an Annotated Translation, with Special Attention to his Influence on Emblem Literature and Iconography." PhD dissertation. University of Pittsburgh, 1970.

Westphal, Merold. *History and Truth in Hegel's* Phenomenology. Bloomington, IN: Indiana University Press, 1998.

Whitehead, Alfred North. *Process and Reality*. New York: Macmillan, 1929.

———. *Science and the Modern World*. New York: Free Press, 1953.

Wilkinson, Lisa Atwood. *Socratic Charis: Philosophy Without the Agon*. Lanham, MD: Lexington Books, 2013.

Witt, R. E. *Isis in the Graeco-Roman World*. Ithaca, NY: Cornell University Press, 1971.

Yates, Frances A. *The Art of Memory*. Chicago: University of Chicago Press, 2001.

———. "The Art of Ramon Lull: An Approach to It through Lull's Theory of the Elements." *Journal of the Warburg and Courtland Institutes* 17 (1954): 115–73.

———. "The Ciceronian Art of Memory." In *Medioevo e Rinascimento: studi in onore di Bruno Nardi*, ed. Firenze: Sansoni, 1955, 873–902.

———. *Giordano Bruno and the Hermetic Tradition*. Chicago: University of Chicago Press, 1991.

———. "Ramon Lull and John Scotus Erigena." *Journal of the Warburg and Courtland Institutes* 23 (1960): 1–44.

Young, Morris N. *Bibliography of Memory*. New York: Chilton Company, 1961.

Zweig, Stefan. *Montaigne*. Trans. Will Stone. London: Pushkin Press, 2015.

Index

Adorno, Theodor W., 22, 24, 167, 168
Agrippa von Nettesheim, Cornelius, 137, 142, 150
St. Albert the Great, 127–31, 133, 137, 154, 157, 192
Alighieri, Dante, 15, 32, 81, 130, 136, 177n2, 187, 192
anamnesis, 263; in Hegel, 222, 240n35, 251, 252; in Plato, 103–8, 114–15, 118, 137, 145, 222, 251, 252
Apel, Karl-Otto, 217
Aristotle, 18, 41, 78n72, 87n21, 95, 115, 124, 127–28, 193, 194, 195, 208n9, 237, 247n9; *De memoria et reminiscentia*, 66n39, 109–14; on memory arts, 113–14, 119–20, 129–30, 187; and Montaigne, 157–63, 165; on recollection, 109, 112–13; relation to Plato, 107–8, 110–13
Arnauld, Antoine, 206
ars combinatoria, 134–36, 248n11
ars critica, 57, 78, 135, 185–86
ars memoria, See mnemotechnic
ars topica, 57, 78, 135, 141, 185, 248n12
Auerbach, Erich, 77, 167n35
St. Augustine of Hippo, 20, 116–18, 119–20, 121n6, 127, 134, 136, 145, 163, 166, 170–71, 187, 192, 239
Aurelius, Marcus, 142
autobiography, 78n71, 171, 230, 233, 236n37, 249
Averröes, 128
Bacon, Francis, 15, 65n36, 89, 90, 196, 225
Bain, Alexander, 87n21

Bakewell, Sarah, 82, 149n1, 150–51, 156n16, 159n22, 172
Bates, Jessica Ann, 249n14, 254n20
Baudier, Dominique, 153, 163
Beck, L. J., 205n1, 212
Bergson, Henri, 39n3, 67; criticism of Kant, 54–56; on memory, 44, 53–60, 61, 62, 64, 209n16, 216n40, 247
Berkeley, George, 44, 186
Berlin, Isaiah, 217
Bernheimer, Richard, 102n4, 142, 145
Blavatsky, H. P., 36n14
Bloch, Ernst, 220n56, 240n35
Bloom, Harold, 125n11
Bolzoni, Lina, 102n4, 130n24, 144n41
Borges, Jorge Luis, 39n3, 82, 83–85, 152, 225n8
Bossuet, Jacques-Bénigne, 197
Bouwsma, William J., 158n20, 198
Bracciolini, Poggio, 120
Brauer, Daniel, 249n13
Bruno, Giordano, 131n26, 133–34, 136, 137, 142, 146, 149–50, 252; influence on Hegel, 57, 222–24; memory arts of, 90, 125, 138–41, 187, 223–24
Byron, George Gordon, Lord, 222n3
Calvin, John, 192
Calvino, Italo, 125n11
Camillo, Giulio, 134, 149–50, 187, 218, 234, 252; memory theater of, 141–46, 172, 177
Campanella, Tomasso, 125
Caplan, Harry, 102n4, 127n12
Carruthers, Mary, 67n45, 78n72, 91, 101–2, 127n12, 129n20, 130

277

Casey, Edward S., 49
Cassirer, Ernst, 18n6, 31n2, 39n3, 68, 73n57, 87n19, 94, 161n24
Castor, Grahame, 163
Cavell, Stanley, 39n3
Charmadas, 39
Charron, Pierre, 23
Cicero, 18–19, 20, 42–43, 119n1, 127, 130, 144–45, 155, 172, 177, 187, 222, 234; *De inventione*, 70, 121, 122; *De oratore*, 120–23; ethics of, 70–72, 129, 154, 157; on forgetting, 79–81; on memory arts, 120–26, 129, 138–39
clairvoyance, 253–54, 255
Clarke, Desmond M., 206n3, 207–8, 212n25, 26
Collingwood, Robin George, 39n3, 93, 104, 255, 257n24
Condillac, Étienne Bonnot, Abbé de, 214
Conrad, Joseph, 77
Cornford, F. M., 18n6
Crites, Stephen, 238
Croce, Benedetto, 93, 220
Cudworth, Ralph, 206n3
Cusa, Nicolas of, 136
Cyrus I, 39, 41
da Vinci, Leonardo, 196
Deleuze, Gilles, 49
democracy, 196–200
Derrida, Jacques, 49
Descartes, René, 15, 21–22, 56, 59, 62, 89, 138, 147, 168, 170, 193–94, 202, 204, 224, 230, 261; criticism of memory arts, 16, 186–87; *Discours de la méthode*, 16, 54, 59n23, 205–6, 212–13, 217; on education, 212–13, 217; *L'Homme*, 208–13; on imagination, 194, 208–10; and *mathesis universalis*, 185, 205–8; on the physiology of memory, 203, 208–15, 219–20; on reflection, 54–55, 186, 231, 243; Vico's criticism of, 209, 217–18, 220
dialectic, 25, 79, 85, 87, 186, 261–62; in Hegel, 22, 220n56, 231–33, 234–36, 244, 247, 251, 254, 257; in Montaigne, 22, 150, 157, 163–68, 172, 178, 182
Dialexis, 119n2
Dioscuri, 119, 121
Donatus, Aelius, 189
Dupré, Louis, 252n19
Durkheim, Émile, 192n17
Eco, Umberto, 36n14, 146, 158n21
education, 105; in Descartes, 212–13, 217; in Hegel, 227, 236, 252; in Montaigne, 151–52, 155–57, 163–64; role of memory in, 11, 101, 108, 114, 124, 155–57, 236, 252
Eliot, T. S., 12, 33, 93–94, 97–98, 178
Ellmann, Richard, 66n37
Ellul, Jacques, 91–93, 95n15, 97, 102
Emerson, Ralph Waldo, 11, 75n64
Engel, William E., 153n13, 180
Epicurus, 79–81, 83
Epimetheus, 32
epistemology, 201–4
Erasmus, Desiderius, 144, 150, 151, 191
Erinnerung, See recollection
essence, 32, 48, 59, 65, 78, 170; in Hegel, 61–64, 242–47
fantasia, See imagination
Feinaigle, Gregor von, 222
Fichte, Johann Gottlieb, 17, 58, 220, 232, 244
Ficino, Marsilio, 39, 73n56, 137
Filmer, Robert, 197
Findlay, John N., 57, 231n18, 241n1, 244, 245, 254, 258

forgetting, 33–34, 42, 46, 78, 79–87, 104; in Hegel, 86–87, 232–33; in Nietzsche, 49–51, 83; in Montaigne, 81–82, 152–53, 163–65, 172

Frame, Donald M., 23, 59n23, 76n65, 77n69, 149, 173n53, 179n7, 180

Francis I, 142, 149

Freud, Sigmund, 46–48, 50, 52n34, 81, 104, 107n9

Friedrich, Hugo, 157n19

Fukuyama, Francis, 258n26

Galilei, Galileo, 193–95

Gall, Franz Joseph, 43

Galton, Francis, 46, 68, 104

Garin, Eugenio, 196n26

Gassendi, Pierre, 193, 211

Gaukroger, Stephen, 209n18

Gombrich, E. H., 130n24, 172–73

Gracián, Baltasar, 83

Grassi, Ernesto, 15n1, 85

Grassi, Orazio, 194

Gulley, Norman, 103, 104n4, 106n7

Gutenberg, Johannes, 188–90

Hajdu, Helga, 102n4, 119n1

Harris, H. S., 222n2, 228, 230, 231n18, 234n21, 236n27, 238, 258n26

Hartle, Ann, 75n62, 155, 159n23, 164, 166

Hazard, Paul, 202n43

Heidegger, Martin, 53

Heisenberg, Werner, 42

Hegel, Georg Wilhelm Friedrich, 17, 21–24, 37, 42, 65, 70, 71, 74n61, 77, 109, 135n8, 167–68, 187, 203–4, 220, 221–59 passim, 261–62; and *anamnesis*, 222, 240n35, 251, 252; criticism on memory arts, 221–25, 236; dialectic of, 22, 220n56, 231–33, 234–36, 244, 247, 251, 254, 257; *Enzyklopädie der philosophischen Wissenschaft*, 221, 246–54; on *Erinnerung*, 59, 61, 63, 76, 168, 220, 221–59 passim; on essence, 61–64, 242–47; on forgetting, 86–87, 232–33; *Grundlinien der Philosophie des Rechts*, 254–56; on imagination, 222–23, 241n2, 248; *Phänomenologie des Geistes*, 43–44, 76, 226–40; on reflection, 57–60, 219, 224, 231, 243–46, 252; on self-knowledge, 230, 236, 237, 239, 252, 258; *Wissenschaft der Logik*, 63–64, 241–46

Henry III, 149

Hermes Trismegistus, 35, 72–73, 77, 137, 139, 145, 175, 251, 252, 261

Herodotus, 34–35

Hesiod, 31–33, 64

Highly Superior Autobiographical Memory (HSAM), See hyperthymesia

Hillgarth, J. N., 134, 136n13

Hobbes, Thomas, 69, 193, 197, 214–15

Hölderlin, Friedrich, 147

Homer, 31, 41, 64, 250

Hume, David, 112n16, 214n33

Hunter, I. M. L., 45, 86

Huxley, Aldous, 22

Hyde, Lewis, 33

hyperthymesia, 82

Hyppolite, Jean, 231n18, 240n34, 242n4, 251

Iamblichus, 19

St. Ignatius of Loyola, 133

imagination, 95, 176, 203; and memory, 17–18, 66–68, 85–86, 123, 133, 160–65, 172, 209, 214, 218; in Aristotle, 110–11, 160, 162, 165; in Descartes, 194, 208–10; in Hegel, 222–23, 241n2, 248; in Montaigne, 160–65, 172; in Vico, 17–18, 66–68, 85, 120, 209, 218

ingegno, See *ingenium*
ingenium, 15, 63, 71n52, 74, 78, 87, 90, 92, 93, 95, 97, 120, 168, 203, 214n33, 234–35, 252, 261; in Vico, 17–18, 65–69, 120, 218, 234
Isis, 34–37, 250, 252–54, 255, 259
Israel, Cynthia, 153n13, 180–81
Jacobi, Friedrich Heinrich, 58, 70, 220
James, William, 46, 51, 79, 87n21
Jaspers, Karl, 39n3, 60, 64, 93, 94n13
Joyce, James, 39n3, 57, 66, 101, 111n13, 125n11, 138, 177n2
Kandel, Eric R., 11n2, 40–41, 44, 48
Kanelos, Peter, 156n17, 181–82
Kant, Immanuel, 21–22, 54, 89, 147, 224, 230n17, 231, 261; and *ars critica*, 185–86; *Critique of Pure Reason*, 201, 218–20; ethical writing of, 71; and reflection, 55–59, 62
Krell, David Farrell, 229n15, 248n12
Kristeller, Paul Oskar, 158n20
Kritzman, Lawrence D., 162
Kuhn, Thomas S., 195–96
La Boétie, Étienne de, 43, 149n3, 153
La Mettrie, Julien Offray de, 194, 206
Lang, Helen S., 108, 111
Lavater, Johann Caspar, 43
Leibniz, Gottfried Wilhelm, 217
Leidi, Thamar Rossi, 220n56
Leonhardt, Jürgen, 189n8
Lille, Alain of, 128
Linnaeus, Carl, 196
Locke, John, 54, 55, 70, 143n38, 197–99, 202, 215–17, 230n17, 243
Lowes, John Livingston, 111n13
Lukács, György, 168
Lull, Ramon, 133–36, 140, 141, 144, 222–23, 248n11

Luria, Aleksandr R., 84–85, 123n9
Luther, Martin, 190–91
MacCulloch, Diarmaid, 190n10
Machiavelli, Niccolò, 23, 198
Magee, Glenn Alexander, 37n15, 73n57, 74n61, 224, 225n6, 241n2, 248n11, 251, 256
Malcolm, Norman, 111n13
Malebranche, Nicolas, 152–53, 163, 186, 215
Marcuse, Herbert, 96n17, 97n19, 235, 236n26, 240n35
Martin, Daniel, 153n13
mathesis universalis, 195; in Descartes, 185, 205–8
memory, passim
memory theater, See Camillo, Giulio
McLuhan, Marshall, 91, 188
Merleau-Ponty, Maurice, 167, 170n46
Mithridates, 39
Mnemosyne, 32–33, 35, 37, 107, 182, 224–25, 249–51
mnemotechnic, 20, 45n16, 79, 82, 119–31 passim, 133, 137, 171, 176, 180–82, 186, 196, 217, 218n49, 261; and Aristotle, 113–14, 119–20, 129–30, 187; in Bruno, 90, 125, 138–41, 187, 223–24; in Camillo, 141–46; in Cicero, 120–26, 129, 138–39; Hegel's criticism of, 221–25, 236; in Lull, 134–36, 140–41, 248n11; Montaigne's criticism of, 150–57; in Quintilian, 120, 124–27, 129, 138, 150; in Thomas and Albert, 127–31
Montaigne, Michel de, 21–25, 36–37, 43, 59, 90, 134, 147–48, 149–83 passim, 185, 187, 220, 221, 222, 225, 230, 254, 261–62; criticism of Aristotle, 157–63, 165; criticism of memory arts, 150–57; dialectic of, 22, 150, 157, 163–68, 172, 178, 182; on education,

151–52, 155–57, 163–64; ethics of, 72, 153–55, 157, 162–68; on forgetting, 81–82, 152–53, 163–65, 172; on *l'humane condition*, 76–77, 169–73; on imagination, 160–65, 172; on self-knowledge, 75–77, 169–73, 258; on writing, 175, 176–83
Moore, Kate Gordon, 116n23
More, Henry, 154n14, 206n3
Muses, 31–37, 41, 46, 51, 62, 65–66, 68, 69–70, 72, 78, 79, 80, 90, 97, 114, 182–83, 219, 249, 250, 252, 254, 259
neurobiology, 40–44, 82
Newton, Isaac, 59, 193
Nietzsche, Friedrich, 49–52, 83, 154
Nuzzo, Angelica, 64, 220n56, 229, 234, 239n33, 240n35, 259n27
Ockham, William of, 101, 188
Orange, William of, 197
Ortega y Gasset, José, 89, 94, 95
Ovid, 68, 155, 164n28
owl of Minerva, 37, 255, 259
Paine, Thomas, 199
Partenio, Bernardino, 144
phrenology, 42–44
physiognomy, 42–44
Pico della Mirandola, Gianfrancesco, 111n13
Pico della Mirandola, Giovanni, 72, 136–37, 142–43, 252
Plato, 19, 20, 31n3, 43n11, 46n18, 69, 79, 158, 187, 190, 203; on *anamnesis*, 103–8, 114–15, 118, 137, 145, 222, 251, 252; *Meno*, 103–5; *Phaedrus*, 91, 105–7, 175; *Philebus*, 107–8; relation to Aristotle, 107–8, 110–13; *Theaetetus*, 107–8, 110; on writing, 175–76, 189
Pliny the Elder, 39

Pliny the Younger, 124
Plotinus, 16, 115–16, 118, 259
Plutarch, 34–37, 114, 119, 187, 250
printing press, 188–90
Prometheus, 32, 35, 145
Protestant Reformation, 186, 190–96
Proteus, 249–50, 252–53, 263
Proust, Marcel, 39n3, 64, 68, 146, 158–59
prudentia, 70–73, 78, 80, 121, 129, 154, 173, 254
Pseudo-Cicero, See Rhetorica ad Herennium
psychoanalysis, 46–48, 104
Pythagoras, 18–19
Quintilian, 11, 119n1, 137, 187, 222, 223; on memory arts, 120, 124–27, 129, 138, 150
Rabelais, François, 150
Ramus, Petrus, 133
Ravenna, Peter of, 133, 139
recollection, 39, 46, 51, 60–64, 69, 74, 78, 80, 81, 83, 96–97, 115, 117, 129, 136, 139, 146, 147, 158, 163, 165, 172, 176, 181, 189, 192, 203, 209n16, 261; in Aristotle, 109, 112–13; contrasted with memory, 109, 112, 241n2, 248–49; in Hegel, 59, 61, 63, 76, 168, 220, 221–59 passim; in Plato, 104–8
reflection, 21–22, 64, 213, 217, 261; barbarism of, 57–59; criticism of, 54–60, 61–63, 78, 92–94, 96, 224, 231; in Descartes, 54–55, 186, 231, 243; in Hegel, 57–60, 219, 224, 231, 243–46, 252; in Kant, 55–58, 219, 224, 231; and technology, 89–90, 92–94, 96
Regius, Raphael, 120
Reiss, Timothy J., 213

Renaissance, 12, 68, 90, 124–25, 127, 131, 133–34, 136–41, 146, 150–51, 154, 158, 186, 187, 196, 198, 214, 217–20, 224, 234
Rhetorica ad Herennium, 113, 120–24, 125, 129–30, 180, 181, 223
Ricci, Matteo, 133
Ricoeur, Paul, 39n3, 49, 52n34
Romberch, Johann Host von, 133
Rorty, Richard, 56n10
Rosen, Stanley, 242n4, 245n6
Rossi, Paolo, 90, 102, 103, 120n4, 127, 133n1, 151, 196n27, 28, 217
Rousseau, Jean–Jacques, 69–70, 152, 157, 164n28, 198
Russell, Bertrand, 202
Russell, Nicolas, 102n4, 177
Sacks, Oliver, 216n41
Saint Victor, Hugh of, 127–28
Santayana, George, 39n3, 81n4
Sarma, Gopal P., 196n28
Schelling, Friedrich Wilhelm Joseph, 17, 220
Schiller, Friedrich von, 239
Schopenhauer, Arthur, 47n24, 65, 87n20
scientific revolution, 193–96
Scipio, Lucius, 39
self-knowledge, 72–78; in Hegel, 230, 236, 237, 239, 252, 258; in Montaigne, 75–77, 169–73; in Socrates, 74–75, 96, 203, 258, 261
Seneca, 39, 67, 81
Shaftesbury, Anthony Ashley Cooper, third Earl of, 75
Shakespeare, William, 143, 170
Shereshevskii, S. V., 84–86, 93, 160
Sibyl (Cumaean), 177, 181
Simonides of Ceos, 39n1, 90, 119, 121
Singer, Dorothea Waley, 137

Smith, John H., 58, 221, 239
Snell, Bruno, 18n6, 31n4, 34n10
Socrates, 19, 42–43, 78, 169, 173, 175, 263; and *anamnesis*, 103–8; and self-knowledge, 74–75, 96, 203, 258, 261
Sorabji, Richard, 111n14, 112–13n16, 113n17
Spinoza, Baruch, 186, 214–15
Stace, W. T., 241n2
Starobinski, Jean, 76n66, 166–67, 178n4
Strauss, Leo, 198n34
technology, 89–98, 164, 188
Tell, Dave, 117n27
Terence, 66, 67, 179
theatrum mundi, 131, 133–46 passim, 168, 224, 234, 261
Themistocles, 79–80
Theuth, See Hermes Trismegistus
St. Thomas Aquinas, 101, 103, 113, 120, 127–31
Tocqueville, Alexis de, 198–99
Todorov, Tzvetan, 169
Valla, Lorenzo, 120
Verene, Donald Phillip, 17n4, 42, 44n12, 68n48, 70n51, 78n71, 94n14, 146; on Hegel, 225, 228n11, 232, 233, 234n22, 24, 238
Vergessen, See forgetting
Verra, Valerio, 220n56
Vico, Giambattista, 86, 111n13, 171, 185, 200, 203, 214n33, 221; barbarism of reflection, 57, 59–60; criticism of Descartes, 209, 217–18, 220; *De antiquissima Italorum sapientia*, 66, 68; on *ingegno*, 17–18, 65–69, 120, 218, 234; on memory, 17–18, 52, 65–69, 73, 85, 189, 218; *Scienza nuova*, 17, 31n1, 57, 65–68, 218

Vieillard Baron, Jean-Louis, 227n10, 251n16
Villey, Pierre, 157n18, 19
Virgil, 177, 230, 250
Vives, Juan Luis, 170–71
Vlastos, Gregory, 105–6
Voegelin, Eric, 39n3
Westphal, Merold, 242n3
Whitehead, Alfred North, 56n10, 62n30, 193, 233
Wilkinson, Lisa Atwood, 33n6
writing, 91, 175–83, 189
Yates, Frances A., 73n57, 89–90, 101, 102, 113n17, 117n27, 118n32, 119–20, 121n5, 6, 124–25, 127n12, 129n20, 130, 134, 136, 144n39, 145n47, 150n4; on Bruno, 137–41 passim
Zeus, 32–33
Zopyrus, 42–43
Zuichemus, Viglius, 144
Zweig, Stefan, 149n1, 169n41

ibidem.eu

Zeitfracht Medien GmbH
Ferdinand-Jühlke-Straße 7,
99095 - DE, Erfurt
produktsicherheit@zeitfracht.de